NONE SHALL
DIVIDE US

NONE SHALL DIVIDE US

**TO SOME HE IS A HERO. THE IRA WANT HIM DEAD.
THIS IS THE TRUE STORY OF THE ARTIST WHO WAS
IRELAND'S MOST NOTORIOUS ASSASSIN...**

MICHAEL STONE

JOHN BLAKE

Published by John Blake Publishing Ltd,
3, Bramber Court, 2 Bramber Road,
London W14 9PB, England

www.blake.co.uk

First published in hardback in 2003
This edition published in 2004

ISBN 1 84454 045 6

All rights reserved. No part of this publication may be reproduced, stored in a
retrieval system, or in any form or by any means, without the prior permission in
writing of the publisher, nor be otherwise circulated in any form of binding or cover
other than that in which it is published and without a similar condition including
this condition being imposed on the subsequent publisher.

British Library Cataloguing-in-Publication Data:

A catalogue record for this book is available from the British Library.

Design by www.envydesign.co.uk

Printed in Great Britain by Bookmarque, Croydon

1 3 5 7 9 10 8 6 4 2

© Text copyright Michael Stone/Karen McManus

Papers used by John Blake Publishing are natural, recyclable products made from
wood grown in sustainable forests. The manufacturing processes conform to the
environmental regulations of the country of origin.

Every attempt has been made to contact the relevant copyright-holders, but some
were unobtainable. We would be grateful if the appropriate people could contact us.

In memory of Margaret Mary Gregg, née Stone

CONTENTS

INTRODUCTION

I FIRST HEARD OF MICHAEL STONE IN MARCH 1988. HIS ATTACK ON THE REPUBLICAN FUNERAL OF THREE IRA VOLUNTEERS SHOT DEAD IN GIBRALTAR IS SEARED ON MY BRAIN.

As a child of the Troubles, for me there are incidents, too many to mention, that stand out for their stark cruelty, their horror and their futility. Milltown is one of them. Although I was young, I could not believe a lone paramilitary would do such a thing. I could not believe a terrorist would gatecrash the funeral of three IRA volunteers killed on active service, but there he was, flat cap and all-weather jacket, lobbing grenades into the crowd and reaching inside his jacket and pulling out a handgun – live on television. I can still hear the crack as the gun was fired, the thuds as the grenades were launched, the sound of women screaming as they grabbed children. I can still see the faces of people as they dived for cover behind gravestones. I remember thinking that nothing, not even funerals, was sacred in the sick, perverted place I called home.

In the days immediately after the Milltown attack the newspapers had a field day about his one-man attack on a high-profile Republican funeral. It took just two days for the UDA, the organisation he joined when he was just sixteen years old, to denounce him. It took just two days for Michael Stone, Loyalist volunteer of seventeen, to lose his identity and become nothing more than labels such as 'Rambo', 'nutter', 'loner', 'madman', 'killing machine' and 'robot' – words used by the print media to describe him. I saw the TV footage and I agreed with their choice of vocabulary. The man was all of these things and more. Only someone insane would even entertain the idea of such a mission.

But sadly the story didn't end at Milltown. It concluded three days later at the funeral of one of Michael's victims, IRA volunteer Kevin Brady. Michael's attack at Milltown was the flame which ignited one of the worst and most barbaric incidents of the entire troubles, the deaths of Corporals Derek Wood and David Howes. The young soldiers served with the Royal Corps of Signals, ironically Michael Stone's great-grandfather's regiment, and were executed on waste ground near the Andersonstown Road in West Belfast. The two were attacked by a forty-strong crowd after straying into Brady's funeral cortège. The crowd attacked because they thought another Michael Stone was attacking them. Republicans heaped on the blame, saying it all went back to Stone's assault, but to right-minded people it was just another senseless death in Ulster's war.

I first met Michael Stone in August 2001. He had been released the previous year after serving twelve years of his life sentence for six murders and a variety of other charges, including attempted murder, conspiracy to murder and possession of firearms and explosives. While serving his sentence he began to paint and fell in love with this new pursuit, which gave him expression and focus in his lonely prison life. Within a year of walking from the Maze Prison a free man he had his first exhibition, in a small gallery in Belfast city centre. The work showcased some of his remarkable prison art, painted on the back of bedside lockers and wardrobe doors, and several post-release paintings. It was a proud moment for Michael Stone and his family, but he accepted with a sad heart that most of the people who turned up at the Engine Room Gallery on the Newtownards Road did so for ghoulish reasons. They wanted to see what sort of pictures a murderer paints, what price he sells them for and who in their right mind would have them. Michael caught my imagination.

I did have fears about meeting this man, a Loyalist folk icon revered in song and verse. I was anxious that my opinions of the man, formed twelve years earlier, would compromise my reactions. I made mental notes to be open-minded but I wasn't prepared for the quiet man who limped down a flight of stairs to greet me; barely able to walk because of the hip injury he sustained in 1988. I was not prepared for the warm handshake that greeted my arrival. I was not prepared for the well-read and intelligent man who enjoys Irish politics and history. I was not prepared for the man who makes a daily superhuman effort to stay alive and admits he is more of a prisoner on the outside than he was inside the Maze.

Most of all, I was not prepared for the man who spoke poignantly about his past as a UDA volunteer and the part he played in the deaths of four men. Nor was I prepared for the man who has the sharpest memory I have ever come across and could recall every heartbeat of his volunteer life with precision. I didn't anticipate liking Michael Stone, but I did.

To my critics, of whom I expect there will be plenty, I would say just one thing: I do not intend this book to be a glorification of the life of Michael Stone. I do not intend this book to glamorise his life as a paramilitary. The book's objective is to show what happens to young men, both Protestant and Catholic, who get sucked into sectarian warfare. It is Michael Stone's story, but it is also the story of a handful of men who lived, and sadly continue to live, similar lives.

Michael Stone's story is shocking but it needs to be told. It will show him to be more than the tabloid labels, more than Rambo, the volunteer, the killer, the crazed gunman, the prisoner and the artist. This is Michael's story.

Karen McManus, 2004

FOREWORD

I AM A PROUD LOYALIST AND THIS WILL NEVER CHANGE. IT IS A STATEMENT OF FACT, NOT A DEFIANT SALUTE. I am British and I am a Loyalist and will be both of these things until I die. At the age of sixteen I put myself forward for a cause I believed in with all my heart. I remain proud of that fact but I am not proud of my actions. I am not proud that four men died by my hand.

I grew up with a sectarian war on my doorstep and I couldn't watch evil things being done, such as Enniskillen, La Mon and the Abercorn, and not do something about it. It is impossible for me to think that I would have never become a volunteer. Before long, terrorism became a way of life for me. I lived on the edge. I knew what my capabilities were. I knew I had the power to take life and to grant mercy, but I was never indiscriminate, unlike the Provisional IRA.

This book is an attempt to explain my actions as a volunteer and a retaliatory soldier. By committing the story of my life to paper, I am taking responsibility for my past. I am acknowledging that I caused pain to four families when I took their loved one away from them.

To the families of Patrick Brady, Thomas McErlean, John Murray and Kevin Brady I am sorry for your loss. I am sorry that you never got to say goodbye to your son, husband, boyfriend, father and brother because of me. I deeply regret the hurt I caused the families of the men I killed. I regret that I had to kill. I believed at the time that it was necessary. There is nothing I can do to take away the pain I have inflicted. There is a lot of hurt out there and I am responsible. Much of that hurt comes from my actions as a paramilitary. I don't see myself as a criminal. I committed crimes as an Ulsterman and a British citizen and that was regrettable but unavoidable.

To the families of Kevin McPolin and Dermot Hackett I am also sorry for your loss.

I didn't choose killing as a career; killing chose me. I hated bullies. When I was a young boy and saw someone being bullied at school or work, I always stepped in. As I grew older and started to form opinions, I realised Republicans were bullies, nothing more and nothing less, who took life after innocent life and no one seemed interested in stopping them. I put myself forward as a volunteer, thinking my actions could change things.

This book is also an attempt to explain the bigger picture: why young men from my community felt duty-bound to take up arms. It is a shocking account of the grim business I was engaged in for almost thirty years. There is nothing romantic about taking a life in defence of your community. It is a cold and brutal act. When a person dies, a little part of you dies too. I want to share that horror as a reminder that we must never look back. All of us must keep our eyes fixed on the road ahead, not the dark paths behind us.

Maturity is a wonderful gift. It is only now as I face the autumn of my life that I really understand. I understand what motivated Republicans. They saw grave injustices being perpetrated on their community and they lashed out. They were angry young Catholic men and no different from me, an angry young Protestant man who saw terrible crimes being perpetrated on his community.

I committed some terrible crimes over the years and I did it in the name of Ulster and in the name of my Britishness. Republicans committed some terrible crimes over the years and they did it in the name of their Irishness. That's the nature of the beast we call war.

Looking back, I can hardly believe that I did those things and lived the life I led. It is like peering into the life of a stranger. But it is my history, the history of Michael Anthony Stone. The person who emerges from these pages is not likeable and he is not attractive. This book shows a young man eaten up with anger and filled with hate for anonymous names on intelligence files. It shows a ruthless man, dedicated to his cause and ready to take life for what he believed in.

This is a true account of my life as a Loyalist volunteer. It is a shock to revisit my past, and writing this book has brought it all back. I have also realised that you can't kill a political persuasion, just a human being. You can't kill an identity, just a much-missed father and son. These people live on in their loved ones.

My war is over. I am no longer willing or able to take a life for what I believe in. I am like an old dinosaur. I hope I can slip into obscurity, but I honestly believe I will die as I lived, with a bullet in my head. When it comes, I hope my death is quick and I hope it is over in seconds. I also hope none of my family or friends are with me when it happens. An old paramilitary saying comes to mind:

NONE SHALL DIVIDE US

If I go forward I die.
If I go back I die.
I'll go forward and die.

Michael Stone

May 2004

The Ballad of Michael Stone

Three taigs flew into Dublin
On a big Gibraltan plane
The Provos planned to bury them
With honour and with fame

The Fenians they were out in force
To see that all went well
But the bravery of a Loyalist
Did shame them all to hell

Michael Stone he was the brave young man
From the Braniel he did come
Who thwarted all the Provos' plans
And killed the rebel scum
With handgun and grenades
He dealt the deadly blow
And the PIRA didn't get to have
Their paramilitary show

The brave young Proddy came
From the east end of the town
He infiltrated West Belfast
And didn't let us down
He stood and did the business
I'm sure you'll all agree
And the day before St Paddy's Day
Went down in history

1

MARY AND CYRIL

I CAME INTO THE WORLD ON 2 APRIL 1955 IN LORDSWOOD HOSPITAL, HARBORNE, BIRMINGHAM, THE FIRST-BORN CHILD OF MARY BRIDGET AND CYRIL STONE. I am a British citizen and proud to be one. I have always cherished my nationality. My family history is complex, but it forms the backbone of my identity. I have two sets of parents: my biological mother and father, Mary Bridget O'Sullivan and her husband Cyril Alfred Stone, and the parents who raised me as their own, Margaret and John Gregg.

I know very little about my biological mother. Mary Bridget O'Sullivan is an Irish name but I do not know if she was an Irish citizen. All I do know is that she spoke with a strong English accent. Mary Bridget was the eldest child in a very large family. Her own mother died when she was very young and she was charged with raising her younger brothers and sisters. My biological father was born in the United Kingdom but spoke with an accent straight from the Shankill Road. He lived in England all his life yet his accent was as strong as if he lived in the heart of West Belfast.

Mary Bridget and Cyril met in the UK and were married at Caxton Hall registry office, London, in 1953. She was just eighteen and he just twenty-one when they exchanged vows. The union lasted only two years, enough time for Mary Bridget to decide motherhood and marriage weren't for her. She walked out on her husband and new baby in September 1955, when I was just five months old. Mary Bridget never again saw the baby boy she left in Cyril's arms. A restless Jack the Lad, Cyril took just minutes to plan his next move: the boat to Belfast to his only sister, Margaret, and her new husband, John, who lived in Ballyhalbert, on the shores of Belfast Lough. He handed his son into the care of the young couple, who raised me as their own, turned on his heels and joined the Merchant Navy.

Margaret and John are the only parents I have ever known. Margaret was the best mother a young boy could wish for. She died in 2001 from heart complications. My father John spent his final years in a nursing home surrounded by ladies who want to marry him. He died in April 2003.

I have just the one photograph of Cyril and Mary Bridget together. It is a symbol of who I am and a poignant reminder that two people brought me into the world but played no part in my upbringing. Yet I am still drawn to them like a nail to a magnet. I am curious about Mary Bridget. I want to know what went on in 1955 when she called time on our little family. The photograph shows a beautiful young girl with dark curls framing her delicate features and wearing smart clothes. She is linking arms with a swarthy man in an overcoat. They look happy. Both are smiling at the camera but I wonder what was going on beneath the surface. When they met, Cyril was a member of the Forces, a full-time reservist in the RAF. By the time I was born, he was driving lorries for a chemical firm, a job which took him all over the UK.

My mother had sparse details about their relationship. She told me Cyril was quick-tempered and possessive and Mary Bridget liked her freedom. It was a stormy marriage and destined to fail. Just a few years before my mother died she told me she met Mary Bridget once. Mum described her as a beautiful and gentle girl who was like a little bird – she just wanted to fly away. That is the memory I carry of the woman who brought me into the world: a little bird who saw her chance of freedom and grabbed it.

I have searched all my adult life for Mary Bridget O'Sullivan, but she has vanished off the face of the earth. I have tried everywhere to find her. Even the Red Cross couldn't help me. Nothing exists after 1955, when my birth was registered. I do regret that I never got to meet Mary Bridget and she knows nothing about the man I became. I do not know what happened to her. She could be dead, she could have remarried or she could have emigrated to America or Australia. I still would like to see her and ask her about her life. I would like to tell her about my own life and would be happier doing this now my own mother is dead. I wouldn't feel that I was betraying my own mother by speaking to Mary Bridget.

My entry into the world was rarely talked about at home. My mother resented Mary Bridget for abandoning her baby and walking out on her family. Mum was old-fashioned. She believed a woman's place was with her children and in the home. From a very young age I was aware that I had a different surname from my brother and sisters, but there was no question of Mum allowing me to change my name from Stone to Gregg. I would ask tentative questions about why my name was different, but the only answer I got was: 'Let sleeping dogs lie.' I never probed. I didn't want to seem ungrateful or unfaithful because I loved her.

My mother was proud of her maiden name and she constantly

said to me, 'Be proud of your name because your married parents gave it to you.'

I am not interested in Mary Bridget's religion, and religious persuasion is not an issue for me. She may have been a Roman Catholic or she may not have been. It doesn't matter. Mary Bridget gave birth to me but she didn't bring me up. Margaret Gregg raised me as her son and within days of my arrival in Northern Ireland had me baptised into the Anglican faith.

When I first put those tentative questions about my biological father, Mum told me that he 'lived far away'. I know she did that to protect me and to make it sound like I hadn't been dumped as a newborn child. Cyril Stone was my mother's only brother and he kept in constant contact over the years, making regular enquiries about his first-born's development. Years later, when I was a grown man, I discovered my mother even sent the odd school photograph to Cyril, who was now living in Birmingham, and he kept all those pictures and placed them side by side with photos of his second family.

I was eleven when my mother decided it was time I knew about my background. She had the perfect opportunity. I was enrolling at secondary school and she feared that if I didn't know the facts I would be bullied and ridiculed in the playground. My elder sisters, Rosemary and Colleen, and elder brother, John, were already pupils there. Just days before I was due to enrol I was handed an old shoebox. Inside there was a bundle of letters and telegrams. They were all addressed to me, had postmarks stretching over an eleven-year period and were stamped with various exotic addresses such as 'Gibraltar Port'. At first I was bewildered. My mother said one thing: 'These letters are from Cyril Stone, who is your father. He is an officer in the Merchant Navy.' The letters are dog-eared and torn around the folds. It proved to me that Cyril Alfred Stone felt something in his heart for the little boy he handed into the care of his sister in the autumn of 1955.

I met Cyril Stone just the once, when I was already a father myself. It was a very strange experience but also a moving one. The meeting answered an unasked question: 'What am I missing out on?' When I met Cyril I realised, with a great sense of relief, that I was missing out on absolutely nothing. I was twenty-eight and it was 1983, the year my grandmother died. Margaret Stone had kept a diary given to me by my mother on the day of my grandmother's funeral. She told me to read it because there are 'things in it you will want to read'. Inside was an address and telephone number for Cyril. He was still living in the Midlands. I rang the number and when he answered I was surprised at the strength of his Belfast accent. I can still hear the conversation we had. I said his name and he answered with, 'Is that you, Michael?'

I told him I was coming to England to see him. He didn't resist, put me off, hang up or refuse to see me. I booked a hotel and my ferry ticket and made my journey to Birmingham. I found his home and with a shaky hand rang the doorbell. He answered the door and there we were – two Stones looking at each other on his doorstep. It was a warm, friendly meeting and I am glad I met him, but I knew he would never take the place of John Gregg, who raised me. Cyril had remarried and had two other children, twins Tracey and Terence. Terence is now a Buddhist monk living in south-east Asia. The whole family welcomed me with open arms. I noticed my school photos sitting alongside pictures of his new family. I was happy to leave Cyril's home and go back to Belfast to the only mother and father I have ever known and loved. The only missing piece in the jigsaw of my early life was Mary Bridget O'Sullivan and I accepted, with great sadness, that I would probably never find her.

2

A BOY FROM
THE BRANIEL

MY EARLY YEARS WERE SPENT IN BALLYHALBERT, ON THE SHORES OF BELFAST LOUGH. In the late 1950s the village was an old-fashioned place with just a handful of houses, the local shops and church, but it had a strong sense of community and family. Everyone knew everyone else and it was a friendly and safe environment in which to bring up children. I remember clearly the walks with my mother along the shore and the gulls which swooped close to our heads in their search for scraps of food. I would grab her hand but was fascinated by their fearless dives.

I was just four when the family moved to the Braniel estate, a new housing complex on the eastern edge of Belfast. More than a thousand new homes were built, making it the biggest development of its kind in Northern Ireland. My mother and father were pleased to get a house at 47 Ravenswood Park. It had a small garden at the back and front, it had a bathroom and my father was near the shipyard where he worked. We were an ordinary, working-class

Protestant family, no different from the families that surrounded us. It was 1959, and fathers went out to work while mothers stayed at home with the children. Dad's job as a steelworker took him out of the house from early morning to dinnertime. Mum never left the house. She had her hands full with two sons and four daughters. Home life was simple. Money was tight because there was just the one wage coming in, but we were happy.

In our home special pictures adorned the walls. Those images celebrated our culture and our loyalty to the young Queen Elizabeth II, our Protestant faith and my family's heritage; a heritage handed down from my grandfather and great-grandfather.

My grandfather was called Cyril Stone and he served in the Royal Corps of Signals. I find it ironic that the two corporals who were murdered at the funeral of Kevin Brady, and one of the men I killed at Milltown, were attached to the Royal Corps of Signals. My great-grandfather was Thomas Stone, an engineer and explorer. He was a fascinating character and spent many years in South Africa laying the railway along the Gold Coast. A photograph of Thomas Stone taken while he was in South Africa as an employee of the British government shows him holding Jacko, his pet baboon. This picture took pride of place in the living room and I was fascinated by the stories my mother would tell about Jacko.

After Thomas Stone finished working abroad he returned to England with his German wife Augusta, Jacko and two live alligators. He disembarked from the boat with the two alligators on leads and Jacko by the hand. The newspaper cuttings from 1936 show him, his massive collection of tribal war spears and his prized juju. Jacko is sitting on his knee. The baboon lived as an additional member of the family. When I was growing up my mother told me stories about life with her grandparents. Jacko was house-trained and lived indoors. He slept indoors and ate with the family. My mother, who paid regular visits to her grandparents as a little girl, said she was terrified of Jacko because he was so big. Eventually my great-grandfather had to kill him, after coming home from work to find his wife cowering in the corner of the kitchen, being attacked by Jacko, who was now fully grown. My great-grandfather and the baboon fought hand to hand: Jacko was strangled and my great-grandfather was covered in bites. The alligators are now in the Museum of Birmingham.

Also on the wall of our home was a framed parchment dated 28 September 1912 which was signed by James 'Soldier' Moore, my other great-grandfather. He served with the Royal Irish Fusiliers. 'Soldier' Moore had put his signature, in his own blood, to a solemn covenant to resist British Home Rule for Ireland. My mother was very proud of that parchment. My family were good, working-class Loyalists who were loyal to the Crown, loyal to their Queen, loyal to their identity and loyal to their British nationality.

As well as my elder brother and two elder sisters, I have two sisters who are younger than me, Sharon and Shirley. One of the first rules of our family, taught to each of us in turn by my mother, was 'Family Comes First'. Years later, when I joined the UDA, I broke that golden family rule. I didn't put my family first and my illegal paramilitary activities became the focus of my entire life. My brother was shy and scholarly as a boy. John loved studying and is now a master draughtsman. He is a quiet family man living in the UK and, although he has never passed judgement on my past life, he often says he doesn't understand how and why I got involved.

As a teenager John was a member of a rock group called Richmond Hill. He was the lead singer of the five-piece group and they played support to the Irish rock acts Thin Lizzy, Rory Gallagher and Horslips. Although he was a quiet lad he had an amazing Joe Cocker-type voice and the band regularly gigged at

Dublin's Baggot Inn. I used to scam my way on to their van whenever I got the chance.

Nowadays my sister Rosemary is a florist, while Colleen is a full-time wife and mother, Sharon an auxiliary nurse and Shirley a care attendant. Although the tables are turned and they now look after me, when we were young I took it upon myself to look after them and protect them from young lads on our estate.

My father worked long hours to keep the family together. As a steelworker at the Harland & Wolff shipyard, he had followed in his own father's footsteps. He was proud to be working class. He was a union man all his life and in his younger days represented boilermen, first as a convenor and then as a shop steward. My mother never left the family home for thirteen years and I mean just that: she never stepped beyond the front door. She didn't even go to the shops herself. Each of us, me included, did the shopping for her on our designated days. Her day, for all those thirteen years, was getting my father to work, getting us ready for school, cleaning, washing, cooking, getting us ready for bed, getting dinner ready for Dad and falling into bed herself. Her day was multiple trips from kitchen to backyard and backyard to kitchen. I don't think she really sat down during all that time. My parents had a long and loving marriage until death separated them in 2001. My lasting memory of the two of them together is Dad buying Mum a new winter coat and taking her into the city for a meal.

My school years – I went to a primary school which was right opposite my home – were not the happiest of my life. I preferred schoolyard games to sitting behind a desk and doing my lessons. It was at primary school that I got the nickname Flint, and it stayed with me until I became a Loyalist volunteer in my teens.

One teacher ensured I would leave school with little education and a dislike bordering on hatred for teachers and educators. Bordering the Braniel estate was a middle-class estate called

Glenview and children from there also attended Braniel Primary. This teacher was a snob: he held a senior position of responsibility but believed working-class kids had no right to education. He ran his school with an iron fist.

I had one encounter with this teacher that shaped the rest of my school life. When I was eight he slapped me in the face, causing my nose to bleed profusely. He beat me because I took a fit of the giggles in the playground when we were lining up to go back into class. I have never forgotten or forgiven the incident. After lunch the bell would ring to tell us it was time for lessons to begin. He had a ritual: you lined up in pairs, took the hand of the boy or girl standing beside you and filed into your classroom. I had a friend called Thomas 'Daz' Dizell. The bell rang and we lined up. I see this teacher striding up and down the lines of children and I take Daz's hand. He laughs, pulls his hand away and sticks his tongue out at me. I start to laugh and the teacher spots us. He walks over to where we are standing and tells us to wait outside his classroom. I am scared because he has a reputation and has been known to beat boys.

In the classroom, Daz is slapped on the palms of his hands with a ruler and ordered back to class. I know I'm next. The teacher walks towards me and I feel a heavy thud on my face that knocks me off my feet. He had hit me with the back of his hand and his knuckles had rammed so hard into my nose it burst a blood vessel. I have always had a weak nose and if I blew it too hard the blood would gush out and take ages to stop. I could see the blood dripping on to the floor and could feel it sliding down the back of my throat. I bolted under his desk, with blood pouring out of my nose, terrified I would get another slap. He screamed and shouted at me. Another teacher – a lady – heard the noise and rushed in. He left, slamming the door behind him, and she put me in a chair, saying just the one thing: 'You made him do that by being bold.' She never cleaned my face or tried to stop the bleeding. I was told to take off all my clothes and I began to cry, asking for my mother. The teacher left me sitting there in my socks and underpants, told me not to move until she came back and locked the door. I could hear her footsteps as she walked up the corridor.

The bleeding had stopped and had dried in my nose and on my face. The teacher eventually came back carrying a plastic bag containing my clothes. She emptied the bag on the floor and placed my trousers, shirt and jumper on a radiator to dry, but it was spring and the heating wasn't switched on. 'You stay here until the end of school, you tell your mother you fell and banged your face,' she said. 'You have sisters here and we can expel all of you.' Once the final bell went, she came back and told me to get dressed. I put on my damp clothes and went home.

My mother was furious with me and wanted to know what happened. I lied and told her I fell in the playground and hurt my nose. I convinced her I'd had an accident. I put on a brave face when I should have told her what that teacher had done. After that, he never let me out of his sight. He asked other teachers to make me sit at the seat nearest the door and he would watch my movements. I was constantly waiting for the next blow or the next punch. I learnt a lesson that day: never tell a secret. I could have told Mum that a teacher had hit me but I didn't. I chose to stay quiet and keep it to myself. Ironically, it is a lesson that was to stay with me in the years to come, when I was operating as a paramilitary. As an eight-year-old I learnt to never spill the beans and never betray anyone.

From that day I have always had a problem with authority figures. When I left my primary school, I enrolled in Lisnasharragh Secondary. My sister Rosemary was already a pupil there and was in the same class as George Best, the football legend. He was head boy and Rosemary had a massive crush on him; in fact all the girls in Lisnasharragh had a soft spot for Best. He had moved from Grosvenor Grammar School and Rosemary told me that years later, at a school reunion party organised by the Democratic Unionist Party councillor Kim Morton, the former headmaster reminisced about George Best and my name also came up in the conversation. Then he said to her, 'Lisnasharragh had one famous pupil and one infamous pupil and I'll leave it up to you to decide which is which.'

My mother, spotting a wild streak in her young son, packed me off to the Army Cadets while I was at the school. I was fourteen and loved the weekend excursions to Orangefield Barracks. My mother thought it would tame me. It didn't. It gave me a taste for weapons and warfare. Every weekend for a year I got to put on a khaki uniform as a junior in the Irish Guards. I trained on real but deactivated weapons. The first I held in my hand was a Webley .45 revolver. The irony of this is not lost on me. Just two short years later I would hold a Webley in my hand once again and swear an oath of allegiance to the Ulster Defence Association, the UDA. I had great fun playing the boy soldier and would pretend my enemies were lurking behind doors and I would take an imaginary pop at them. The year culminated in a weekend exercise on the Isle of Man and the training in the use of live ammunition that I got there taught me to respect firearms.

But I still had to finish my schooling. I got into trouble at Lisnasharragh Secondary because I wouldn't do as I was told. I hated the teachers and thought they were all the same. I had no intention of doing exams, so I didn't see the point in being there. I hold the teacher at my primary school responsible for this tough-kid attitude. I wanted to leave school but the authorities wouldn't let me because I was only fifteen. So I engineered fights to get expelled. The brawls were easy. Too many big-mouthed boys would ask questions about my family, why I had a different surname from my sisters, why I was Stone and the girls were Gregg. I told them it was none of their business and used my fists and my feet to ram the message home.

My ploy worked and at fifteen and a half, a good six months before I could legally leave school, I was released by Lisnasharragh. They were glad to be rid of the tough troublemaker who continually disrupted the school. I was glad to be free of them. I hadn't a qualification to my name. My education was basic, to say the least. The past ten years sitting behind desks and looking at blackboards had been a complete waste of time, apart from school girlfriends.

In the early days the Braniel estate was mixed. Catholic families lived side by side with their Protestant neighbours. There was no reason for it to be any other way. Catholic families were exactly like mine, with fathers who worked and mothers who stayed at home. Their homes were exactly like mine except they had different pictures on their walls. There was a long-haired Jesus Christ exposing his heart and a picture of a woman in a blue veil standing on a burning bush in her bare feet and I couldn't understand why she was smiling and not screaming in pain. In one home there was a well that a Catholic pal would dip his finger into and touch his forehead, chest and shoulders before leaving the house. Boys like him were my friends. I kicked footballs and played games with them. Politics, religion and nationality had nothing to do with our fun, even though Northern Ireland was just a few short years away from full-scale sectarian warfare.

When I wasn't playing street games with my good pal, Tim and other friends, I was involved in activities at St Bridget's church hall. I was taken to Sunday service regularly and joined the Junior Boys' Brigade. I sang in the local choir and, to my mother's delight, was poached by St John's in Orangefield to sing in their much bigger and better-known choir. The rector, who had great hopes for me, taught me to read music. I even appeared on the BBC's *Songs of Praise* in a red surplice and snow-white ruffle. The singing stopped when I became leader of a junior street gang and was more interested in using my fists and feet than my angelic voice.

3

STREET FIGHTER

IT WAS 1970. THE FABRIC OF NORTHERN IRISH LIFE WAS UNRAVELLING FAST. Catholic agitation was escalating and three years after the formation of the Civil Rights movement in the province they were still shouting in a collective voice. They said they wanted changes, they demanded reform and were fed up with being treated as second-class citizens. They said it was their basic human right to have a job, education and decent housing. I was fifteen and not interested in a group of strangers moaning about their lot. I was more interested in street life and carving a niche for myself as the local bad boy.

The same year the Civil Rights activists were making waves for the establishment, I was making waves of my own – as the leader of a ruthless street gang. We called ourselves the Hole in the Wall Gang and we formed to defend our turf, and our girls, from neighbouring gangs. The Hole in the Wall wasn't sectarian. I can put my hand on my heart and say that, because half of the gang

17

was Catholic. The Hole in the Wall had nothing to do with vigilantism and keeping Catholics out, but it had everything to do with keeping rival street gangs in line. If they strayed into our territory they had to obey the rules and the golden rule was no flirting with our girls. They also had to behave – no anti-social antics, no trashing of local property – and show respect for the local gang. And if they didn't keep our rules there would be hell to pay.

As a teenage boy I ruled the 'middle Braniel' with an iron will and at fifteen I was already showing signs of the man I would become. There were fights every weekend and sometimes on weekday evenings with the Braniel's two other gangs – Terminus and Lower – who felt our tough justice. I also enjoyed leading the gang into rival turf in Castlereagh, Corduff and Tullycarnet in a bid to lure gangs from these areas back to my patch for a real fight. I had tough street rules and was proud of my 'nine to ninety' rule: any male from a ganged-up area who was between those ages was fair game.

The gang had weapons. There were no guns but we did carry small flick knives, and during a scrap we would use anything that came to hand, including lumps of wood and bricks. We even strapped coins to the inside of our hands. Our uniform was distinctive and made up of jeans and ox-blood-red Doctor Marten's boots. It was our badge. The gang lasted a year. It disbanded when the Troubles erupted and the Braniel became a tinderbox. Catholic families were forced to flee, grab what belongings they could and run for their lives. They had windows broken and threats shouted at them, but the houses were never burnt. That was a deliberate ploy to keep it ready for the new Protestant family who were waiting to move in, after being kicked out of another part of the city. All over Belfast thousands of displaced families were on the move, intimidated out of the areas they called home. Areas once mixed now became ghettos. Northern Ireland had drawn her sectarian battle lines.

Overnight the Braniel became almost exclusively Protestant. Only a handful of Catholic families chose to stay. A good friend of mine was one of the final victims, and when his family left I broke up the gang. To this day he probably thinks his family was forced to flee because Protestants didn't want them on their estate. The truth is, they were forced to flee because an angry young Catholic set fire to a wheelie bin and pushed it up against the family's back door in a fit of rage. Two nights before they were forced to leave, a gang from an estate in Woodstock in East Belfast had come into the Braniel to target Catholic families. They had escaped, but another friend Tim was targeted. He was furious that his house was trashed and my other friend's was untouched, so he set the wheelie bin on fire and calmly walked away. I witnessed the incident. When I tackled him about what he was doing he just said, 'I'm not leaving on my own. He can come with me.'

They were gone that evening. They didn't even take their furniture. They were terrified they would be ambushed if they hung around packing up. The family moved to Twinbrook and so did Tim.

Like many young boys, I followed my father into Harland & Wolff, but it would not be long before I would be in trouble again and fired for assaulting a workmate. In working-class Protestant families it was more than tradition for a boy to follow his father into the world-famous yard. It was obligatory. I had left school just weeks before and was just four months off sixteen. I started as a 'hammer boy' in the blacksmith shop at the Deep Water dock. I loved my new job and looked forward to going into work in the mornings. I felt grown up.

One of my duties in the blacksmith shop was to direct a massive steam-driven sledgehammer on to sheets of white-hot metal. Hammered into smaller, workable sizes, these were then fashioned by the craftsmen into fittings for the ships. I loved the Deep Water. I worked hard and kept myself out of bother. The highlight of my working day was mealtimes, when I would slope off and fish for mackerel and mullet using home-made harpoons made from welding rods. I felt like Huckleberry Finn.

My good behaviour lasted just a couple of months. One lunchtime I put a mullet on an anvil and hit it with the hammer, splattering fish guts all over the men and their lunch. The men wanted to paint my balls with red lead and I would have been in agony for a month. I had to stay away from the yard for a week.

Within the year Harland & Wolff indentured me. I was signed up as an apprentice steelworker. I wasn't looking forward to being cooped up in a classroom and hated the move from the freedom of the Deep Water to the dark indoor enclosures of the training school. I knew it was a job for life and I knew it would be safe and secure employment until my retirement, but I didn't want it. My wild and reckless streak kicked in and I began looking for a way out.

There were a lot of hard men in the yard. These men had to be tough, and some were doing terrible jobs. 'Stagers', for instance, were the men who erected the scaffolding around the ships and boats. They had to be physically and emotionally tough. There were a lot of deaths, about six a year: guys falling from a height and being sliced in two when they hit the scaffolding. Young apprentices learnt very quickly that if you messed with these guys they would turf you into the Deep Water.

Most workers had a go at making 'old rattlies', home-made sub-machine guns, in the yard machinery shop. They were basic but worked. Loyalist paramilitaries used them in the early days and they were fine for a couple of rounds before becoming volatile. They tended to jam or even explode unexpectedly.

I hated the training school, being indoors and being told what to do. Small groups of apprentices would work together at the one bench, sharing equipment and machinery, and every day we had something new to build or learn. Brian Moorehead, who was murdered by the Shankill Butchers, sat at the bench next to mine and so did Danny McDowell, a young lad from East Belfast. Danny was quiet and I was brash, but we ended up pals. I looked out for him because older men, who should have known better, picked on him.

One day, about five months into our apprenticeship, he was thumped in the face and called an 'East Belfast bastard' by a man from the Shankill. Danny told me about it at the morning teabreak. I hated bullies, despising them from the day that teacher thumped me, so I told Danny he had to stand up to them. Danny shook his head and said he couldn't because that would only make things worse. So I vowed to do something about it. If Danny couldn't help himself, then I would help him. I chose lunchtime and followed the man who thumped Danny into the toilets.

He was a big lad with Afro-type hair that stood like a halo around his head. I would make sure he didn't act the bully any more. He was wearing hairspray. I recognised the smell. It was the same one my mother wore. He had a cigarette lighter in his hand, one of the plastic Zippo type that had just hit the shops. I asked him if I could see it. He handed it over. I lit it and whoomph, his hair went up like a burning bush. He screamed. I kneed him in the stomach and he fell, hitting his head on one of the urinals. I kicked him a couple of times and warned him that if he ever assaulted my friend again he would get a chisel in the neck. He lay on the ground blubbering like a baby. An instructor heard the commotion and ran in. I was hauled before my bosses and the union representative. Danny and the bully were also present. My friend never opened his mouth. He stood hanging his head and refused to look at anyone. I was disappointed. He refused to confirm that he had been punched and to my disgust the bully kept crying and saying, 'Stone attacked me, Stone attacked me.'

As far as the authorities were concerned, it was an unprovoked, one-sided attack. I was suspended. The Harland & Wolff bosses called the Harbour Police and I was removed from the premises. They arrived in a small police van with just two seats in the front. In the back they kept their Alsatians, and I had to sit on the floor on newspaper they had put down for the dogs. When we got to the front gate of the shipyard the Harbour Police let me out. I preferred to walk the length of Queen's Road rather than stay a minute longer in the van.

There were terrible rows at home over the suspension and my father kept saying, 'Michael, I am a union man. You can't do this.'

I was reinstated four weeks later but I turned it down. My father was disappointed because John was doing really well in his apprenticeship at the shipyard. I had my eye on other pursuits. Danny never lasted at the yard and that doesn't surprise me. He couldn't stand up for himself. I heard he is now working as a caretaker in a block of flats in East Belfast.

By the end of 1970 the Provisional IRA had begun their indiscriminate bombing campaign. The following year they started to target soldiers and policemen. I was beginning to sit up and take notice. Like many young Loyalist men, I recognised that there had to be a response to the Republican assault and there had to be a counter-attack. Some chose to defend their country wearing the uniform of the police force or the newly formed Ulster Defence Regiment. The rest of us chose the paramilitaries.

On 6 February 1971 an IRA unit from the Ardoyne shot dead three young British Army soldiers in the Belfast hills. The three, who were Scottish and had just arrived in Northern Ireland, died in an horrific way. Aged just seventeen, eighteen and twenty-three, the squaddies were off duty and drinking in a bar in the city centre. Two young and pretty girls lured them to a fake party but, instead of being driven to the late-night party, the trio were taken to a lonely spot in the hills outside the city and shot one by one in the head. The youngest was just a year older than me. In memory of the Scottish soldiers, young Loyalists in the Shankill set up 'Tartan gangs'. They wanted to cause trouble for Catholics because, in their eyes, Catholics supported the IRA and it was the IRA who had murdered three young men.

Soon other Loyalist areas were following and the Braniel, in turn, formed its own gang. We had a uniform like the Hole in the Wall Gang: denims and DM boots. The only difference was the small piece of tartan sewn into the collars of our denim jackets. But our Tartan gang was different from the Hole in the Wall in another, important way: it was a paramilitary street gang and it was sectarian. The Braniel Tartan was run along proper military lines and made the Hole in the Wall look like babies having a water-pistol fight. It was organised and structured. We copied the military and had a general to lead the team. There were deputy leaders, or sergeants, and we had officers – the gang members.

I was General of the Braniel Tartan and had 140 teenagers in my gang. I was known as the 'heavy digger' – fast fists, hard fists, first in and last out. Every weekend I would lead my Braniel Tartan into the city centre. We would meet with other Tartan gangs, such as Young Newtown or Woodstock, and rampage through Belfast. Any Catholics stupid enough to stray into our path would be shoved through glass windows or beaten up. Every weekend the Catholic shop opposite the church on Castle Street would be trashed. The *Belfast Telegraph* newspaper described it as a 'sea of denim moving through the city centre'. It must have been an unnerving sight to passers-by because, on any weekend, there would be five hundred or more Tartan gang members on the streets. It was as the General of the Braniel Tartan that I came to the attention of Tommy Herron. For many months the UDA leader just watched me and made no approach.

It was 1971 and Northern Ireland was literally exploding all over the place. That was the year that sectarian strife touched my family. I have a cousin, Wesley Lambe, who lived in Farringdon Gardens, on the edge of the Catholic Ardoyne area of the city. He was unmarried and, an only child, lived with and cared for his wheelchair-bound mother and frail father. It was a weekday evening when Wesley was alerted by his Protestant neighbours that Republicans were on their way to burn them out. His neighbours fled, taking what belongings they could carry, and Wesley and his ailing parents were left facing a Republican mob. His mother and father watched, helpless, as the mob beat him and put a revolver to his head, chanting, 'Kill the Orange bastards.' Wesley said one Catholic woman who lived in the same street shouted at the mob, 'Leave him alone, he's only a big softie who looks after his ma and da.'

The mob did let him go and he walked up the street, away from the home and area he loved, pushing his mother in a wheelchair and with his father holding his hand. He told me he cried as he made that last journey from Farringdon Gardens, the place he always called home. I listened to him sobbing as he told me his story in the front room of our family home. I felt pity for the man as he related how he thought he was going to die, but pity turned to anger when he said he thought his father would die from the shock. Wesley's experience touched a raw nerve. I was furious.

This sectarian attack on my family sowed the seeds of hatred and resentment that would stay with me for most of my adult life. The seeds took root, pushing me nearer and nearer to the big paramilitary organisations. I began to take an interest in what was going on around me. I bought newspapers and listened to news bulletins. I familiarised myself with the deteriorating situation. I vowed to never forget the sobs of a grown man who thought that he was going to die and his parents would be left with no one to care for them. I knew someone, somewhere sanctioned this activity and, just like the school bullies I despised, they had to be sorted out.

But worse was to come. Once again my family would be touched by sectarian violence and this time loved ones would be injured and killed. Harry Beggs and his sister, Doreen Beggs, were frequent visitors to our family home. Harry, an educated young man, was blown to bits in the electricity showroom where he worked in August 1971. He died saving the lives of two young female colleagues. Seven months later Doreen took her two little children into the city centre on a Saturday afternoon shopping trip. They stopped for some dinner in the Abercorn, a popular restaurant in Cornmarket. It was 4.30 and the place was packed with women and kids. A bomb ripped through the restaurant, killing two women and injuring seventy others. Doreen and her two youngsters were among the seriously wounded, suffering severe leg injuries. The bomb was planted by members of West Belfast's 1st Battalion of the IRA, who hid it under a table. The warning was phoned from a pub on the Falls Road, just two minutes before the bomb went off. The two women who died were Catholics.

When the IRA blew up a popular restaurant in Belfast city centre they pushed me into the arms of the UDA. I knew, when that bomb went off in March 1972, that I was on a path of no return that would eventually take me to prison, or to my death.

Loyalist

When I was just a boy
This bloody war was begun
With a rebellious violence
Which killed and stunned.
Indiscriminate terrorists
Still slash and scar
With sectarian attacks
On Protestant bars.
Bombs of destruction
Tear the heart out of my city.
Bloody Friday, Enniskillen,
They never showed any pity.
Republican death squads
Spawned from hell.
In ethnic-cleansing, they do excel.
These hooded cowards
With hate-filled eyes
Create the horror
Ignore the cries.
Now a man
I've answered the call.
I am an Ulster Freedom Fighter, defender of all.

4

FOR GOD AND ULSTER

TOMMY HERRON WATCHED MY FLOURISHING STREET CAREER WITH INTEREST. HE LIVED ON THE BRANIEL ESTATE AND SAW POTENTIAL IN THE ROUGH-AND-TOUGH KID WHO EXCELLED IN HIS ROLE AS LEADER OF THE TARTAN GANG. I sorted out the 'anti-socials', those who terrorised old people, trashed their neighbours' properties and were a nuisance in the area. I gave offenders one chance. They were warned verbally, but there were no second chances. I never 'kneecapped' anyone, but beatings were a regular occurrence. Tommy Herron later told me it was my ability to keep the anti-socials under control that brought me to his attention. He said he was impressed with my street skills, which belonged to a man older than sixteen.

A one-time security guard, Herron was a powerful and ruthless man who ran the East Belfast brigade of the UDA from a tiny office on the Newtownards Road. He was also vice-chairman of the Association, and this made him one of the most important and powerful figures in the early development of the UDA. He was a big, muscular man and always expensively dressed in a suit and tie and a long camel coat. Herron appeared frequently on television and gave countless press conferences, sometimes in a combat jacket and forage cap, at that time the standard UDA uniform. He was abrupt and he was rash, and he liked to shout and raise his voice, but when he talked, he talked sense. When Tommy Herron spoke I sat up and took notice.

I first met him in 1972. Although it was thirty years ago, I can still see him in my mind's eye. It was a weekend evening in early summer when his car pulled up. In the middle of the Braniel estate was a small grassed area where kids would play and teenagers would congregate. I had my Alsatian, Wolf, with me. About ten of us, including a couple of girls, were larking about, when a silver Zodiac car pulled up alongside us and stopped. A man wearing a sharp suit got out, followed by two men. They wore dark glasses and were obviously there as personal security. The man in the sharp suit approached me, looked at me and then finally addressed me.

'Hello, kid, I want a word with you.'

I didn't answer him. I had no idea who he was. He spoke again.

'Listen, kid, I'm moving into the area. I know you live in Ravenswood Park. I know it's your area. What's it like to live here?'

I didn't know who the man was, but he looked important. His car was flash; he had expensive clothes and two bodyguards. Whoever he was, he knew my name and where I lived. He handed me an address in Ravenswood Crescent and instructed me to visit over the following weeks. I had no intention of going anywhere near his house. Two weeks later I found out who he was. He was on television, wearing a combat jacket, forage cap and dark glasses. The TV reporter addressed him as Tommy Herron, UDA Supreme Commander. I was livid. I didn't want the UDA, whoever they were, moving into my turf. I asked around, to find out if anybody knew anything about him, but no one did, except one lad. The only thing he said was, Herron was capable of blowing your head off.

I still had the UDA leader's address, so I went to see him. I wanted to find out exactly what he wanted from me. I knew he wasn't just passing the time of day when he stopped his flash car to speak to me. He wanted something and I knew it involved me. I rang his doorbell and he invited me in. He came straight to the point.

'I want to start a squad in this area. I need good men. I have moved here from South Belfast to protect my family. I am looking for a couple of good guys. I think you will fit the bill. Do you have any mates that you trust?'

I told him I had several and he asked me another question.

'Can you use a gun?'

'Yes, I used to play at soldiers when I was an Army Cadet.'

'What about this?'

He handed me, butt first, a 9mm Star pistol. It was his own weapon. Before he handed it over he cocked it and flicked on the safety catch. I took the pistol, released the magazine, cocked it, cleared it, leaving the working parts open, reloaded and put the safety catch on. He said he was impressed.

'Will you meet me next week?' he asked.

I said I would, and he gave me a day and a time. It was to be at Davison's Quarry in the Castlereagh Hills. He told me to bring four friends but only guys I trusted. He also told me not to be late because he hated bad timekeepers. A week later I stood in Davison's Quarry with four friends, waiting for Herron to turn up. It was full of rusty car bodies and oil drums. The ground was overgrown and uneven, causing little pools of muddy water to form. My four mates and I skimmed stones as we waited. A blue van pulled up and one of Herron's gorillas got out first, followed by the UDA leader. Herron nodded at me and walked to the back of the van. He opened the door and out jumped a mongrel dog. It was an Alsatian cross and had a rope around its neck, which Herron used as a makeshift lead.

The rope took me by surprise. Knowing Herron loved dogs, I thought it was a strange way to restrain one of his prized pets. I squatted and rubbed the dog behind its ears and asked Herron what its name was. I was told that it didn't have a name and the dog didn't need one. It was a male dog and wanted to play. Herron let it off the lead and it made a dash for a stick thrown by one of the mates I brought with me. For thirty minutes Herron watched us play with the dog, then he called a halt to the play and ordered each of us to line up.

I was fourth in line.

He handed the first boy a .22-calibre pistol, a low-velocity weapon that makes very little noise but is deadly on impact. 'Do you want to be a member of the UDA?' he said.

'Yes, sir.'

'Shoot the dog.'

The boy's chin dropped. Herron never spoke.

'I can't do it, sir,' the lad said, and handed the gun back.

Herron moved to the second boy, then the third, but neither touched the weapon.

He handed it to me and repeated the order. I looked him straight in the eye, fully expecting him to say he was teasing and that he was just having a bit of fun, but I knew by his expression that he was serious and he wanted the animal shot on the spot. The gun still lay in the flat of his palm, barrel pointing away from me. I took it and released the safety catch.

My mates were looking at me, then at Herron and back to me again. The dog was in front of me. It was panting, its tongue hanging out. Its tail wagged back and forth. It took me just seconds to lift that gun and aim it at the dog's head. To my left I could hear one mate shouting, 'No, Flint, don't kill it, don't do that', but I blanked out his words. I distracted the dog by shouting, 'What's that?' and as it looked away I pulled the trigger, putting a bullet into its head. The dog dropped, spun around on the ground, shuddered for a few seconds and then lay still. I could see a trickle of blood seeping from under its crumpled body. Just a few minutes ago it was playing with me. It believed I was a friend. I heard a scream, which pulled me back from my thoughts, and I looked behind me. My mates had bolted in horror. The gun was still in my hand. I handed it back to Herron. He said nothing. His face was expressionless. I spoke first.

'I love dogs. I didn't want to kill it.'

'Why did you raise your hand and cover your face, Flint?'

I had used my hand as a visor to protect my face, eyes and mouth from the blood and tissue that would shoot out when the bullet entered the dog's head. The animal was at point-blank range.

'I didn't want bits of brain and skull spraying my face.'

'The dog was a test. You did well.'

I didn't feel that I did well. I felt terrible. I'd killed a living thing. I'd killed an animal that had a face and eyes and thought I was its friend. Herron got back into his van and rolled down the window. He said to me, 'If you couldn't kill the dog, then you're not capable of killing a human being.' And with that he was gone.

The following week I was sworn into the UDA. The ceremony took place in Braniel community centre. The only people present were Herron and myself and two guards of honour who wore the obligatory black leather jacket and sunglasses. They stood either side of a small table draped with the Union Jack. On top were a Bible and a Webley pistol. None of the four mates I'd brought to the quarry that day had impressed Herron, so I was on my own. We weren't disturbed. Tommy had fixed it with the guy who ran the community hall that we would have our privacy for the fifteen minutes it took to swear me in. Herron spoke to me for an hour beforehand. He ordered me to march in and stand to attention in front of him. He told me exactly what to say during the ceremony.

'You understand what you are committing to.'

'Yes, I want to defend my community, my family and my country.'

'Do you know what that means? It doesn't make you a hero. When you make this commitment, there are only two outcomes: death or prison. Do you understand that you could end up being killed or spending the rest of your life behind bars? Do you understand that there are no medals, no victory salutes and no pats on the back?'

Herron handed me the Webley and the Bible. I swore on the open Bible to be a faithful and honourable member of the Ulster Defence Association. I swore to defend my community. I promised to be a guardian of my people and to fight to protect them with every drop of my Loyalist blood. The service was over in minutes. I felt good. I was on a high. I was swept away by the romanticism of it all. It didn't enter my head that I had just committed myself to a life of violence. I was in love with the idea of being the great defender, the knight in shining armour looking after my people.

My training began the following week in Davison's Quarry, initially with Herron's two weapons, the Star and a shotgun. Tommy Herron was a colourful and enigmatic character and I enjoyed his company. He also loved dogs and had a massive pure black Alsatian called Satan. He was my mentor and taught me everything I know about being a paramilitary. He schooled me in firearms, explosives and forensics. He taught me the special skills that I have used all my active-service life. He trained me in interrogation and how to survive it.

From the day I was sworn in, it was Herron who trained me. He taught me how to shoot but admitted I had little to learn. He honed my pistol, revolver, rifle and shotgun skills. He showed me how to open and split a shotgun cartridge and smear it with axle grease so that it would effortlessly punch through reinforced doors and metal. He showed me how to doctor cartridges and make them more deadly by opening the top and dripping candle wax into it, then closing the cartridge again. The bullet would remain intact on impact and cause horrific wounds to human flesh. Undoctored cartridges spread on impact, which makes them less deadly. They injure but don't always kill. Herron was shown how to make other deadly cartridges by using mercury from a thermometer or garlic purée in the tip of the cartridge. On entering the flesh the garlic or mercury gets into the bloodstream and causes blood poisoning within seconds.

Just weeks after being sworn into the UDA, I learned what Tommy Herron was capable of. It was one of my many and regular training days and, as usual, it was just the two of us in the derelict quarry. I got to work setting up the oil drums to practise my shooting skills and, as I worked, Herron went to the boot of his Zodiac and took out his shotgun. I had my back to him and glanced round when I heard him shout at me, 'You know kid, you should never trust anyone in this game.'

His words stopped me in my tracks but his actions – raising the shotgun to his shoulder and levelling the gun at me – almost stopped my heart. I heard the crack as the gun went off, then the wall of pain as it hit me in the chest. Tommy Herron, my mentor and my friend, had shot me. I saw it coming. I knew he was going to use the gun on me but I was powerless to do anything. It happened in a split second. I didn't even have time to duck or drop to the ground. The force of the impact threw me backwards and I landed on my back with a rough thud. I lay on the ground, immobilised by pain, thinking I was seriously injured and about to die. My body felt like it had been hit with a sledgehammer. I forced my arm to move, putting my hand on the wound to stop the flow of blood, but there was none. There wasn't even a tear or rip in the denim jacket I was wearing. I sat up, my body still throbbing, and looked at the ground. There was a pool of dry rice mixed in with the dirt and the sand. I had no idea how the white rice came to be scattered around my body. Meanwhile, Tommy Herron never took his eyes off me. I stood up, awkwardly and with a lot of difficulty, and began a slow hobble towards Herron and the quarry entrance. As I passed him I said, 'Fuck you and fuck this.'

Herron started to laugh. It echoed around the quarry face and he shouted after me, 'Come back, kid, it's all part of your training.' When I looked back to where he was standing, Herron was doubled over with laughter.

Later he told me he had doctored the shotgun cartridge to teach me a lesson – a lesson that could mean the difference between being done for robbery and being done for murder. One of my duties as a UDA volunteer was the procurement of funds and that meant robbing banks and post offices. With robberies come have-a-go heroes, and Herron warned me that doctoring a shotgun cartridge and filling it with grains of rice would be the difference between stunning and immobilising a wannabe hero and killing them.

Herron introduced me to a secret gun club in North Down. I was just seventeen years old. Judges, barristers and policemen were among the members of this state-of-the-art shooting gallery. The G-Club was underground, hidden beneath a well-known local landmark. Membership was closed: you couldn't walk in off the street and join. It didn't advertise: you had to be invited. The club had a rifle range, moving targets and pop-up targets and was equipped with .303 rifles and .22 target pistols.

Through Herron I learnt to be an assassin. I learnt to be an independent soldier. He taught me how to kill without a gun. He showed me how to garrotte a person with the brake cable of a pushbike by looping it in a specific way. It was foolproof and guaranteed to cause instant death. I learnt about anatomy and how to use knives. He showed me how to stab by inserting the knife and twisting up and in. Just sticking a blade into flesh would not cause death, he told me. You have to know where the vital organs are and puncture them in order to precipitate death. I was shown that any instrument and any implement could be turned into a deadly weapon. Perspex can be fashioned into a blade and a piece of plastic or wood such as a knitting needle or even a pencil can be used to kill. He showed me the exact spot on the neck to kill someone by what he called 'scrambling their brains'. The procedure didn't cause a massive blood loss, just a tiny surface puncture mark.

Herron taught me to be self-sufficient when I was on the road. Even when staying in trusted safe houses there were golden rules: carry your own bed linen and your own towels, wear Vaseline on eyebrows and eyelashes, coat the hair in gel or wax, wear tight-fitting kitchen gloves at all times, eat Mars bar sandwiches and only drink water. He told me to carry plastic bags and take my solid waste home and burn all clothes after an operation including footwear. Once back from active service, burn everything.

He pioneered interrogation schools by bringing hand-picked men from other areas to train me in surviving long, tough sessions at the hands of the RUC. His technique was simple. He ordered two volunteers to be the security forces, who would try to get a confession from me, the pretend suspect. He would stand in a corner of the room and watch, but he never spoke. The 'cops' would beat, kick and threaten me. They split my lip, my internal organs were kicked and my neck was almost broken with the weight of heavy, wet towels lashed across it. Sometimes someone's nose would get broken in these exercises. Herron had recreated what happened in holding centres like Castlereagh. The volunteers worked in pairs: good cop and bad cop. One would shout abuse and scream threats to get a result. The other would calmly try to reason and appeal to my vulnerable side. The sole object of the exercise was to not reveal the phrase given by Herron at the start of the session. Grown men broke down. I broke down.

It was elite services training, I know that now. Herron had turned me into an assassin primed for every eventuality and every situation. He taught me skills for protecting myself but he was also thinking of his own safety. He had me earmarked for my first job in the UDA – as his bodyguard.

I asked him from whom or what he needed protection.

He answered, 'Everybody, kid, especially our own.'

5

TOMMY HERRON

WHEN I WASN'T IN THE QUARRY BEING TRAINED I SPENT MOST OF MY TIME AT TOMMY HERRON'S HOME, SITTING ON THE STAIRS LISTENING, LEARNING AND TALKING TO HIM. He liked the stairs. He called them his neutral space and he always kept his legally held weapon within reach. Herron confessed that he was on constant alert for a gunman who might break in his front door and open fire. He would laugh and say he would do his best to blow their brains out first. Many of my new associates thought he was bad-tempered, stern, unapproachable and unpredictable. To me he was a father figure. He took a personal interest in my fledgling UDA career and I wanted to impress him. He singled me out for special attention and I wanted to repay the compliment. Under his guardianship, I thrived.

With Herron's guidance my training became more intense and more specialised. He taught me martial arts and unarmed combat. He taught me how to punch someone in the heart to stop it beating and cause rapid death. In his mind the business of killing had to be swift and it had to be clean. I asked Herron where he learnt his skills and he just laughed in my face and told me to mind my own fucking business. To this day I believe he was a trained assassin and can only speculate as to where he learnt the skills he handed down to me.

It may seem unbelievable to some but Herron had a soft side and he liked to look after those he cared about and who were close to him. One day, as we practised shooting in the quarry, he said to me, 'If you are ever in trouble and you need to leave Northern Ireland, call this number.' On the paper was a name and a London telephone number. When I rang it a female voice answered. I asked for the person and was told he wasn't available but to ring back on a certain day and at a certain time. When I finally spoke to the man, I told him I was a friend of Tommy Herron's and that he'd given me the name and number plus a guarantee of help if ever it was needed. The voice on the other end of the phone said he could find me work anywhere in the world. He said he supplied top-grade 'security' for select clients all over the world. He asked whether I wanted to be on his books and I said yes. The man was hiring mercenaries.

I was enjoying my new life in the ranks of the UDA. I felt I had found what was missing in my life. In the first weeks after joining very little was asked of me by my superiors. I knew that time would change that. I knew it was inevitable that I would soon be on the road on active service. In the meantime I shadowed Tommy Herron. While I acted as his bodyguard, I was also learning. He had four men acting as his personal security, including me, and he rotated us at random.

I chanced upon a photograph of Herron recently and it awakened old memories. He's been dead almost thirty years now but I can still hear his gruff voice. It was an old newspaper cutting illustrated by a very bad picture. In it he is frowning and looks like he is ready to blow someone's head off. The photo revealed nothing about his personality and character. Herron was a hothead. He was rash and quick-tempered and probably *would* have blown someone's head off, but he was also an intelligent and astute soldier. Neither the article nor the photograph showed anything of the Herron I knew and portrayed nothing of the man I remember, a man with a sharp brain, impressive intellect and remarkable powers of persuasion. Listening to Tommy speak, I really believed anything and everything was possible. Even the media were seduced by his charisma. Journalists flocked to his press briefings. He knew how to handle them and when he held court, anything was possible. Once he produced rubber bullets that he said had been doctored by the British Army. There had been rioting in East Belfast and four bullets were found with razor blades, four-inch nails and batteries attached to them. One was even split and rebuilt using fine wire. On impact it would have turned into a deadly bolas.

We spent a lot of time together in Davison's Quarry and he liked to show off his shooting skills. He loved emptying magazine after magazine into oil drums and the bodies of scrapped cars. He had a good eye and could even shoot in circles or in rows. He would roll up his sleeves, coolly take aim and say to me, 'Watch this.' He was a first-class shot.

The Ulster Defence Association remains one of Ulster's biggest paramilitary organisations and was legal until 1992, when the then Secretary of State, Sir Patrick Mayhew, proscribed it. It was formed in 1971, when Ulster was on the brink of all-out civil war, as an umbrella body for Loyalist 'defence associations' springing up in Protestant areas of Belfast, Lisburn, Newtownabbey and Dundonald. It adopted a motto, *Quis Separabit*, roughly translated as 'None Shall Divide Us', and the UDA quickly became a formidable force in Loyalist districts. Many young Loyalists saw the UDA as a replacement for the B Specials, a part-time paramilitary force that was abolished in 1969, and offered their support by the truckload. The UDA was distinctly working class and organised along military lines. When I joined, in 1972, it had a membership of forty thousand.

The UDA has had a varied history and its thirty-year existence is littered with violence, strong-arm tactics in support of Loyalist protests and journeys into political thinking. Tommy Herron was an architect of all of these things, especially the Loyalist street protests. He told me he got a kick out of watching thousands of men assembling in combat gear and making themselves ready for action. In 1972 thousands of UDA men, many wearing masks, marched through Belfast city centre. I was one of them. Herron was one of the chief organisers. As I walked with my fellow Loyalists I felt I was living up to the solemn promise I'd recently made. I was making a difference. I was making a contribution. I was a defender of my community and here was the proof: my combat uniform and mask and a triumphant march through the streets of my city.

Herron was once again at the helm in July 1972, when plans to erect barricades between the Springfield Road and Shankill Road led to eight thousand UDA men, in full uniform and carrying iron bars, confronting three hundred members of the security forces. It was an ugly situation, the Protestant community turning on its police force. Herron regarded the offensive as a spectacular example of the speed and efficiency that an 'army' could be assembled at short notice. It was his intention to build on this in the months to come but his murder changed everything.

He particularly hated the Welsh Guards because they called all of us 'Paddies'. He always encouraged us to get a riot going with them. Herron had a master plan for his young recruits: you get caught, you get sent to prison and you then get to finish the rest of your training in the 'University of Terror' – Long Kesh.

In my new role as a UDA volunteer many things were expected

of me, including the procurement of funds and weapons. That meant I stole cars and took part in robberies. Three weeks before my seventeenth birthday I appeared before a resident Magistrate at Newtownards Petty Sessions. I was found guilty of handling stolen goods from two robberies and was given a twelve-month conditional discharge and ordered to pay compensation. My new life had begun.

No sooner had I walked from Newtownards Court when my superiors ordered me to steal weapons and ammunition from a sports shop in Comber, County Down. An accomplice stole a car; we broke into the shop after dark and took three shotguns and several thousand rounds of ammunition. I only got caught because my sidekick, high on adrenalin after the robbery, couldn't keep his mouth shut. He bragged about the robbery to his girlfriend, she told her father, who was a policeman, and he was lifted and questioned. He even squealed on me. I got lifted and was charged. He went to court and got a suspended sentence. I went to court, Saintfield Petty Sessions, in June 1972, and was charged with possession of firearms and ammunition. I pleaded guilty.

Judge Martin McBirney asked me why I stole guns and bullets and I told him I needed to sell them to make a few quid to pay a debt. I didn't tell him I was a member of the UDA and had been ordered to steal the guns by my superiors because they were needed for war. I was sentenced to six months in prison. Judge McBirney ordered prison because I was under licence from my last court appearance. He died very shortly afterwards when a Provo unit burst into his home and shot him dead as he ate breakfast with his wife.

My first experience of jail was the Women's Prison in Armagh. I was on remand before being moved to Long Kesh, and shared a cell with two Republicans. I was the only Loyalist prisoner there. One of my cellmates, Fish, was doing time for a sniper attack using an M1 carbine on the Army sangar at Ardoyne. The three of us even played football together in the yard. The other two knew I was a Protestant because my cell card had my name and religion written on it, but I told them I was in for theft and they left me alone. Given my age, I should have been sent to Millisle Young Offenders Centre, but the police knew I was a bad boy and had me sent to the Kesh.

There I remember entering one of the large Nissen huts, which held up to forty prisoners. It was a mixed unit and we were kept in these 'holding' areas while we waited to be claimed by our organisations. There were groups of mostly young lads huddled together. In those days new prisoners were not immediately claimed by their groups. Each of us had to be assessed by men on the inside who passed messages to men on the outside to make sure we were who we said we were and not Special Branch plants. A network of coded messages confirmed our identities. While we waited for confirmation, Loyalists and Republicans lived together in the same huts. It was survival, but strangely there were never any cases of one side assaulting the other.

Within four weeks of entering Long Kesh I was accepted by the UDA leadership and moved to the Loyalist compounds. I was just a young lad and here I was doing my six months alongside men doing big time for murder and attempted murder. I never met Gusty Spence, but I did hear plenty about him. I did see him once, though, striding through the prison in a three-piece suit carrying a briefcase and accompanied by two prison officials. I thought he was one of the prison directors until someone put me straight. Spence, a UVF volunteer, was overall commander of the Loyalist internees and serving twenty years for the murder of Peter Ward. He was a strict disciplinarian and ran the University of Terror along military lines. Spence was deeply resented by the UDA prisoners. We saw him as hijacking the whole Loyalist cause.

I served four months before I was released. Those four months turned me into a man – a cliché but true. I learnt things in the Kesh

I couldn't have learnt outside, and they complemented my training under Tommy Herron. The first thing I learnt was that I was militarily enthusiastic but naive. I spent my four months listening and learning from those who had practical skills I could use on my release. Through these men I learnt about active service. I learnt about explosives from bomb makers. I learnt patience by simply helping veteran Loyalist John Havern with his leatherwork. I learnt about my own history and also the history of my enemies. I now had clarity, determination and focus. I was back on the streets of East Belfast in October 1972 ready for action.

I was only out of prison three months when I was back behind bars. I needed a getaway car and was charged with 'taking and driving away a motor vehicle' and fined two hundred pounds. After refusing to pay the fine I was given a three-month sentence. I deliberately made the decision to go to jail rather than pay. I needed time away from the paramilitaries. I needed to step back. A teenager called Michael Wilson had been shot dead. He was Tommy Herron's young brother-in-law and I had alarm bells ringing very loudly in my head.

Michael Wilson was ambushed as he slept in the house he shared with his sister, Hillary, and Herron. He was actually sleeping in Herron's bed at the time because after an attack by a group of nationalists on the Short Strand his arm and shoulder were in plaster and his single bed was too small for the cast. Swapping bedrooms cost him his life. Two gunmen appeared at the Herrons' front door in Ravenswood Crescent, asked for Tommy and were told by his wife he wasn't in. Refusing to take no for an answer, they pushed their way into the hall and again asked for Tommy. His panic-stricken wife said he was out. One gunman held her in the front hall, put a gun to her head and the other rushed upstairs. He shot the sleeping Michael Wilson in the mistaken belief he was Herron. I was on an errand to the local shop and as I returned to the house saw the two men making their escape. One even got on a passing bus. The police were on the scene in seconds. Hillary was standing in the front garden screaming her head off. The children were running around the garden in a panic and a policeman was trying to catch them. The police wouldn't let me into the house.

The death of the eighteen-year-old Wilson devastated Herron. Afterwards he went around in a daze. There was speculation that he knew about the killing and even organised it, but I know this to be untrue. The rumour was started by Loyalists in South Belfast who couldn't wait to dance on Herron's grave. Before Wilson was even buried, those same men had already hatched a plan to kill Herron himself. I asked him if he wanted retaliation against the IRA for the death of Wilson. I told him it was easily organised. He said just one thing to me: 'Wrong side, kid.'

Herron now became a stranger to me; he wasn't the man I'd known. He told me he was resigned to his own death and knew it was only a matter of time before his brother-in-law's killers caught up with him. He actually excused me from my bodyguard duties, saying he didn't need me any more. Disappear and keep your head down, he told me. Herron, who never left home without his Star pistol, started to go out without it. He even wandered the streets of East Belfast without security or his bodyguards.

Tommy Herron died in September 1973, three months after his brother-in-law, ambushed by Loyalists on a quiet road in County Down. His body was found outside Drumbo and his legally held firearm was still in its holster. He had taken a lift with someone he knew and obviously trusted. They drove for a few miles but a gunman was secretly hidden in the boot. As soon as the car stopped, the gunman pushed the back seat forward and shot him in the head. Herron didn't stand a chance. His body was dumped in a lonely ditch and lay undiscovered for days.

Many of his close associates fled to England, America and even Australia, terrified they would be next. I wanted retribution for his death. I started to look for targets and went to Shandon golf course, where arms had been stashed, but the hide had been emptied. I had no weapons. The Braniel unit had run away and I was the last remaining member of the unit that Herron had set up.

I went to Herron's funeral. The gunmen were there, and the men who organised his execution. The South Belfast brigade wanted Herron removed from the picture and had ganged up on other brigades to get their way. To convince the other members of the UDA's Inner Council, South Belfast put out a rumour that the American journalist Herron that was romantically involved with was a CIA plant. The rumour took on a life of its own and it freaked out the UDA hierarchy. It was the final nail in Herron's coffin.

Many years later I was told that the two gunmen were ordered by their brigadier to kill Herron or face death themselves. In the UDA, volunteers did what they were told.

6

RED HAND COMMANDO

WITH HERRON'S DEATH, THE BRANIEL UDA WAS DECIMATED. FOR ME IT WAS TIME TO BECOME ANONYMOUS AND INVISIBLE. I'd listened to Herron's advice, and now I made a decision to disappear. I never resigned or left the UDA; I removed myself from the picture by seconding myself to the Red Hand Commando's newly formed unit in the Braniel. The Red Hand Commando, founded in 1972, was close to the UVF and limited its territory to Belfast.

Sammy Cinnamond was the Commander of the Red Hand Commando on the estate. He was a good Loyalist and a good friend. He made the initial approach by saying he was sorry to hear about the death of Tommy Herron. He then asked me what my immediate plans were. I told him I didn't have any. He persisted with his questioning and asked if I was staying in the area. He then came straight to the point: was I interested in crossing over to the Red Hand Commando?

The Red Hand Commando met in Braniel Community

Centre once a week and its midweek slot was sandwiched between disco-dancing classes and other community activities. They called themselves the Braniel Fishing and Shooting Club and had a notice pinned up in the reception area. There were thirty men in the group, including an RUC reservist and a former British Army soldier.

I went along to a meeting, but that first night I told Sammy Cinnamond that I couldn't swear an oath of allegiance to the Red Hand because I'd already sworn to remain a member of the UDA until the day I died. But he said that was fine and I could make a solemn promise to the Red Hand instead. He explained that he'd fixed it with a UDA brigadier 'up the country' so that I could be seconded to the Red Hand for as long as I wanted. All Cinnamond insisted on was that I put my hand on the Bible, pick up the Walther gun and swear an oath to 'never betray my Loyalist comrades'.

I did make that promise. I swore on the open Bible to never betray my brothers-in-arms. I thought of Tommy Herron and hoped he wouldn't think I had let him down by moving sideways. And as I said those words I hoped he understood that although I was now 'UDA deactivated', my promise to protect my community and my people would continue under a different guise. It was January 1974, four months after Herron's death.

After the ceremony a suitcase was dragged from behind a chair. Inside was a tartan blanket and underneath the blanket was an assortment of 'old rattlies' that had been secretly made at the Harland & Wolff shipyard. Cinnamond nodded at them and said, 'That's your equipment, that's what you need to do your job.' I was introduced to another man, called 'the Armourer' because he was in charge of the unit's weapons. He was a former British Army soldier and an expert bomb maker. The IRA was targeting Protestant bars almost every night and the Braniel Red Hand Commando retaliated. The Armourer masterminded the unit's city-centre bombing campaign, including attacks on the nationalist bars Paddy Lamb's and the Hillfoot. He was very skilled and didn't need large amounts of explosives to create a big bang. He looked at the building to assess exactly what type of explosive and how much was needed and where it should be placed for maximum impact. The Armourer could 'car park' buildings with the smallest bombs.

The Red Hand Commando had a small office on the Upper Newtownards Road and one of my first duties for the group was protecting William Craig, the leader of the Vanguard Unionist Progressive Party. Craig had no idea I shadowed him. I was always 'suitably attired' and for a year I shadowed him when he attended and addressed VUPP meetings. The party was mostly ex-members of the Ulster Unionist Party who were disillusioned with the policies of its leaders, Terence O'Neill, James Chichester Clarke and Brian Faulkner. Craig, an MP for East Belfast, was also a former Home Affairs Minister in the 1966 Stormont government.

In 1976, I married Marlene Leckey. Together we had three sons – Michael, Jason and Gary – but within two years the marriage started to break down. I was away a lot on active service, and, with all the late nights and weekends away, it became very difficult for her. I left the marital home after two years of marriage and move into rented accommodation. We could not be officially divorced until a legal timeframe had elapsed, and in 1983 we divorced on the grounds of my unreasonable behaviour. By then, I was living with the woman who would become my second wife, Leigh-Ann Shaw.

In 1978, I took six months off from the Red Hand and joined the Royal Irish Regiment at Ballymena. I did so with the permission of my superiors and to do a specific job. I joined to learn how to use anti-tank weaponry because a shipment was due, although at the time I did not know this. When the Army asked me why I wanted to join, I said I fancied a change of career. When I asked if we could train on anti-tank weapons, I was told those munitions were at least a year away. Six months was the minimum amount of service permitted, and I made a decision to use my time wisely to forge a network of contacts that I could call on in the months and years ahead.

Sammy Cinnamond was a quiet and logical man. He once asked me how I felt about the Catholic families who lived on the Braniel. Even though it was a Protestant housing estate, thirteen Catholic families were still choosing to live there. In my eyes, I told him, those families were not a problem, and I was being truthful. I was thinking of the Maines, an old couple who lived near my mother. I told Sammy that I didn't want anyone touching them because they were quiet, good, church-going people. Sammy agreed and said, 'The thirteen Roman Catholic families are very welcome in the Braniel. No harm will come to them and they are safe – that is until the day the IRA comes into this area and ambushes a Protestant family. They are my insurance policy and, just like an insurance policy, if I have to cash it in I will.' Sammy didn't elaborate but I got his drift. I knew he was talking about retaliation if anything happened to a Loyalist family on the estate.

Through Sammy Cinnamond and the Red Hand Commando I was introduced to two other men, John McKeague and John Bingham. I met McKeague just once, in a Loyalist club on the Ravenhill Road. Sammy introduced us and McKeague and I spoke for a few minutes. I was initially taken aback by his shock of blond hair but immediately understood why people said he was a member of the Red Handbag Commando. McKeague was blatantly homosexual. A hard-working Loyalist, he even printed his own political papers on his own press and he ran the Woodvale Defence Association like a military operation.

John Bingham was a different sort of operator. He was the West Belfast Commander of the UVF, which had strong links to the Red Hand Commando. Sammy had made the initial introductions but then given me free rein to initially liaise and work with him.

Bingham was a pigeon fancier and our first meeting was conducted in the pigeon shed at the back of his home in Ballysillan. He wanted to exchange ideas with me. As we chatted we discovered we had a mutual interest in dogs and operationally our work had crossed over in previous years. We had a lot in common. He asked me to be present at a meeting scheduled for the following week. He added that it was important for me to meet this group of people. I agreed. I wanted to work with this man.

One weekday morning Bingham took me to a house on the outskirts of Belfast. As we travelled there he told me I had to make a presentation to three educated, wealthy, right-wing, German businessmen. They had travelled from Munich and were interested in the Loyalist cause. I had no time to prepare. I had to speak off the cuff. Bingham briefed me further, saying they had considerable funds at their disposal and were prepared to funnel the cash in our direction if we said the magic combination of words. The funding would be ours if we could give them harrowing first-hand accounts of our war with the IRA. It was my job to convince these men that Loyalist paramilitaries were a good investment.

We arrived at the designated place and the Germans were already waiting for us. I was initially taken aback by them. They had word-perfect English and were intelligent and articulate. I told them about Republican violence. I told them about Harry Beggs being blown to bits in the electricity showroom where he worked. I told them about his sister Doreen and her two kids, mutilated by a no-warning blast in the Abercorn restaurant. I told them about indiscriminate bombs and bullets and the targeting of our police force. They listened. They never spoke, except to say thank you. My presentation must have worked. The money was donated.

Three weeks later John Bingham, Sammy Cinnamond and I made another journey. It was a to a secret location on the outskirts of Belfast nicknamed 'The Farm'. By the time we arrived two Israeli visitors were already present. It was the second part of a two-tier deal first negotiated with the Germans. The two men were members of the elite Israeli intelligence agency Mossad, and, like the three German businessmen, wanted to help us. They told us that if we could supply the cash, they would supply the munitions. Already the funding had been confirmed and received from the Germans and we could now choose and pay for what we needed.

Bingham wanted me to go to Israel and link up with the two Mossad men to complete the deal. I told him I couldn't make the journey because I didn't have a passport. He opened the small case he was carrying. 'Which nationality do you want to be?' he said, and showed me seven passports with the official seals and stamps from the country of origin. There were two British, one Irish, two German and two from the Middle East. Bingham said he wanted to go but couldn't because MI5 were watching him. I declined the trip to Israel. If MI5 were watching Bingham, then I would be putting myself in the spotlight if I went in his place. He also tried to tempt me with a shorter trip, saying he needed someone to go to Brussels. I told him I was a military man and my job was working as an operative, on the road on active service. I said intelligence and research were not what I wanted to do.

To be honest, I was now getting involved in a different league and I felt out of my depth. I had seconded myself to the Red Hand in order to stay anonymous, not parade myself in front of the security and intelligence agencies. When I told Bingham that both of the trips were out of the question, he accepted my decision with no further questions. He made the journey to Israel himself. It was both a fact-finding mission and the final part of the arms deal. Bingham was so well organised that he was even furnished with 'end-user' certificates to help him get the munitions through customs.

Years later, after I was released from prison, an Israeli journalist interviewed me about the Peace Process. The reporter, a man in his sixties, said he knew me and that we had met previously. I shook my head and told him he must be mistaken because I didn't know any Israeli journalists. He whispered in my ear, 'I was one of the two men you met in the 1970s to discuss weapons.'

John Bingham was a humble man. He wasn't into the trappings of power and wealth, unlike many of the Loyalists holding rank at the time. Bingham was intelligent and astute. He lived in a working-class area and drove a clapped-out old banger. He liked to walk in the Black Mountain with his mother's Labrador and I would occasionally join him for walks, taking my pitbull terrier, Buster, with me. It was during one of these walks that the security forces photographed us. I didn't know about the picture until my arrest and the snap of us walking our dogs was shown to me by detectives.

I was coming up to twenty-three when the IRA bombed the La Mon House Hotel in February 1978. I was horrified at the slaughter of innocent people caused by the blast, which came without warning. The La Mon bombing was an important step in a journey that would eventually lead me to the Republican Plot at Milltown cemetery, almost ten years later, with grenades around my waist and a Browning in my hand. Twelve people were killed. Seven of the dead were women and there were three married couples among the toll. All the victims were attending the annual dinner dance of the Irish Collie Club. The hotel was packed with four hundred people enjoying a Friday night out when the place was turned into a fireball after the IRA attached cans of petrol to the window grilles. The device, set to go off in fifty-eight minutes, was designed to sweep through the room like a flame-thrower. As it went off, it blew out the window and sprayed the room with blazing petrol, which had been mixed with sugar to make sure it stuck to whatever it touched. The people inside didn't have a chance. Some stumbled out of the hotel or jumped out of the windows with their hair, skin and clothes on fire. Those who didn't survive shrivelled in the intense heat, so that their bodies looked like tiny children. It took two hours for six units of the fire brigade to bring the blaze under control. They were removing the bodies when I arrived on the scene.

I had been ordered to La Mon by my Red Hand superiors to see what I could do to help the emergency services. As I walked through the car park and saw the sad procession as firemen carried body after body from the charred and smoking building, I realised there was nothing I could do to help the living or the dead. Tarpaulin covered the dead. I wanted to see the carnage for myself. I don't know how I managed to get past the RUC patrol and through the cordoned-off area, but suddenly I was standing by a row of covered bodies. I gently pulled back one cover and quickly replaced it. It was a horrific sight. What I saw in those five seconds has stayed with me for the rest of my life. I can only describe it as looking like a lump of charred wood. I couldn't tell what gender the person was, there were no limbs and what was left of the face was a mouth wide open in a silent scream. I wondered what sort of person would do this to a human being. I could feel anger rising in the pit of my stomach. I wanted revenge. I wanted retribution of a similar kind. I was burning with rage and hatred for the people who had done this. I wanted the Republican community to pay dearly for this atrocity. I knew then that picking off a Catholic here or a nationalist there wasn't revenge. It had to be retaliation in kind, something with a massive body count and deaths in double figures. Republicans had brought war to our doorstep. I wanted to bring war to their doorsteps and I could find people to help me.

I spoke to Sammy Cinnamond and he advised me to sit tight, but I didn't agree with him. I told him about the charred remains of the young men and women. I told him La Mon was a sectarian strike and as Loyalists we were duty-bound to retaliate. He cautioned me to be patient and to not sink to the same depths as the IRA because that wasn't 'our style'.

Weeks went by. There was the sickening cycle of tit-for-tat shootings but nothing to match the horror of La Mon. In truth, the Red Hand was frightened of the public consequences of a big strike on the Republican community. In the late 1970s IRA bombs were going off at an alarming rate. I was frightened for my family and friends. When you left your home you ran the serious risk of getting injured or killed. I didn't want loved ones to live like this. The IRA had to be stopped. I saw the Provos as rabid dogs, and in civilised countries rabid dogs are destroyed on the spot. I didn't see my government or the authorities doing anything to stop these evil dogs of war. I thought back to when I was sixteen and had promised to defend my community in its hour of need.

My community was crying out for help. It was time for me to honour my promise.

7

NONE SHALL
DIVIDE US

I SPENT TEN YEARS SECONDED TO THE RED HAND COMMANDO, BUT IN 1984 I DECIDED IT WAS TIME TO REACTIVATE MYSELF WITH THE UDA, THE ORGANISATION I HAD SWORN ALLEGIANCE TO BACK IN MY TEENS. I had an interesting and informative time with the Red Hand, but I needed to get back to the UDA. My all-out war with Republicans was shifting up a gear. There were rumblings of a new joint agreement, a political process being cooked up by Whitehall bigwigs. There were even rumours that Dublin wanted a say in how Ulster was governed. I knew it was time for me to come in from the cold and my first port of call was Andy Tyrie, the Supreme Commander of the UDA.

Tyrie's office was in UDA headquarters in Gawn Street, on the corner of the Newtownards Road in East Belfast. Before I went in I had a good look at the buildings facing and overlooking the premises. One caught my eye. It was a flat above a bakery and it looked vacant because it had whited-out windows, but in one corner was a clean spot about the size of a fifty-pence piece. It intrigued me and I mentally noted it.

Surprisingly, the main door of UDA headquarters hadn't any security features. It wasn't even locked. Anybody, rival Loyalists or a Provo hit squad, could have walked in off the street, pushed open the door, climbed the stairs and shot their way into Tyrie's office. Inside the only other person present was Billy Elliot, brigadier of East Belfast. I stood at the desk and asked to see Tyrie. I was told that an impromptu meeting was impossible and I needed an appointment. I raised my voice, insisting I wanted to see Tyrie. Again I was refused. So I jumped the desk, but before I could even put my hand on the door, Tyrie was standing in front of me with a bewildered look on his face.

I spoke first. 'My name is Michael Stone. You don't know me. I am a former member of the UDA and although I have not been active for a few years I have always regarded myself as a UDA man.'

Tyrie asked me what I had in mind. I told him I wanted to return to military action in a unit based outside the city. I said Belfast, especially the east of the city, was out of the question. I gave him a telephone number where he could contact me and told him I expected to hear from him within days. Tyrie said he couldn't help me personally but that he would let the 'right people' know about my enquiries. Within forty-eight hours I had a phone number; it was the Mid-Ulster brigadier's. I met the brigadier and told him I wanted to assassinate known IRA terrorists and Sinn Fein activists. He told me that was 'very ambitious' and he would prefer me to concentrate on fund-raising. I told him to forget it. I said if I rob banks, then I keep the cash for myself.

I kept a low profile for four weeks before going back to see Tyrie. Nothing had changed at Gawn Street: UDA headquarters was still an open building and could have been attacked at any time. Tyrie said he was sorry that the contact didn't work out. He said he would put me in contact with others. As I left I told him he needed to sort out his in-house security. I explained that the building was open to attack, his life was compromised and he needed to check the building opposite with the whited-out windows. I told him it looked suspicious. Tyrie did have the flat above the bakery looked at. It was empty, but he later discovered the security forces did have a camera on UDA HQ, monitoring all movement of people coming and going.

Within weeks I had a new associate. He was the brigadier for South Belfast, John McMichael, and our paths first crossed at a venue in that part of the city. He was at a fund-raising event for prisoners and their families and I was at a different function. I refused to work with time-wasters or the tea-and-biscuits paramilitaries. I wanted to work with professionals. McMichael was a professional and we got on instantly. I knew I would enjoy working with him.

I am proud to call John McMichael my friend. He was a giant among Loyalist men but sadly he didn't get to fulfil his potential. He was an astute military and political man and for many years he played a magnificent double-hander as the UFF's Commander and also as leader of the UDA's foray into political activity. As brigadier for South Belfast he often discussed tactics and operations with me. We also discussed politics. McMichael knew that in the long term it was going to be politics and dialogue that would solve the Ulster problem. He was a man ahead of his time.

I am also proud of the fact that this solid and dependable soldier was one of my military associates. He was the only UDA man who had my home telephone number. We didn't meet regularly, both preferring impromptu arrangements. We spoke in code and devised a language based on doggy talk such as 'the dog's off his food' or 'the dog's gone walkies' to disguise our work. If I needed anything, McMichael would provide it because he knew I would use it. He knew I wasn't all talk and no action. His base was a snooker hall in Lisburn, County Antrim. It was from this location that I was given munitions used in some of my operations. McMichael never offered me 'sanctions', or targets. He never offered me intelligence. He never said, 'I want this man killed' or 'This man is your target.' Instead he would ask if I was operating in his area and, if so, would offer assistance. Sometimes he even pulled back his own men so as not to jeopardise my operations. We did discuss targets and we did discuss names seen on montages and intelligence files, but he never, ever handed me a file and told me that person had to be sanctioned.

I was given information on potential targets from the UFF's intelligence officers. The same intelligence was shared throughout the UFF, so the files I saw were also seen elsewhere. They always arrived in the same way, in an A4 brown manila envelope. I wore gloves when I was handling them. Inside were video grabs, pictures, Ordnance Survey maps, aerial shots and documents. There were also RUC mugshots and photographs of targets taken in prison. The files were very professional. I never questioned where they came from but it was obvious UFF intelligence officers had connections with the security forces. It wasn't my position to grill my colleagues and I never wanted to question where the intelligence came from. I accepted what was on offer and made the best use of it.

From day one I made it very clear to McMichael that I wouldn't undertake just any sanction. The target had to have Republican history and be a heavy hitter. He had to have a profile or hold rank. I insisted on having watertight evidence that all potential targets were active in the PIRA or Sinn Fein. I told him I wouldn't be sectarian and I wouldn't kill Catholics just for being Catholic. I said if I wanted to be sectarian I could have picked from hundreds of innocent Catholics walking the streets of Belfast. I told McMichael I wanted the IRA men and their political representatives in Sinn Fein. He laughed and said he liked my passion and commitment. There was no question of the UFF targeting innocent Catholics, McMichael pledged. He said the Catholic community had nothing to fear. I promised I would never be indiscriminate or sectarian, unlike the PIRA. I would never place a no-warning bomb among innocent civilians or randomly spray a place filled with nationalists.

8

REPUBLICAN TARGETS

OWEN CARRON WAS MY FIRST TARGET AS A REACTIVATED UDA MEMBER, AND I STALKED HIM FOR FOUR WEEKS. Carron was a Sinn Fein politician and a former MP for Fermanagh-South Tyrone. He first came to prominence as the election agent of the Republican hunger striker and martyr Bobby Sands. Ironically, Sands's cousin was a boyhood friend of mine. When Sands died in the Maze in May 1981, the first of ten IRA men to starve to death over the next four months, Carron stood in the Westminster by-election and won the seat. Although he had lost his seat in 1983 he remained a member of the Northern Ireland Assembly and had a constituency office in the centre of Enniskillen, which is where I planned to execute him.

McMichael agreed that Carron was a good political target. A UFF intelligence officer supplied me with his file and told me he was a leading Republican in the area. I knew Carron's life as well as Carron knew it himself. I knew every second of his day. I knew where he lived and had his full address. I knew he had two dogs, a cocker spaniel and a Labrador, and that there was a double garage to the left of the house as you looked at it. I knew that all over the house and garden he had the best security and surveillance equipment money could buy. He had cameras and sensors. He even had tin cans tied to a tripwire strung across the field at the back of his house to alert him to the security forces that watched his every move.

The UFF provided me with local contacts and a safe house. I ruled out attacking him at his home because he had too much security and I could not get close enough to kill him without being spotted or killed myself. My best option was his constituency advice clinic in the centre of Enniskillen. My own research showed the advice centre was the weakest link in his daily routine and the only place where I could get close enough to kill him. Carron's routine was simple. Every day he visited his advice centre with his associate James Joseph Murphy, nicknamed 'Mexican Joe' because of his long hair and droopy moustache.

I planned to kill Carron first and then Mexican Joe, and I wanted to assassinate them outside the office. I knew a girl worked on the reception desk and I knew I would also have to shoot her. If constituents were in the room, unfortunately they too would have to be shot. If I was forced to go inside it would be a clean sweep, clearing each room as I worked through the building. My weapons were a .45 semi-automatic Colt pistol loaded with dum-dum bullets and a sawn-off shotgun loaded with solid shot cartridges.

I knew something else about Owen Carron: he carried a personal issue weapon. It was a .22-calibre Star pistol and the RUC gave him a licence to carry it for his personal protection. As a former member of parliament it meant he was entitled to carry one. I know for a fact that he wanted a 9mm pistol but the RUC refused. He then asked for a .38 revolver and that too was refused by the RUC. He was eventually given a licence for the .22, one of the lowest-calibre weapons, and I knew he carried that. The Colt and the shotgun were more than able to take on a small .22 Star.

I chose Christmas Eve as the date and told my UFF associates to prepare a car to my exact specifications. Two cars were to be used in the operation: one a Ford Cortina legitimately owned by one of my accomplices who would later report it as stolen, and the second a stolen vehicle. Concrete blocks were placed in the boot of the Cortina and cushions filled with sand across the back window. It was the simplest and most effective way of bullet-proofing the car if the security forces opened fire.

I drove the car myself and parked opposite the Sinn Fein advice centre. My back-up man was parked a mile away, scanning the police airways with a special radio obtained from a member of the RUC. I'd chosen to do the hit alone by approaching Carron on foot, putting one round into his chest and a second into his head. I would use the pistol on Mexican Joe. I had a window of seconds to do the job. I did not want to have to go into the advice centre, but if I had to I would, and had mentally prepared myself for the possibility of shooting the young secretary.

I sat in the car and waited. There was no sign of Carron. Just then a group of workmen pulled up behind me in a van, took out a compressor and began their noisy work on the car park next door to the advice centre. I remember thinking that the noise of the drill would tone it down for me. Thirty minutes turned into sixty, and Carron still hadn't arrived. Neither had Mexican Joe. Just as I turned the ignition, my back-up man pulled up alongside me, told me to abort the operation and to get out of the area as fast as I could. When we met at a safe location he told me that Carron had been caught red-handed with an AK47. The news had been broadcast on the police frequency and picked up by my associate's scanner. I had got out in the nick of time because the RUC searched the advice centre just minutes after I left.

I distinctly remember the news footage of Carron as he was

released from Crumlin Road jail. He had been given bail to fight the Westminster by-election in the Fermanagh-South Tyrone constituency and I remember thinking the authorities were stupid to release him because the first chance he got he'd jump the border. Carron did go on the run in the Irish Republic and was captured, but the British government failed in their bid to extradite him. He claimed he was on a 'Michael Stone hit list' and the RUC were involved in wanting him killed. The Irish government listened and refused to extradite him. I regret that I did not assassinate Owen Carron. The fact he was caught with an automatic rifle was proof enough for me.

It was November 1984. The year was almost over and the UFF was responsible for just one death. Republicans had killed forty-nine people. I vowed that by New Year's Eve the UFF would be able to add at least one more figure to their year total. Nineteen eighty-five would bring a major change for the UFF. It would see the start of an all-out assault on the Republican movement. In the meantime I was frustrated. Carron hadn't worked out. I needed to kickstart the UFF's new campaign.

An intelligence officer gave me a montage of mugshots of ten men and asked me to pick one. I studied the ten faces and decided on number one. It was my intention to work my way through the whole sheet. Number one was Patrick Brady. I chose him on a Thursday evening. The following morning he was dead. Brady was a milk deliveryman for Kennedy Brothers' Dairy in South Belfast. He was thirty-five, married with two daughters and lived near the Upper Falls Road.

After I chose Brady, the intelligence officer handed me an individual file in a brown envelope. It was a substantial file and expertly put together. I told the UFF that I would only agree to the sanction if the file proved Brady was a legitimate target, otherwise I wouldn't do it. It contained photographs and documents confirming exactly what I needed to know. Brady was a legitimate target. He was a member of Sinn Fein. Some of the papers in his file were very professional. There were notes on people that he met and associated with, along with times and places. It gave the name of his wife and two daughters. Best of all were the grainy black and white photographs, grabbed from a video of the most recent Sinn Fein annual conference in Dublin, clearly showing Brady standing on stage beside Gerry Adams and Martin McGuinness.

The file also showed that Brady used his milk run to gather information in West Belfast. I agreed to the sanction. From the file, I had a clear profile of his every move, from house to car and car to work. It took him just five minutes to drive from his home in St James's Crescent in West Belfast to the dairy on the Boucher Road, where he would pick up his milk float and do his round. The file showed him to be a big man, at least twenty stone. I knew he wouldn't be able to run away from me. I was fit. If he did try to escape, I could catch him.

I burnt his file in a dustbin in my backyard and, as the flames destroyed the pictures and notes, I mentally chose my weapons. It had to be a big gun like a shotgun. It would take more than a revolver or a pistol to kill this heavy man. I chose a Remington 45 pistol and a Remington automatic shotgun using number-four cartridges. The weapons were sourced privately. I had two men to accompany me on the hit, one an experienced operator and a young lad who was to be blooded on his first sanction. The young driver and myself did a dry run the night before using a clean car. I told him nothing about the hit. I didn't want him to have any time to think about it. I assessed the possibility of killing the target at his home but decided against it. I knew I had a window of time to carry out the sanction. Luck was on my side. Milkmen started work early, and that meant my escape routes would be traffic-free and the security forces thin on the ground.

In the early hours of 16 November I made my way on foot to the nearby Stormont Hotel. I knew I could get a car in the hotel car park because the odd tourist and businessman chose the place for overnight stays. I picked a brown Ford Cortina, hot-wired it in seconds and calmly drove off, tooting my horn at the night watchman. He waved back, thinking I was a member of the night staff going home.

At Braniel Primary, I collected the first of my associates. The young lad was hiding in bushes and had the weapons that I had collected and given to him the night before. They were wrapped in a tartan blanket and placed on the back seat. I moved into the passenger seat and the youngster took the wheel. Full of enthusiasm, he drove off and asked what the job was. It was his first operation on active service and I didn't want to unnerve him. I told him it was a robbery and we were going to rob the payroll clerk who worked for the dairy on the Boucher Road. I explained to him the drill: we pull up, we park the car, we rob the dairy, we leave. Later, when the operation was completed, I would explain everything to him.

On the outskirts of the city we picked up the second member of the squad. I crawled into the back seat and he got in the front. Dressed in his trademark boiler suit, gloves and monkey hat, he was an experienced volunteer who knew the drill. If my gun failed, he would open fire on the target. If we were attacked by Republicans or the security forces, it was his job to return fire. He shocked me by announcing he wanted to get out of the car and couldn't go through with the operation. I looked at him and asked him to repeat what he'd said. He said he didn't want to be involved and wanted out of the car.

The driver started to slow down and I could hear the panic rising in his teenage voice when he asked what was wrong. The back-up man repeated his request. The car was doing fifty miles per hour. I told him if he wanted to go, then he was free to go; all he had to do was open the door and jump. I said the car wasn't slowing or stopping for him just because he had taken a fit of the 'girlies'. His hand was on the door handle. I told him to think about what he was doing and that he could change his mind, but he shook his head violently. I yelled at him to open the door and jump. And he did. He sprang from his seat on to the open road. I heard the bounce as he hit the tarmac but I didn't look back. He was big and ugly enough to look after himself.

He had let me down. I was determined that he wouldn't compromise the sanction. I was determined the target would be assassinated even with an unblooded volunteer as my deputy. The poor lad was confused and kept asking, 'What's up?' and 'Why did he panic?' I told him I would explain later. In fact, I had no idea why the back-up man chickened out and so had no explanation for the driver. The back-up man had been on sanctions before, but I was clueless about his behaviour. I put the pistol on the seat between the driver's legs, the barrel pointing forward. I felt his fear, so I joked with him about not moving in case he blew his testicles off. He laughed, but it was a nervous laugh.

We were on the Boucher Road and had arrived with time to spare. I told my driver we were looking for a white Volvo 340. It was still dark. I told the lad to drive to St James's Crescent and there we saw Brady's Volvo parked outside his red-brick terraced house. I explained that the man we wanted was a wages clerk who kept the payroll money overnight and we were going to jump him as he set off to work. A police Land Rover pulled up alongside us. I urged the youngster not to panic and to give a little nod of acknowledgement, and the Land Rover kept moving. We left St James's Crescent to take up position at the dairy, and parked directly opposite it. The radio was on, playing a tune called 'Blue Monday'. The volume shot up and the driver turned around to look at me, saying he loved the song and was going to buy the single later that day.

Out of the corner of my eye I caught the white Volvo and all my senses kicked in. The radio was flicked off. I told the driver to gently pull up alongside the car. This had to be timed to perfection. We couldn't linger. Brady had to be shot on the street. I couldn't follow him into the dairy. I had also been ordered to shoot Brady's young helper, and chose the lighter revolver for this part of the operation. The shotgun was loaded and sat on my lap. I waited for my moment. We pulled up alongside the Volvo. I wound down the window. At this point Brady was out of the car and at the passenger side. He couldn't lock his door from his side and walked round to the other side to use the key.

Brady's move gave me an extra five seconds. I heard the driver say, 'Let's go, jump out, that's our man', but I didn't jump out. I had a perfect line of vision. The barrel of the shotgun was perched on the open window. I could see the target clearly and he knew what was about to happen because he dropped his car keys and tried to run. I zeroed in with the Remington and fired. I hit him once in the chest and I heard him call for his mother. As he fell, I shot him once in the head. I twisted in the car seat and pointed the shotgun at his helper, who was standing with his mouth open in shock. He was standing under a street lamp and I could see his face clearly in the light. Paul Anthony Hughes was a very young, skinny kid who looked about twelve. I had my orders to shoot him, but I couldn't do it. I later learnt he was a stand-in helper. I fired one shot into the wall and screamed at the driver to get moving, boot to the floor.

Tyres spinning, we sped towards Tate's Avenue. I loaded the shotgun with three more cartridges. This extra firepower was a precaution in case we got into difficulties with the Army or police. Driving along Shaw's Bridge, we were passed by several police cars going at top speed, obviously making their way to the scene of the shooting. The driver never spoke. His hands were clamped to the steering wheel. It was a frosty morning and I felt the car slide from under us when we hit some black ice. I told the lad to slow down, but he never acknowledged me. The car kept gaining speed. I told him again to slow down, and the car skidded to a halt. He looked at me. He didn't speak. He just looked like he was about to burst into tears.

'The money … what about the robbery? I thought it was a robbery for the UFF.'

'You have done your first hit. We executed a Republican.'

I felt like a bastard. The youngster was thrown in at the deep end and had been blooded without even a second's notice. He just shook his head and drove on. We dumped the car in a lovers' lane near the Upper Braniel Road and walked across fields for a couple of miles before going our separate ways. I put the weapons in the hide on Shandon golf course. I arrived back home at 8am and changed my clothes in the shed. I always kept spare trousers and shirts there for a quick change after coming back from active service. Leigh-Ann was up, getting breakfast for our baby son. I needed her out of the house, so after Daryl was fed I gave her money and asked her to do some shopping. The fire had been kept burning overnight and I burnt all my clothes. I took a bath, scrubbing every inch of my skin and hair. It was the only way to destroy the cordite residue that had been absorbed into my skin.

In my paramilitary life I had a ritual. I never looked at newspapers and I never watched television reports. The radio was my only source of news. Mid-morning bulletins confirmed Patrick Brady's death, and that same day the UFF claimed responsibility for the murder in a telephone call to Downtown Radio. I tried to look at Brady's death in a detached way. He was a soldier and I was a soldier, and in war soldiers die. I didn't want to expose myself to the human aspect, the grieving widow and the weeping children, because that's when it becomes real. That is when a target becomes a human being. The grief and pain of the target's loved ones would be enough to make me stop. I wasn't a trophy Loyalist, unlike many of my colleagues. I tried to look at it as a job that had to be done. I tried to see the target as a target, not a human being, but when I pulled the trigger a little part of me died too. I tried not to feel anything, but I did. Only a monster would feel nothing. When you take a man's life you lose part of yourself and part of your humanity for ever.

But that night I did see the *Belfast Telegraph*. On the front page was a picture of the body of Patrick Brady lying on the road covered with a blanket. The headline told how the UFF claimed responsibility for his murder. John McMichael's brigade claimed it. Leigh-Ann showed me the paper and said it was a terrible crime and she felt sorry for his poor wife and daughters. I agreed with her. Another dead body on our streets was a sad and terrible thing. Reaction to Brady's death was swift. Sinn Fein admitted he was a member of their organisation but his funeral bore no paramilitary trappings. Mourners included Gerry Adams and his closest adviser, Danny Morrison.

A few weeks later I met both of the men who accompanied me on the sanction. I gave the driver fifteen hundred quid out of my own pocket and told him the UFF wanted him to have it. I apologised for his baptism of fire and he said he understood. I never worked with the lad again and I understand he never took part in another UFF operation. The back-up man's paramilitary career was also finished and he never again worked on active service. No one would touch him after he jumped from the car, because no one trusted him. He had bottled it and now had paramilitary baggage. When we met he told me that he was in his forties and active service was a young man's game. He told me he was too old and too tired and he couldn't run the risk of being shot or sent to prison. He said he knew the time was right for him to leave. We shook hands and parted. I never saw the man again.

After my arrest following Milltown in March 1988, Tommy 'Tucker' Lyttle, brigadier of the West Belfast UDA, would publicly deny that I had anything to do with Paddy Brady. He told the press that the man responsible was a hired mercenary and not a member of the UDA/UFF. Brady's wife even repeated this in a subsequent television interview. Her husband's name appeared on a UFF intelligence file circulating in South Belfast. It was a UFF-sanctioned operation.

After Brady I dedicated myself to the elimination of known Sinn Fein and PIRA operatives. It was my intention to work my way through the montage. Number two on the sheet was Robert McAllister. My attempt on his life would take place on the same day as my wedding to my second wife, Leigh-Ann Shaw. She was just nineteen when we married, and came from a middle-class area called Glenview, bordering the Braniel estate, and had been living with me for some time after my break-up from Marlene.

Robert McAllister's son was serving a prison sentence for having information useful to terrorists. The lad had been caught with the car registrations of several senior Loyalists, including John McMichael and Supreme Commander Andy Tyrie. The intelligence file told me his father and grandmother lived on the Ormeau Road. I was ordered to assassinate Robert McAllister. John McMichael supplied me with a Mills 36 hand grenade for the job. I took it from his base in the snooker hall at Lisburn, concealing it in a tub of chocolate doggy treats, and transported it to my arms hide hidden in the door panel of my car. The grenade was a Second World War weapon, brutal and effective. The Mills 36 was dubbed the 'chocolate bar' because of the tiny fragments of metal which spread when detonated and also because, like a chocolate bar, 'everyone gets a bit'.

But I had a problem. I had seen a file on McAllister's son, but I wasn't sure about McAllister himself. In my heart I was uncomfortable with the operation. I had promised to target only Republicans and active Sinn Fein members. Robert McAllister was neither.

My attempt on McAllister's life came right in the middle of

political unrest. From July 1985 there had been sporadic violence in Protestant areas when the RUC prevented Orangemen marching through streets in Portadown. The political climate was also hotting up. There was more and more dialogue between London and Dublin and that made my blood boil.

I checked McAllister's house and decided the only option was to blow up the car by attaching the grenade to the steering column with cables. I didn't want to go into the house and kill the target there. He lived with his elderly mother. I didn't want her to be harmed in crossfire or to witness the execution. At four o'clock on the morning of my wedding to Leigh-Ann Shaw, I wired McAllister's car. I slid under the bonnet and attached the Mills using a pushbike brake cable, but I needed a second cable. I didn't have one and was forced to improvise with my bootlace, which I tied to the grenade pin. When the car was put in gear, the Mills would explode. Men who worked in the nearby Ormeau bakery were arriving for work and some had to pass McAllister's car, parked on a sidestreet near his home. As I worked quickly and quietly to attach the Mills, one stopped and spoke. He said, 'Hiya, Rob, having problems with the motor again?', but kept walking. Hours later I exchanged vows with Leigh-Ann and took time from the wedding celebrations to listen to the radio news. The bomb never exploded. It was spotted by one of McAllister's colleagues as he arrived for work later that day. I saw the footage of the car being towed away by a police vehicle to be detonated by an Army bomb-disposal unit.

Unknown to me, UFF intelligence officers had in fact targeted McAllister because they couldn't get to their real target, his son. So they got to the son by trying to kill his father.

My marriage to Leigh-Ann fared little better than my first marriage. We had two children together – Daryl and Lucy – but our marriage started to fall apart within six months. I wasn't committed to her, and started seeing someone else. But it took a long time for the divorce to go through.

Politically, Northern Ireland was moving up a gear and my paramilitary life was also shifting into top gear. In November 1985 the Anglo-Irish Agreement was signed at Hillsborough Castle, the official residence of Northern Ireland's Secretary of State. The signatories were the British Prime Minister, Margaret Thatcher, and the Irish Premier, Dr Garrett Fitzgerald. In my eyes it was the beginning of the end of Northern Ireland's British status. The political pundits dressed it up, saying it was the most far-reaching political development since 1921, when Northern Ireland was created. I disagreed. It was Northern Ireland's death knell. The communiqué issued after the signing said the aims were to promote peace and stability, the reconciliation of the two traditions, the creation of a new climate of friendship and co-operation in combating terrorism. The radical feature of the Agreement was that it set up a joint ministerial conference of British and Irish ministers backed by a permanent secretariat at Maryfield. I was incensed; Protestants and Loyalists were being led by the nose to a united Ireland. We were being handed, wholesale, over to Dublin.

Exactly a week later a huge crowd estimated to be a hundred thousand strong packed the streets around Belfast City Hall to hear their political leaders, united as they had never been, attack the great betrayal. Loudest of all was the Reverend Ian Paisley, seen by thousands of Loyalists as the prophet whose words had come true. He summed up the anger and emotion felt by all of us with three simple words: 'Never, Never, Never.' I have never been a Paisley fan. He rants and raves and he shouts and screams, but he never takes action. Paisley never goes beyond opening his big gob. The UDA dubbed him the 'Grand Old Duke of York' – he marches his men to the top of the hill and then marches them back down again. Paisley has never had the guts to go over the top.

I was now working as a self-employed builder and it provided the perfect cover for my paramilitary activities. I remember Leigh-

Ann thinking I was working too hard and not spending enough time with her. She described me as the most boring man she had ever met. What she didn't know was that I was chasing Republicans all over Northern Ireland. I avoided all contact with paramilitaries except John McMichael and a handful of other trusted freelancers and associates living throughout the province. I dubbed myself the 'minimalist soldier' and kept a low profile. Loyalism was still recovering from the 'supergrass' trials that took place between 1981 and 1986. In these, 'converted' terrorists, such as the Loyalist Budgie Allen and the Republican Christopher Black, would bring accusations against fellow terrorists, who would in turn be arrested and tried. I avoided unnecessary contact with unnecessary people. This way, if more supergrasses were to emerge, I couldn't be implicated in anything because nobody knew me.

9

TAKING THE RAP

AS A RESULT OF MY ARREST ON 16 MARCH 1988, I WAS CHARGED, TRIED AND SENTENCED TO LIFE FOR THE MURDERS OF SIX MEN. But two of them I didn't kill. I can hear the chorus of 'He would say that', but I confessed to the murder of Kevin McPolin to protect the unit who carried out the operation. I wanted to divert suspicion away from them. I said I killed Dermot Hackett to try to help a teenager wrongly charged with Hackett's murder.

Kevin McPolin was a twenty-six-year-old Catholic carpenter who was killed in November 1985. He died after being ambushed as he sat in his car on a housing executive estate in Lisburn. John McMichael's South Belfast unit of the UFF shot McPolin as he waited to start work renovating pensioners' bungalows on the Old Warren estate. The victim was shot at close range through the windscreen with a shotgun. Stumbling from his car, he collapsed and died in the arms of a school patrolman as horrified children looked on.

After my arrest I was questioned not just about Milltown but about a total of twenty-eight murders, including the death of Kevin McPolin. My RUC interrogators put it to me that his death had all the signs of my *modus operandi*, including a shotgun used at close quarters and the target ambushed at work. My answer to their question was simple: 'I killed him. He was a legitimate target.' The truth is, I knew nothing about this young man. I had never seen an intelligence file on him and knew absolutely nothing about him or his background. I didn't even know his name until it was put to me under questioning at Musgrave Park Hospital, and I can't even recall the news bulletins about his death. I confessed to McPolin's murder in order to protect the South Belfast brigade, as they were a new unit beginning to find their feet. I knew my confession would allow them to carry on their work free from suspicion. I was going down for life. The charges relating to Milltown alone ensured I would spend at least thirty years behind bars, so another murder on my charge sheet wasn't going to make a difference to the overall outcome. It was a classic illustration of the old paramilitary saying 'in for one or 101'. With murder carrying a life sentence in Northern Ireland, a convicted murderer would get the same sentence no matter how many people he had killed.

My confession also gave the McPolin family closure. They saw the man who 'murdered' their loved one confessing, going to court and going to prison for his death. I am sure this helped them as they grieved for their son and brother and I am sorry that now, eighteen years later, their pain is going to come flooding back and hit them like a giant tidal wave.

In custody, the police had to talk me through every detail about McPolin's murder. They had to hold my hand like I was a five-year-old. My interrogators were forced to drop clues and leave hints and give me just enough information to weave into a credible version of events. The RUC knew I didn't kill McPolin and they even laughed at some of my answers to their questions, but I was grabbing in the dark trying to picture myself there. The police questioned and probed, trying to get me to slip up and make mistakes saying, 'Are you sure about this?' and 'Was it not like that?' One detective couldn't continue and left the room shouting, 'We are telling him everything. The fucker didn't do it.' I managed to convince the police I did do it and the murder of Kevin McPolin was added to my charge sheet.

In prison I spoke to the man who pulled the trigger. He told me he had read McPolin's file and killed him because he was a Republican. He also thanked me for taking the rap, and confirmed that his unit was able to continue operating suspicion-free after McPolin's death.

Dermot Hackett died in May 1987 after being ambushed by the North Belfast brigade of the UFF. He perished in a hail of gunfire on a lonely road outside Omagh, County Tyrone. I first heard of Dermot Hackett early that same year. He was a family man with a young daughter of nine. He was a Mother's Pride bread deliveryman and lived in Castlederg, a tiny village in County Tyrone. I believe he was involved in charity work and gave much of his free time to the St Vincent de Paul organisation. But Hackett had a secret. He used his bread run to transport guns for the IRA. I had seen his intelligence file. It was the usual collection of photographs and information. It showed he used his delivery van to move weapons around the lonely roads of South Tyrone.

At the time of Hackett's death, Bishop Edward Daly accused the security forces of harassing Hackett whenever he left home. Bishop Daly said the constant pressure brought the young father to the attention of Loyalist paramilitaries, who used the opportunity to execute him. His cousin, a member of the SDLP, had protested to the RUC about the attention Hackett received every time he left his home and a prominent member of the same party, Denis Haughey, had also made representations on his behalf. Hackett travelled the lonely network of roads for his work and was often pulled over and searched by the security forces. They constantly stopped him because they wanted to catch him red-handed with guns and bullets hidden among the loaves and cakes. The security forces knew he was active and it was for the same reason he was targeted by the UFF. After his death the Hackett family denied that he was involved or active in the Republican movement, but the intelligence I saw on him proved otherwise. I agreed to assassinate Dermot Hackett and was given his file. I burnt it after memorising the details it contained.

I took a lift to the area, based myself in a safe house and did a dry run. Two young volunteers were made available for the sanction and both were to be blooded on the hit. They told me they had stolen a car, an Opel Manta, and garaged it until the day of the operation. A Sterling Mk 5 sub-machine gun and another weapon would be made available on the day. I pulled out of the operation. In my eyes, Hackett wasn't a big enough target.

There is another more important reason why I pulled out of the assassination of Dermot Hackett. Everything was in place. I had seen his file, had weapons and transport organised and was ready to go. I even did a dry run and sat in the lonely lay-by chosen as the place.

Seven days before the operation was scheduled to go ahead, the mid-Ulster brigadier had a strange and interesting conversation with me. I can still recall every word of it. 'We will have no problems with this operation. I can guarantee it.'

'Why?'

'I have contacts in the security forces and they have assured me there will be no activity in that area on Saturday morning. They know about the operation and they will let your team get in and out safely. They will be in the area and, if any stray units chance upon the scene or off-duty members of the force are out and about, they'll block off the road.'

I told him that it had taken three weeks to set up the operation and, as a result of his relationship with local security forces, my security was compromised. I told him I wouldn't do it.

A week later Hackett was dead.

The two young volunteers assigned to the operation had a friend called Peter Deary. He was seventeen years old, collected money for Loyalist Prisoners' Aid and wasn't involved in active service. The

Manta stolen for the operation had an expensive radio. The two volunteers ripped it out and give it to their friend Deary, who had a clapped-out old banger with no radio. A few weeks after Hackett's death, Deary was stopped by the RUC for having no road tax and insurance. They noticed an expensive radio system in his car and knew it didn't belong in the banger. It was checked and the owner of the Manta confirmed it was his. Deary was hauled in for questioning and broke down under interrogation, was arrested and charged with the murder of Dermot Hackett. The police threw the book at him because he knew about an old arms hide and about other stolen items.

Northern Ireland has a bizarre law called Thompson's Law. This means it is irrelevant whether you pull the trigger or are standing nearby, whether you are the back-up man or the getaway driver. Murder is murder and you do life for it. Young Deary was remanded in custody to await his trial. I knew he wasn't involved in the Hackett murder. I told the RUC I killed Dermot Hackett to try to get Deary off, but it didn't work.

I confessed to the murder in Musgrave Park Hospital and, unlike the murder of Kevin McPolin, I knew I could convince the police that I was the gunman. I had seen Hackett's file and had even done a dry run. I could name the weapons and give the police explicit detail only someone close to the operation could provide, but there was a problem with my fake confession: the Opel Manta. During questioning the police asked me if I'd used a car and I deliberately threw swerves to confuse them. First I told them I was a passenger on a motorbike. They were puzzled and asked me how I managed to strike the cab of the bread van, which was substantially higher than a bike. I told my interrogators that I got the driver to overtake the van, I aimed at the driver's side of the vehicle with the sub-machine gun in an out and upwards motion and then opened fire. I said the Manta was a cover. One detective wasn't convinced. He kept shaking his head and asked whether I shot out and upwards. I confirmed this was correct, saying, 'I leant out of the window, pointed up and fired at the cab.' The police were puzzled. They told me my story didn't add up. They said they understood everything else, the weapons and the route, but they couldn't work out the car. I thought they were playing games with me. The fake confession was eventually accepted by the RUC and Dermot Hackett's name was added to my charge sheet.

It was a year later before I understood the RUC's confusion. The answer to the puzzle was contained in my depositions. The police scene-of-crime photographs clearly showed the Manta – complete with sunroof. The UFF volunteer who had shot Hackett had stood up through the sunroof, aiming straight at the cab of the delivery van. The sub-machine gun wasn't aimed out and up like I said it was, but parallel with the cab. Forensic evidence showed that the trajectory of the bullets, which penetrated Hackett's body and even his feet, could only have gone one way: out and straight across on the same level as the cab of the van. Deary signed for the car after admitting his link to the getaway car through the radio and was jailed for murder in 1988. He faced the Secretary of State's Pleasure for something he had no hand in and even though I tried I couldn't save his skin. Paramilitary godfathers shouldn't use kids.

I remember when I was in prison there was a television programme about the murder of Dermot Hackett. His widow spoke about her husband and she was very gracious in her grief. I realised that her husband lived on in his wife and daughter. She spoke softly and lovingly about her husband and said she wanted to invite me into her home and ask why I murdered her husband. In 2000, the year of my release from prison, Hackett's daughter said she was leaving Northern Ireland for a new life in America because she couldn't bear to be in the same country as me, the man who killed her father. I was sad about that and sad for her that she felt she couldn't stay at home because I was walking the streets of Northern Ireland a free man.

10

MARTIN McGUINNESS

MARTIN McGUINNESS. THE HEAD OF THE REPUBLICAN SNAKE AND ENEMY NUMBER ONE. I personally held him responsible for atrocities like Enniskillen and Kingsmills and I wanted him wiped off the face of the earth. I asked my intelligence officers to get me his file and they duly presented it. It was an archive stretching back twenty years. It contained hundreds of photographs showing McGuinness in a variety of different looks over the years. In some he was wearing the trademark tweed jacket with leather elbow patches, in others he was just a teenager with long hair or a man in his twenties with dyed hair and a moustache. The file also included official photographs. I knew he drove a burnt-orange Volkswagen Jetta. I had his house number in Londonderry's Brandywell estate. I knew about his wife and kids.

The file contained detail on his every movement. I knew he collected his newspapers from a small shop in Bishopgate Street and he never paid cash, always put it on account. I knew he signed on every second Thursday afternoon with his brother Frank and

DHSS officials allowed him a three-hour flexibility slot because he was a security risk. I knew that he bulk-shopped with his wife in Curley's supermarket after his dole cheque came through. I knew he walked his daughter Grainne to school and I knew he was a football fan and followed his favourite team, Derry City FC, going to every home match. Martin McGuinness had several routines and I intended to exploit every opportunity until I succeeded. The entire file was handed back to UFF intelligence officers. I wasn't allowed to destroy it.

I spent six months stalking McGuinness. I wanted him dead before Sinn Fein's Ard Fheis, its annual general meeting, and I had another plan in mind at the same time: to spark an internal row among the Republican movement. I wanted to use a Republican weapon and decided on an AR15 Armalite. I knew the UFF had one in their possession and John McMichael swapped four revolvers for it. The rifle ended up in the hands of Loyalists via Loyalist hoods, who got it from Republican hoods, who stole it from the Provos. The security forces had been watching the arms hide with instructions to arrest or shoot on sight whoever came to pick it up. Republicans heard the hide was being watched and left the gun. Republican hoods waited for a while, moved in and passed it on to Loyalist hoods. The rifle had been used in a number of sniper attacks and I knew ballistic tests would show it to be an IRA weapon. I wanted the Republican movement to wonder what the hell was happening if a high-ranking official was shot with one of their own weapons. I wanted to spark an internal feud. I also chose a Smith & Wesson .38 revolver.

McMichael put me in touch with a UDA commander in Londonderry. At our first meeting he said it had been eleven years since the UFF had attacked Republicans in Londonderry, although the IRA had been active. He then added, 'If you kill him [McGuinness], I am a dead man.' I told him that was war and he said he understood why I was in Londonderry and what I must do.

He said he would help me. This man was willing to take the risk and put his life on the line for Loyalism. He supplied my safe houses and accompanied me on all dry runs. He helped fine-tune options for the assassination and even went into the Brandywell with me to do a recce of McGuinness's house. We bought Derry City FC scarves and wrapped them around our necks. We bought a football and kicked it around the streets outside McGuinness's home. Our pretend football game allowed us to assess the house and evaluate our options. I was an angry man. If McGuinness walked out of his house, I was going to pump him full of lead. It wouldn't matter who saw me or who witnessed the shooting. The job would be done.

Standing facing his home, it was obvious to me that McGuinness had installed extra security. The windows had the telltale blue-green tint of reinforced glass. I could see his bathroom and had a clear line of fire from the street below. I decided against the window shot because I could not be totally sure the figure silhouetted against the window was McGuinness himself, his wife, his child or a visitor to his home. McGuinness was my target, not his family.

As a final check I went back to the Brandywell after dark. I took a small folding ladder and climbed into the football pitch which bordered the side of his house. I walked around the grounds looking for possible vantage points to strike the house, but none presented themselves. The football pitched was overlooked by a British Army sangar. I ruled out assassinating McGuinness at his home.

Plan B was the newsagents in Bishopgate Street in the city centre. I wanted to strike as McGuinness left the shop with bundles of papers under his arm. New shops were being built directly across from the road and I knew the builders wouldn't be around at the weekend. The hit had to take place on a Saturday or Sunday. I planned to hide among the builders' equipment on a motorbike, kill McGuinness with the Armalite, drop it and drive off and meet my driver on the outskirts of Londonderry. The motorbike would be dumped just across the border in County Donegal.

The Armalite would cause havoc among local Republicans. I wanted the snake to start eating itself. I wanted the Republican movement to implode in an internal feud. I decided on a Saturday to coincide with a Derry City home match. I decided to operate alone. I could move and operate more easily under cover of the massive crowd decked out in their uniform of red and white. McGuinness loved his football and attended every match that was played at the nearby ground. I opted for a car rather than the motorbike and the idea was to hit him with the .38 as he went into the newsagents, then switch to the Armalite to finish him off. I dressed as a football fan, wrapping the red and white scarf around my neck and wearing a coloured monkey hat. With two eyeholes cut in it, the hat would double as a mask. As I made my getaway, it would give me a quick disguise.

I waited for McGuinness to show. He never altered his newspaper run, and hadn't missed a home match for twenty years, but where the hell was he? The Army had a lookout post on Strand Road and I knew I could be seen. A foot patrol walked past the car and one of the soldiers bent down and looked in at me. I thought the game was up, but they continued walking and I drove out of the city. I met my associate at a safe house and asked him if he knew what was going on. He said there was a major problem with the operation and it would be in my interests to go back to Belfast.

Unknown to me, Tucker Lyttle, the West Belfast UDA brigadier, had sent three volunteers to Londonderry to 'kill' McGuinness at the dole office. When I say 'kill', I mean Lyttle wanted it to look like a real UFF operation, even though it wasn't. His three volunteers were game for the sanction and were carrying two Sterlings. They were also going to kill Frank McGuinness and two other men who signed on with the

McGuinness brothers at the same time, but they were pulled back to Belfast at the last minute. As a member of the UDA's Inner Council, Lyttle knew about my attempt to kill McGuinness because all sanctions had to be passed by the Inner Council, but he stood up at the meeting and insisted his volunteers would do the job. Lyttle was a tout and he needed to give the impression he was involved in big operations. He needed to keep his cover. In reality he wanted to fuck things up. He reported back to the Inner Council that the operation wasn't feasible and 'we should leave well alone'. Lyttle knew that with McGuinness's death his own death warrant would be signed.

He spent most of his time socialising in Republican West Belfast and racing his prized greyhounds in Dunmore stadium in the heart of Provoland with his Republican pals. He even drank in IRA bars. Lyttle knew the assassination of Martin McGuinness would mean all bets were off and he would automatically become a target. He knew his Provo pals would turn on him. He spilled the beans to his RUC handlers. I am absolutely certain McGuinness was tipped off and deliberately changed his routine because he knew he was a target.

My options to assassinate McGuinness were reduced. His house and the newsagents were ruled out. I couldn't kill him at the dole office because the then Mid-Ulster brigadier had been photographed, by the Army, with an off-duty RUC officer. They were in the RUC man's car watching McGuinness as he arrived to sign on.

I would let things sit for a while before going back to Londonderry and trying my other option: his daughter's primary school. McGuinness was a marked man. He would be assassinated and his death would be claimed by one of the Loyalist paramilitaries I associated with. I was not letting anyone stand in my way. Several weeks later I returned to Londonderry and met up with my associate. In a car registered in his name we sat outside the school. It was a dry run, but if McGuinness appeared I was going to shoot him with the .38 revolver hidden between my legs.

By now my associate was beginning to panic a little and told me I was 'on my own' as he couldn't risk drawing attention to himself. I was prepared to cowboy it if McGuinness showed. He did turn up, but I didn't shoot him. He was walking hand in hand with his little girl. He bent down and hugged her and she threw her arms around his neck and kissed him back before running up the lane to school. I couldn't shoot Martin McGuinness in front of his daughter. I couldn't live with the responsibility of forcing a little girl to watch her father die. I left Londonderry and returned to Belfast.

I am not a gangster or a criminal. I don't assassinate targets in front of their wives and children. I have never burst into a man's home and shot him in front of his family. When my time comes, and it will, I do not want my family to be around. I wouldn't want them to be caught in a hail of bullets or executed just because they are mine. I saw my own family reflected in his daughter and she stopped me in my tracks. I saw the human side to Martin McGuinness and I couldn't pull the trigger. His little girl saved his life. McGuinness had got away from me. Later, he would get away at Milltown too. I read he boasted about leaping over gravestones as he pursued me. I have seen photographs of him crouched on all fours, mouth open in a scream, terrified look on his face, hiding behind a gravestone. It proved he had blood running through his veins.

Martin McGuinness is still ever present in my life. He is constantly on the news and is now a minister in our government. He is in charge of the education of my children and grandchildren, but I can watch and listen to him now. Years ago I would have shot the screen.

It was an open secret among Loyalists that Tucker Lyttle had

Special Branch handlers. With him on the UDA's Inner Council and blabbing to his RUC handlers, I was banging my head against a brick wall. Big operations were never going to succeed. There were a lot of dirty games, counter-intelligence and misinformation generated by career Loyalists like Lyttle who were more interested in retaining their lavish lifestyle than the war with Republicans. I am in no doubt that he compromised the attempt to assassinate McGuinness by telling his Special Branch handlers what was discussed at the Inner Council. I am in no doubt that his actions ultimately led to McGuinness becoming aware that there was a genuine attempt to take him out. John McMichael had warned me about Lyttle several times. He told me he didn't think twice about sacrificing Loyalist volunteers. I was beginning to understand exactly what that meant.

11

THE POPPY DAY MASSACRE

McGUINNESS LEFT ME WITH A SOUR TASTE IN MY MOUTH. I WAS DISAPPOINTED THAT THE MAN WAS STILL ALIVE, BUT I WAS DETERMINED MY WORK WOULD CONTINUE. Intelligence was coming to me thick and fast and my list of targets was growing by the day. Peter Joseph Bateson was an IRA man from Magherafelt in County Londonderry. When he came to my attention he had been out of prison just two years.

He was one of the IRA's most feared and dedicated volunteers, a golden boy who was ruthless, organised and highly motivated. He was a cradle-to-grave Republican whose family was steeped in Irish politics.

Bateson had served only half of a twenty-year term for attempted murder. The RUC finally caught up with him in 1977 and he was charged for his part in the attack on three policemen in 1974. Despite being ambushed in their patrol car, the three officers escaped with their lives and were able to identify Bateson from RUC 'wanted' posters. I knew he socialised in the Elk bar, where he met his five-man active-service unit every Monday night. I knew where his girlfriend lived, her name and what she did for a living. I knew where Bateson lived. I stalked him for six weeks.

I wanted to kill him in the Elk. I chose an AK47 because I knew I would have to shoot round me to make the operation a success and a pistol would be useless in this situation. In addition, an intelligence officer warned me that Special Branch were watching Bateson and were likely also to be in the Elk. If I opened fire on Bateson and his unit, they would open fire on me. I decided to blow him up.

I chose two RDG5 grenades with five-second fuses to make my bomb. I filled a plastic bottle with sugar and oil and taped the grenades either side of it. This was then attached to a litre of petrol. The device was to be attached to the steering column of Bateson's car. Each grenade contained six ounces of TNT. The combination of petrol and explosives would cause a massive fireball. Bateson would die in the blast and then be incinerated.

It was a two-man job. The back-up man had a scanner that picked up RUC broadcasts on the security forces' movements in the area. We knew, even before the security forces on the ground, when the RUC and Army were on the move. We knew which areas were hot and which were cold. For two nights I sat in the car park of the Elk waiting for Bateson to show. I also kept my personal weapon, a Ruger, in my pocket, and if he arrived in the car park I wouldn't hesitate to pump him full of lead. I had spent six weeks organising this operation but Bateson never appeared. I don't know if he was tipped off. I don't know if was coincidence, but according to his file, which stretched back many years, it was the first Monday-night meeting he had missed.

I was disappointed that Bateson had slipped through my

fingers. I was suffering from what Vietnam veterans called the dreaded 'cluster fucks'. A string of operations weren't working out: Bateson didn't happen because he didn't show; McGuinness didn't happen because Tucker Lyttle compromised the operation; and Robert McAllister was also a no-result.

One year after my thwarted attempt on his life, Bateson was caught red-handed by the security forces with a bomb. He was about to explode a massive Semtex device weighing eighty-five pounds, which he had planted in a drain near Army living quarters. The IRA had a policy of attacking the families of security forces. Bateson was caught with the control wire in his hand, dressed in overalls and hiding in undergrowth. When he was asked what he was doing, he is reported to have said he was on a death list and in hiding. Bateson got his second jail term, this time twenty-five years. He was a dedicated Republican soldier.

The next name on the UFF montage was a taxi driver called John James Bloomfield. He lived in Ballynahinch and was the owner of JJ Taxis in the town. His file had him marked as an intelligence officer for the IRA who used his taxi to watch the security forces at Ballykinler Army base. Bloomfield categorically denied this in court. I made one attempt on his life and had previously tried to lure him to his death with a request to pick up a fare at the Royal Ascot disco in Carryduff, but he failed to bite. I made the phone call to a number given to me by intelligence officers, but he knew something was up. On the phone he was very coy and nervous. He wanted to know where I got the number, and I said a girl I met in the disco. He wasn't convinced and told me he couldn't pick me up. So I went back to the drawing board. I waited a few months and got a female acquaintance to make a call to Bloomfield requesting a pick-up from the Spa restaurant, to go to Newcastle, County Down. He fell for it. With a girl caller, Bloomfield had no reason to suspect a ploy.

I waited for Bloomfield in the car park of the Spa. I was armed with a 9mm Luger and a shotgun, but he got away. Even though I fired a hail of bullets, he escaped without being injured. Bloomfield was a skilled driver, and his ability to drive saved his life. I tried to block his exit, but he accelerated at me and drove off into the night. Unknown to me, the car used for the operation had been hijacked in another part of the county and a woman driver, Agnes Dickson, had been taken hostage. The volunteers put her in the boot and she came with us on the operation. I knew nothing about this until after the event. By putting the woman in the boot of the car used in the attempt on Bloomfield's life, the volunteers had turned her into a human shield. I don't know the lady but she has my sincere apologies for her horrific experience.

I was never indiscriminate or sectarian, never like the PIRA, targeting innocent people as they did in Enniskillen on Remembrance Sunday. To my mind the 'Poppy Day' massacre is one of the horror stories of the Troubles. Eleven innocent people were killed. Countless numbers were maimed. It was 11 November 1987 and people had gathered in the town to pay tribute to the dead of two world wars when the IRA struck. In my eyes it was sacrilegious. The IRA said it was a mistake and the bomb was for the security forces. I thought it was a pathetic attempt to justify a sectarian attack on civilians. These people were gathered at the cenotaph to pay homage to the men who fought fascism in Europe. Meanwhile modern-day fascists had plotted to take their lives. It was a big body count and I was horrified.

On the same day as the Enniskillen massacre, another large IRA bomb failed to go off. It was also on the route of a Poppy Day commemoration, in another border town. At the time Republicans tried to write it off as a one-off and a mistake, but I didn't believe them. They knew exactly what they were doing.

I wanted revenge. I wanted to do something so terrible it would be burnt for ever into the minds and hearts of the Republican movement. It had to be something spectacular and it had to be unforgettable. My attack had to be a shock to the collective Republican consciousness and I knew there was only one way: to wipe out the entire Republican hierarchy.

Six weeks before the Enniskillen bomb, an off-duty RUC man had been shot dead. The shooting was part of an IRA operation, a spectacular double whammy to eradicate high-profile members of the RUC and the government. The young officer was to be interred at Roselawn cemetery, a quiet and peaceful place on the outskirts of Belfast where members of my family have been laid to rest. The Secretary of State, Tom King, and the Chief Constable of the RUC, Sir John Hermon, were expected at his funeral. The IRA planted a bomb at the gate lodge of the cemetery and detonated it just as the cortège was passing. It weighed three hundred and fifty pounds, an unusual size even by the IRA's standards. The booster, charged with Semtex, failed to ignite the bomb but still caused an explosion scattering debris and bits of car over the mourners. Miraculously, no one was killed, but several people, including members of the dead officer's family, were injured.

The Provos staged a spectacular assault. They killed a policeman and used him as bait. They killed a secondary target in order to attract the primary target. They knew important people would come to the dead officer's funeral and they exploited mercilessly this window of opportunity. It was a very radical move as it eliminated the need for an around-the-country chase. I could modify this idea for my own operations. I would kill my enemy and make his comrades come to me.

I still wanted to eliminate the IRA leadership. I could not make a further attempt on Martin McGuinness's life. Tucker Lyttle had closed that opportunity for good, and if I were to try I would probably end up dead. But I could get him at Milltown if I targeted and killed the right Republican. A new plan began to form in my head.

12

TOUTS
INCORPORATED

THE POPPY DAY MASSACRE IN ENNISKILLEN STRENGTHENED MY RESOLVE AND I SWORE TO AVENGE THE DEATHS OF THE ELEVEN INNOCENT CIVILIANS. McMichael and I vowed to work even more closely masterminding a strike so horrific the Republican movement would never recover.

But time was running out for John McMichael. Just like Tommy Herron, McMichael knew he ran risks. We often met in the car park of the Old Crow pub in Comber, County Down, for our regular meetings. One evening he was quiet and withdrawn, not his usual self. When I asked him if there was something in particular that was bothering him, he nodded. He gave me two names. One was Jim Craig, the UDA's fund-raiser-in-chief and a gangster and criminal posing as a Loyalist. The other was McMichael's quartermaster. He said to me, 'If anything ever happens to me the first name is responsible and the second name will help you.' McMichael was telling me that if he was killed, and he believed his days were numbered, Jim Craig would be behind it and his quartermaster would provide a weapon for a retaliatory strike. I told him I had never killed or wounded a Loyalist before and his answer was short and to the point: 'You will.'

McMichael constantly warned me about Tucker Lyttle and on this particular night he took the time to ram the point home. I distinctly remember him saying, 'Tucker is a tout, so never tell him anything, don't befriend him and keep him away from your UDA business.' He knew Lyttle had Special Branch handlers and was the weakest link in the UDA's Inner Council. Also, he knew that Lyttle had a better and more intimate working relationship with his Special Branch handlers than his Loyalist brothers. McMichael wasn't telling me anything I hadn't discovered for myself. I had first-hand experience of Tucker the Traitor.

John McMichael was killed on 22 December 1987. It was a massive personal blow to me and for the second time in my life I was robbed of a good friend and ally. He died after the IRA booby-trapped his car. The device exploded outside his Lisburn home. McMichael was conscious after the blast but died on the way to the hospital. He suffered terrible injuries. The IRA had been given the intelligence on McMichael by Jim Craig, the man he suspected would try to have him killed. Craig even organised and supplied the safe house for the Provo unit.

On 26 December a special service for John McMichael was held in Dromore, County Down. A UDA colour party fired a volley of shots over his coffin in honour of his life and work. The small town was sealed off at midnight on Christmas night to allow members to prepare the square and to prevent people from straying in on the proceedings. The shots were fired into the air just hours before the funeral. The Supreme Commander of the UDA, Andy Tyrie, summed up the feelings of most of us when he said, 'John was killed because he was the best person we had and the Republican movement didn't like him. I didn't have anybody as astute in politics as he was. They also didn't like him because he was being listened to and they knew the loss we would incur when he was killed.'

John McMichael was buried with UDA but few paramilitary honours in his home town. Andy Tyrie carried the coffin, which was draped in the Union Jack and UDA flag. A guard of honour, formed by local members of the Apprentice Boys, escorted the coffin. I didn't go to the funeral. I knew Special Branch would be watching and photographing every person and every vehicle arriving for the service, within a half-mile radius. John McMichael was my friend, but I couldn't run the risk of being seen or photographed by the security forces. My work as a volunteer depended on staying anonymous.

The timing of John McMichael's death couldn't have come at a worse time. I was on a roll, chasing senior Republicans all over Northern Ireland, and was particularly preoccupied with finding a way to eliminate the Republican hierarchy. I know McMichael was also masterminding his own operations to hit senior Republican figures. He was the brains behind the UDA's aggressive offensive against prominent Republicans, including Bernadette McAliskey. He prided himself on being a man at war with militant Republicanism.

But there was a fly in the ointment. Jim Craig. I nicknamed him 'the don' because he swaggered around Loyalist West Belfast as if he was a Mafia boss. He always had a cigar in his mouth, wore an expensive overcoat and had gold jewellery on his neck, wrist and fingers. He was a man of middle UDA rank who thought he *was* the UDA. He patronised volunteers. One young man told me that Craig stopped him on the Shankill Road, took a look at the man's wife, engaged the couple in idle chit-chat, then pulled out a wad of notes big enough to choke a donkey. The young volunteer said it looked like thousands of pounds held together in a rubber band. Craig pulled off two or three fifty-pound notes, handed them to the girl and told her to 'buy herself a nice dress because you need one'. He then swaggered off, leaving the couple open-mouthed in disbelief. The young volunteer said he felt two inches tall.

Craig didn't like McMichael. He hated his investigations into extortion and gangsterism. Craig was up to his neck in McMichael's death and I was going to kill him for it. Over the years several Loyalists have said to me that Craig and two other men were in a van nearby and watched as the bomb detonated under McMichael's car. Within hours of McMichael's death, Craig had raided his office and stolen hundreds of documents. I wanted to avenge the death of my friend and colleague and I was, of course, acting on his personal wishes. Initially I wanted to look for Craig on the streets of West Belfast, with a clean weapon, probably an AK47, sourced from the quartermaster for South Belfast, and just gun him down on the street. A statement would be given to a newsroom claiming the death on behalf of a fictional Loyalist group, but weeks rolled into one and I was busy chasing Republicans, so Craig was put on ice.

Then Milltown happened. It was my intention that, once that major operation was over, Craig would be stiffed and I knew exactly what I was going to do. I would lure him away from the relative safety of his turf with a plan that would appeal to his greed. I would have a hole already dug and as he approached the meeting place, I'd shoot him, dump his body in the hole, cover him in lime and leave him to dissolve and rot. When Craig had John McMichael killed he deprived Loyalism of its best weapon for taking on the IRA and winning. When McMichael was murdered our best chance of winning the war also died. McMichael was the prototype of a tough new breed of Loyalist. He would have no dealings with brigadiers and commanders who had long-standing deals with the security forces and the Provos. He said it 'bastardised' the name of the UDA. He had his sights on Craig. Killing Republicans was something the UDA took pride in, but there was an aspect to the organisation which left a bad taste in McMichael's mouth: extortion, gangsterism and racketeering. McMichael was seen as a purist. He got abuse from the old-school UDA who turned a blind eye to this sort of activity.

Jim Craig was the biggest racketeer in the UDA and enjoyed his self-appointed title of fund-raiser-in-chief. John McMichael was compiling a report on extortion and Craig's name cropped up at every turn. Craig bullied hundreds of building firms all over the city. He told them they needed protection and protection cost money. Firms, fearful for the safety of their workers, would hand over thousands of pounds on a regular basis.

McMichael's report also investigated Craig's role in the death of two UDA men, Billy 'Bucky' McCullough and Billy Quee. Craig had both of these men murdered and even watched their executions from a safe distance. He called McCullough and Quee his 'bridges to be burnt'. McMichael found that Craig, although a Loyalist, had conspired with both the IRA and INLA over the deaths of these two men and several other Loyalists. McMichael's intelligence had also uncovered a trail linking Craig to a senior Republican in West Belfast and the death of Shankill Butcher and UVF leader Lenny Murphy. The intelligence showed that Craig had provided a safe house for the IRA unit in the Loyalist Glencairn estate where Murphy lived. The notorious Loyalist was shot as he stood at his front door.

There was also the matter of the phone call Craig made after McMichael ordered the assassination of Gerry Adams. Senior Republicans asked Craig why Adams was a target when it was contrary to the unspoken agreement that the leadership was not to be touched. Craig was conspiring to kill Loyalists and carving up areas with his Provo pals and this wheeler-dealer attitude infuriated McMichael. His internal investigation was going to expose Craig for what he was, a hood and a gangster. Once the findings were complete and it was presented to the Inner Council, Craig would be executed.

Craig knew the noose was beginning to tighten around his neck, and passed information to Republicans leading to John McMichael's death. Before the report was finalised and put to the Inner Council, racketeering was raised at an Inner Council meeting. Craig, furious at the charges put to him, pulled out his gun, waved it around and pointed it at McMichael's head. At the top of his voice he categorically denied he was a gangster and racketeer. He said he never worked hand in glove with the IRA or INLA. By brandishing his gun Craig made matters worse that evening. The Inner Council had an unspoken rule: no guns were to be carried during the meeting. Craig broke that rule. If the police had crashed the meeting, he would have thrown his gun into the middle of the room and every single one of the Inner Council members would have been arrested and done for possession.

I learnt from a former member of the Inner Council about the day Craig sealed his own fate. There was a robbery in Portadown, County Armagh. It was a big heist. The UFF unit was dressed in RUC uniforms stolen weeks earlier from a dry cleaner's in Belfast. The unit raided the bank and calmly walked away with eight boxes of cash, each containing about twenty-two thousand pounds. At the Inner Council meeting Craig proposed each member of the Inner Council take a cut from the robbery to cover personal expenses. Tucker Lyttle backed the motion. Three brigadiers refused: Andy Tyrie, John McMichael and the man who told me the story. Craig pushed Tyrie, saying, 'If we take it, you must take it too.' Tyrie refused outright, saying that as Supreme Commander he would not be compromised. McMichael also refused, but the money appeared at his front door disguised as a parcel. At the next Inner Council meeting he handed back the money and said he couldn't and wouldn't take it. Craig stood up and personally addressed McMichael, saying, 'If you don't take the cash, none of us can. If you hand it back, we all have to hand it back.' McMichael told the assembled brigadiers that he was giving the money to his quartermaster.

Craig was happy because he got to keep his slice of the funds. The brigadier told me he himself reluctantly accepted the cash and spent a couple of thousand pounds on his house and his family but then felt guilty. He returned what was left of the cash and Jim Craig said he was more than happy to 'relieve' him of his guilt and took the remaining cash for himself. McMichael was cleaning out the UDA closet. Craig didn't like it and he had McMichael killed.

Jim Craig was no Loyalist. He was an unscrupulous gangster, a hood in a suit and gold chain. I was on remand when he was killed in October 1988. An associate of Craig's asked for advice on how to handle him. He said the UDA didn't want to kill Craig because he generated cash, so I told him about the robbery, the boxes of cash and the cuts Craig insisted on keeping. I warned him about the brigadier for East Belfast, known to have been turned by the Army, and that Craig's downfall would be his greed. A message was relayed back to me to say that the UFF had agreed to 'get rid' of Craig and I was glad to hear it. A few weeks later there was a robbery in Belfast city centre. Several thousand pounds' worth of gold was stolen. A Belfast unit told Craig they had jewellery they wanted to get rid of quickly and if he had a spare thirty thousand pounds he could have the lot. Craig bragged that he wouldn't give a penny more than ten thousand and demanded to see samples.

A meeting was arranged in the Castle Inn in East Belfast. Craig went on his own. He was so greedy he refused to bring any of his henchmen. When the deal was done he flashed his cash and bought drinks on the house. Not that there were many people having a drink that night, just a couple of pensioners. Word had got out to stay away. I am told Craig had just finished a game of pool and was at the bar talking to a pensioner when the gunmen burst in. They were wearing boiler suits. Several rounds were fired and Craig was hit in the lower body and chest. Unfortunately, the old man Craig was talking to was also killed. Victor Rainey thought it was a Provo unit and threw himself in front of Craig to try to protect him, which is tragic.

The volunteers had been ordered to take Craig's thick gold bracelet after killing him. It was going to be used, along with the massive wad of notes he kept in his pocket, as proof he was nothing but a gangster who bastardised the name of Loyalism. The volunteers tried to remove the bracelet but couldn't. It was welded to his wrist, as we say in Belfast. At the time of Craig's death I was on remand in the Prisoner Segregation Unit of Crumlin Road jail. News filtered through the wings that he had been killed. I remember the whoops of joy that filtered through the 'Crum', right down to the PSU. I heard the chants of 'Old doggy-box head is dead.' I smiled to myself. John McMichael finally had the justice he deserved.

McMichael had a young son, Gary, who wanted to carry the political baton his father had held for many years. After my arrest Gary and his aunt, John McMichael's sister, came to see me in prison. They were very distressed about newspaper reports linking McMichael to me. The brigadier of South Belfast who inherited the area after McMichael's death urged me to deny my relationship with my late friend. He said I should do it for 'the sake of internal UDA politics and for the McMichael family'. I was shocked. McMichael's sister and son were pleasant and courteous to me, but his sister cried a lot. His son was diplomatic and shifted uncomfortably in his chair when he addressed me. In front of McMichael's grieving family I denied my relationship with the man I called my friend. I told them I never knew, never worked with him and never met John McMichael in my life. His son wanted something in writing, a statement he could read out to the press and I agreed to their wishes out of respect for the family.

My statement appeared in the *Sunday Life* as a two-page story. I felt insulted. Was I not good enough to know the man or was he not good enough to know me? I told a lie. I felt like Judas Iscariot. I denied my friend and associate. John was a good commander of the UFF. He was also an astute politician who had the skills and intelligence to make the UDA a political force to be reckoned with. Sadly, he didn't get to reach his potential. I am sorry I denied John McMichael in front of his family and I am glad to have the opportunity to put the record straight. I did know John McMichael. I worked with John McMichael on a regular basis. Operationally, our work brought us into close contact and he was a trusted friend and ally.

I was sad that McMichael wasn't around to see the UDA closet getting its clear-out, but I knew that if he had been he would have been happy to see the back of Craig.

It is ironic that the UDA's biggest tout got rid of the UDA's biggest gangster in a personal feud. Tucker Lyttle ordered the execution of Jim Craig. The UDA said Craig was executed for treason, and he was, but the real reason was that things had got personal between Tucker and Craig. Someone very close to Tucker was having an affair with Craig; Tucker was infuriated because the girl was underage. Tucker and Craig had words, Craig was warned off but ignored the threats. Tucker didn't warn him again and had him killed.

Tucker Lyttle was the UDA spokesperson for fifteen years. He had a senior position in the organisation, holding the rank of brigadier for West Belfast. Tucker had a secret. He was a Special Branch informer and had several handlers. He cosied up to his RUC bosses and sold out his Loyalist brothers. To those of us who knew him, he was affectionately known as 'Tucker the Fucker'. He was despised for bringing the Loyalist cause into disrepute with his covert relationship with the RUC.

He is the stuff of legend, but for all the wrong reasons. One story tells how he accompanied Loyalist icon Glen Barr to Libya to see Colonel Gaddafi's men. The two were to make representations for financial assistance to set up an independent Ulster. The story goes that they ended up staying in the same hotel as Republicans who were in Libya to secure weapons for their armed struggle. A fight broke out and Tucker ran for his life. He grabbed a taxi, made straight for the airport and never looked back. He didn't even take his suitcase. Tucker began his paramilitary career running vigilante groups in Protestant West Belfast and rose to leadership as the right-hand man of the UDA's first leader, Charles Hurding Smith. He liked to dabble in politics and founded the New Ulster Political Research Group with Glen Barr and Andy Tyrie, but he did not impress voters, who abandoned him in their droves at the polls. In the mid-1980s he became a brigadier and under his stewardship most military activity ceased. But he fell out of favour with the young Turks, a new breed of ruthless men who saw merit in eliminating members of the IRA and Sinn Fein.

Tucker's pride and joy were his greyhounds, which he raced in Dunmore Stadium in the heart of Republican West Belfast. One of his dogs, which he bought just weeks before Milltown, was worth five thousand pounds. It was worthless after Milltown because he had nowhere to race it. He couldn't run the risk of going into Republican West Belfast: run the risk that his Provo pals might turn on him. Before Milltown he did what he liked. After Milltown he couldn't put a step in Republican West Belfast. Tucker resented the Loyalist cause interfering with his social life and that's why, after my arrest, he put out the rumour that I was 'too extreme' and not a member of the UDA. I had tried to assassinate the Sinn Fein leadership and that did not go down well.

His UDA career came to an end when he brought the full force of a major police investigation on the UDA. In 1989, the year I began my life sentence, he tried to justify the shooting of a Catholic man by passing a security-forces intelligence file to journalists. The outcry led to the establishment of the Stevens

Inquiry to investigate collusion between the security forces and Loyalist paramilitaries. A year later he was arrested after his fingerprint was found on one of the restricted files. He pleaded guilty and was sentenced to six years.

I had one unexpected visit from Tucker when I was in prison. I hadn't asked to see him but he insisted he wanted to see me. It was a Saturday. News of his arrival was relayed through a Shankill Road prisoner. I asked him what Tucker wanted. I didn't get an answer. It was early summer and the weather was warm. I made my way to the yard for a lift to take me to the visiting wing. Saturday is a busy day and lots of men were waiting for transport. I found it unusual that the bus, which usually comes every fifteen minutes or so, wasn't around. The lads were agitated. A prison van pulled up and the lads cheered, but only I was allowed on board. The cheers turned to shouts and abuse. When I walked into the visiting area it was empty. I was the only one there. Normally at mid-morning on Saturday the room is packed with people, but now it was empty except for six prison officers lined up at one end. Sitting at a table was Tucker.

I sat on a chair facing him and we silently acknowledged one another. Tucker was after something. I asked the prison officers to leave us. They ignored me. They hovered just two feet away, which meant they could hear every word of our conversation.

'I don't mind them here. They are just doing their jobs,' Tucker said.

I studied his face, letting him do the talking.

'I need to know about Milltown.'

'It is a need-to-know basis.'

Tucker shifted in his seat. His face was red and I could feel his anger.

'I had a guy come to me recently, Stone. He was in tears. He was young and he cried like a baby. He said he killed Kevin McPolin.'

'He is telling stories.'

'He wanted to get it off his chest. He said he was sorry for killing Kevin McPolin and has nightmares about the man.'

'I was convicted of the murder of McPolin. Why are you here?'

Tucker reached into his jacket and pulled out a small notebook. The sweat was pouring down his face. It was a warm summer's day but he was wearing a jumper, a jacket and an overcoat. He was also wearing his bullet-proof vest. I wanted to leap over the table and break his neck.

'Why are you wearing the vest? Are you afraid of me?'

'You can't be too careful. I need to know more about Milltown.'

'It is a need-to-know basis. Always has been.'

'When you went up to assassinate Martin McGuinness did you meet the Brigadier for Londonderry?'

'Who is he?'

'I know you met him.'

'Are you fishing for information?'

'I need to know about the safe houses and the weapons. Who provided them?'

I never answered him. He blustered that he held UDA rank and was entitled to answers.

'It is need-to-know and you don't need to know.'

'What about the brigadiers. Tell me, who sanctioned Milltown?'

'Need-to-know.'

'When you were arrested, I did not know you were on a UFF-sanctioned operation.'

'My intelligence tells me you met a tabloid Sunday newspaper journalist on the peace line, at a chip shop, and told him to put out the following statement, "Michael Stone is too extreme to be a Loyalist paramilitary. Michael Stone approached us but he was too extreme for the UDA and we turned him down." How extreme can you be when you are taking human life?'

'I did not know you belonged to us.'

'When I get out of here I am coming to see you.'

He left. I never saw him again. I asked one of the prison officers escorting me back to the wing why I had the visiting suite to myself. He made no reply. When I said I was making a formal complaint they told me not to bother, saying they were in the visiting suite 'at the request of your visitor'. Tucker had the whole jail locked down just to see me.

Two months later the Brigadier for Londonderry was dead. The IRA shot him as he sat in his living room talking to two RUC detectives who were there to warn him about his personal safety. The IRA active-service unit stood at a wall and shot through the window. The two detectives lay on the ground. They didn't give chase and they didn't return fire. Tucker had the Brigadier for Londonderry killed.

Tucker died in October 1995 from a massive heart attack while playing pool in Millisle. His death notices made interesting reading. At the time the young Johnny Adair was in charge of the UDA's C Company in the Lower Shankill, and his battalion placed one as coming from Tucker's 'friends in Tenant Street and Ladas Drive', two well-known Belfast RUC stations. I am glad Tucker Lyttle is dead. Like Jim Craig, he bastardised the UDA. He was a career Loyalist, feeding the press, meeting Republicans and meeting his police handlers.

13

THE BIG BALL
IS ROLLING

ENNISKILLEN CONTINUED TO WEIGH HEAVY ON MY MIND AND NOW THAT JOHN MCMICHAEL WAS DEAD I FELT IT WAS UP TO ME TO CONTINUE THE WORK HE STARTED AND AVENGE THE DEATHS OF INNOCENT CIVILIANS. By early 1988 there still had been no retaliation for the atrocity, but I knew it was only a matter of time. I wanted Republicans to pay. I wanted something so terrible it would be for ever stamped on their collective heart. It had to be something spectacular and unforgettable, something they would remember for generations to come.

I continued to stalk Republicans whose names and details appeared on intelligence files given to me by UFF intelligence officers. I continued to pursue my master plan: to use a high-profile Republican as bait and lure his comrades to his funeral. Sooner or later, luck and fate would be on my side. I had also adopted a strict new set of personal rules. It was at this time that I decided I would keep Tucker Lyttle out of the loop. He would never know what my plans were and so wouldn't be in a position to compromise any more operations or my security.

I set my sights on John Joseph Davey. He was a sixty-year-old Sinn Fein councillor. Davey was married with three children and lived a life steeped in Republican traditions. In the 1950s and 1970s he was interred in Long Kesh. In his later years he was an active and devoted member of Sinn Fein and a well-known local politician on Magherafelt District Council. I had seen his intelligence file, which contained the usual assortment of photographs and video images, but one picture caught my eye. It was a large black and white photo of him carrying the coffin of an IRA man from Toome who drove off a bridge while being chased by the security forces. There were also notes from speeches Davey made about 'driving Orange scum into the sea'. He was an old-school Republican but a target. An old-fashioned family man who had a routine, he always returned home for his meals. I would exploit this window of opportunity. A weekday in early February was decided for the sanction.

Davey's home was in the middle of the countryside, surrounded by fields. It was miles from anywhere. I wanted to strike as he left the house. I would disable his car with a Sterling sub-machine gun. The Ruger pistol would deliver the death shots. The telephone wires linking his family to the outside world were cut to allow me extra time to escape from the scene. I hid in the bushes surrounding the remote house, waiting for Davey to appear. He appeared in the pool of light that illuminated his front door, got into his car and drove into the lane. I waited for the Sterling to start rattling, but it didn't. It had jammed. This gave Davey a chance to escape with his life. I fired shots from the Ruger but his early IRA training kicked in and he rolled away from the car in the defensive manoeuvre and, although I kept firing, no bullets struck his body. I ran after him, but an alarm went off, then lights came on, so I disappeared into the dark.

Almost a year to the day later, Davey was shot dead by the Mid-Ulster brigade of the UVF. He was ambushed near his home after attending a council meeting. The gunman had been blooded by me and was my back-up man on my failed attempt on Davey's life. The young gunman hid behind a pillar and opened up with an AK47. Davey was cut to shreds. I got the news when I was on remand in the solitary wing of Crumlin Road jail. I was proud my protégé went back and finished the job. He even carried out the hit to the last detail, as instructed by me a year earlier. He torched the car and left the weapon in the burning wreck. The associate who supplied the weapon didn't want it back. He had a lot of munitions at his disposal.

After Davey, I turned my attention to John Augustin O'Kane. I was determined to have my target as bait for a high-profile Republican funeral. Farmer O'Kane was from Kilrea, County Armagh, and lived with Davey's sister, Annalena. He had a twenty-seven-acre farm on the outskirts of the village. O'Kane only occupied the farm dwelling during the lambing season, but during the rest of the year he paid regular visits. He kept a cock and hens in one shed and there was animal feed and dog kennels in another. A third outbuilding was used for rearing chickens.

I constructed a bomb in Belfast. It was a percussion-cap grenade that I intended attaching with a hook and wire to the door of the henhouse. On the inside of the doorframe, I fixed a small hook to the wood. I then attached the wire to a bolt at the back of the grenade's fly-off levers, tested the tension of the wire to make sure the device detonated at the exact moment after O'Kane pushed open the door. I'd set a nine-second delay, so it would explode when he was deep inside the shed. Things didn't go according to plan. O'Kane didn't push open the door, but Stephen Kennedy, his nephew, did and the device exploded, causing eye injuries. I was surprised to find out later that there were also kids at the farm at the time. I didn't see any on my dry runs, but that day happened to be a school holiday. They weren't physically hurt, but all the same I had angry words for my contacts.

One year later, Kennedy lifted a bail of hay at his farm. It had been booby-trapped with an RDG5 grenade by a unit I had trained. As he moved the bail he heard the grenade click and ran for his life. He escaped serious injury for a second time.

THE BIG BALL IS ROLLING

The Game

Dad's resting after dinner, gone the hard day's toil.
Manually breaking the earth, rhythmically
shovelling the soil.

The television is humming as he slumbers in his chair.
Mum's gone to run an errand, so he'd better beware.
Two mischievous little eyes watch in a calculating way.
It's young Darryl aged four, he's determined to play.
Armed with weapons of plastic, a gun and a knife.
Man's well-rehearsed ritual, in the taking of life.

Darryl wants to have fun, so he plans his attack.
He'll pounce on his quarry with a punch and a smack.
Pick the right moment, when he's deep in his slumber.
A scream and a shout as he strikes Dad like thunder.
That instinctive reaction wakes Dad with a start.
'Christ, it's only the nipper' as hand goes to heart.
The youngster, now puzzled, beats a hasty retreat.
Dad looks angry, as he gets to his feet.

The game now commences, mission search and destroy.
Both hysterical with laughter, this man and his boy.
The battle is relentless, over chairs, under beds.
An inevitable conclusion, poor Dad lies dead.
Those imaginary projectiles, from a toy plastic gun
Have concluded this battle, the victor – the son.
The deceased playing possum is refusing to budge.
Darryl kneels by his father, first a touch, then a nudge.

The boy is frightened by stillness,
not sure what he's done.
'I was only playing, Daddy, it was only fun.'
His pleas go unheeded, gone the fun and the joy.
So cruel to torment his beautiful boy.
'Please get up, Daddy, please don't die.'
A surge of emotion, he has started to cry.
Comforting arms embrace him, Dad's eyes
fill with tears.
A re-enactment of reality. Damned rebellious years.

14

CHAIN REACTION

I DIDN'T GET MY REPUBLICAN BAIT, BUT FATE WAS TO DEAL ME AN AMAZING HAND ON 6 MARCH 1988. IRONICALLY, THE BRITISH GOVERNMENT WOULD SET ME UP WITH THE PERFECT SCENARIO, THREE DEAD IRA HEROES. The SAS shot dead the three in Gibraltar. The two men and a woman were planning a murderous attack on innocent people. The British government said the target was a military band that played in front of the Governor's residence during the ceremonial changing of the guard, but men, women and children bystanders would have been caught in the blast. It said the soldiers acted because they were in danger. The dead IRA members – Sean Savage, Mairead Farrell and Danny McCann – were posing as holidaymakers on the Rock. Rumours circulated that there was a fourth member of the active-service unit, who fled for her life when the shooting started.

The authorities made political capital out of the Gibraltar incident. Praise was heaped on the SAS men for killing three terrorists who were out to take human life. The government showed the IRA who was boss, and then came the embarrassment when no weapons or bombs were found in the car. A device was found the next day, in a car in nearby Marbella, but the SAS still came under fire, accused of having a licence to kill. The three deaths on the Rock became a notorious propaganda weapon for the IRA, and the Republican movement has never forgotten it.

Those deaths had an impact on my associates and myself. We were pleased the British Army's elite had eliminated three ruthless killers and saved scores of innocent lives. We were glad when Sinn Fein had problems getting the bodies home. Its leadership had to plead with the Irish government for a specially chartered plane after Spanish ground staff refused to handle the bodies. I listened to every media broadcast and discovered they would be flown to Dublin and taken by road to Belfast. I hoped Loyalists would turn out by the thousand and throw missiles at the cortège, and they did. They threw bricks and missiles from overhead motorway walkways.

I scanned the death notices in the *Irish News* for details of the triple funeral. The funeral service would form the backbone of my operation. The three gunned down in Gibraltar would be buried with full military honours at the Republican Plot in Milltown cemetery, in the heart of West Belfast. This is Sinn Fein/IRA's cenotaph, where the remains of many Republican soldiers are buried, a historic and emotional place for all Republicans. Martin McGuinness would be there and so would Gerry Adams. The mourners would be a who's who of the IRA. The leadership was about to get the shock of its life.

I went to see a senior member of the UDA and told him I wanted official clearance to undertake a special operation. I said the sanction was in retaliation for the Poppy Day massacre at Enniskillen and other atrocities carried out by the IRA. The brigadier said he needed to know the exact details of what I had in mind, including the names of the targets, where it would happen and my weapons of choice. I refused point-blank to tell him anything. I told the brigadier the operation was 'something special'.

He insisted he needed more information. I stood firm and refused to give any details, saying my personal safety depended on the confidentiality of the operation. When he said again he needed more information before he could OK the sanction, I told him: McGuinness and Adams, within ten days. He promised to come back to me within twenty-four hours of consulting his colleagues. When he came back he said I had official UFF clearance to sanction Adams and McGuinness. He also informed me of the official codeword for claiming responsibility, but I would never have claimed responsibility. I wasn't stupid. I knew that calls were made to the Samaritans and newsrooms and that those calls were recorded.

I now had ten days to prepare. Top of my list was munitions. I had my two personal weapons, the Ruger and the Armalite, but I needed something different. I couldn't stick an Armalite up my coat and use it at the Republican Plot. I had to have different weapons and new weapons, and I knew exactly who could help me. I took a train to Coleraine to see an associate I was sure could help me. I knew he could supply the munitions I needed to make my contribution at the IRA's cenotaph. I always used public transport when visiting contacts and associates. Buses and trains were the ideal way of getting around Northern Ireland suspicion-free. Buses and trains were never stopped and searched by the security forces but cars were. Taking a car posed too high a risk.

I was met in Coleraine by my associate and informed I was going on a drive. I took a seat in the last car of a three-car convoy and our journey began. Each car was linked to the others via walkie-talkie. We drove for miles. Two hours later the car stopped. I was back in roughly the same area where our journey had begun earlier in the day. It was a farm in the middle of nowhere. I was introduced to 'Mr A' in the hay shed of his sprawling property. Mr A was a leading figure in Ulster Resistance, which was launched in 1986 in response to the controversial Anglo-Irish Agreement. He invited me to sit down. Next to where I was seated was a massive item covered in tarpaulin. I pulled back the covers and there was part of a large arms shipment that had arrived from South Africa via contacts of Brian Nelson. Nelson was a high-ranking UDA/UFF man who was also a British Army agent. The shipment was split three ways – between the UDA, the UVF and Ulster Resistance – and each got a one-third share. Contained in Ulster Resistance's share were AK47s, RPGs, rocket launchers, 9mm revolvers and grenades. I had never seen so many weapons in one place at one time.

There was also another container, about four feet long, and Mr A asked me if I wanted to see something special. It was an FIM/92A Stinger, a £50,000 surface-to-air rocket launcher, which he said arrived in the shipment by mistake. Mr A told me the Stinger 'just arrived, out of the blue'. He said it was going back to South Africa, but I don't know if it was returned or not.

Mr A didn't say much except to tell me to take whatever I needed and to use it well. I could have walked away from that remote hay shed with five revolvers, five rifles and twenty grenades, but I took enough to carry on my person without raising suspicion. Instead of being greedy, I took seven grenades, one Browning pistol, a box of 9mm rounds and two extra magazines. I wrapped the detonators in tin foil and placed them in my outside pockets. I wanted to prevent them from getting warm against my body and igniting. I put the Browning down the waistband of my trousers. I now had my weapons.

My associate drove me to a safe house. In the kitchen I raided the cupboard for food. I put biscuits, bread and milk in two plastic bags and hid the grenades and the gun among them. On top I placed a carton of eggs.

I was to be driven back to Belfast by my contact, but when I got into the back seat a stranger was behind the steering wheel. I had never seen him before. My associate told me to 'not worry about vehicle checkpoints'. The car drove off. The driver, one hand on the steering wheel, held up his RUC warrant card. If we were stopped at a checkpoint he would show his pass and we would be waved through. My associate left me at the Albert clock in the centre of Belfast and I walked to the bus stop to get the number 24 home. It arrived. I paid my fare, took a seat at the back and got off just yards from the house. As I walked up the garden path I realised I was taking my weapons of war home with me. I hid the grenade and pistol in the dog kennels. If the house was raided, the cops would never get near them – my dogs would eat them alive.

Later I watched the news. I watched in disgust as the Irish police saluted the three bodies as they were removed from the belly of the plane. I felt anger rising in the pit of my stomach as they escorted the massive convoy as it left the airport to begin its journey northwards. The Irish people had given the IRA dead a hero's welcome, and that made my blood boil.

The countdown had begun. The bodies were back home and would be buried within the next three days. I chose my back-up team. It was to be a three-man squad consisting of me, a driver and a back-up gunman. The others were not members of the UFF but part of a trusted network of freelancers and associates I had nurtured all over the province. The original plan was that the back-up man would accompany me into the cemetery and cover me as I made my move on Adams and McGuinness. He would be armed with an automatic rifle that had a folding stock for easy concealment. He would also have three of the seven grenades, which would enable him to perform a crossfire operation. He was young, with some experience of active service, but he believed in the cause. He had fire in his belly. He told me he understood the importance of the operation and was prepared to die at my side if it came to it.

My driver was someone I had worked with before and trusted with my life. He was my protégé and I had trained and blooded him. On 8 March I did a recce with my driver. I had specialist associates. One gave me aerial shots of the cemetery and another gave me street maps which had the exact placing of the Army sangars, or lookout posts, overlooking Milltown cemetery. This information was vital. I needed to know if I would be observed in the cemetery and leaving it after the attack.

While my driver explored a variety of escape-route options in his car, I took a look around the cemetery. First I went to the Roll of Honour. Names were inscribed on the black marble, honouring those who died for their great cause. I knew the cortège would have to pass it. I smiled to myself at the poetic irony of it. The coffins of three dead martyrs would pass and, as mourners grieve for their fallen comrades, the IRA leadership dies with a clean shot to the head. This would be their Enniskillen, an insult to their war dead.

I thought about using a bomb to cause maximum chaos and injury. I thought of booby-trapping the open grave at the nearby Republican Plot with a hair-trigger pressure plate that would go off as soon as the coffins were lowered into it. I abandoned the idea because I thought it was too indiscriminate. It sounded too much like Enniskillen. I realised to do that, to prime the open grave, as mourners looked on, would be to stoop lower than the Provos. It would be sacrilegious to butcher people as they mourned their dead, even if the dead and the mourners were Republicans. I would be better than McGuinness and his people. My actions on 16 March would prove I was no indiscriminate sectarian killer. I had three targets, Gerry Adams, Martin McGuinness and Danny Morrison. Ordinary people were not the targets, but if they became involved, then so be it.

I checked the immediate area around the Republican Plot by foot. I checked all my routes. I walked slowly around the central path and measured the distance to the chain-link fence that separated an industrial complex from the graveyard. I also measured from the chain-link fence to the motorway, where my getaway car would be waiting. I needed precision. The whole operation relied on split-second timing. I went back and redid the journey, this time at a faster pace. I searched for places where I could position myself and not be outflanked by Republicans who no doubt would do their best to catch me as I made my escape.

The whole operation had now begun to take shape. I visualised it and in my mind's eye I saw it all crystal-clear. I shoot Adams and McGuinness, drop a few grenades to panic and confuse people and in the mayhem I escape to the motorway, where my associates and I make our escape.

I started to fine-tune everything. I chose my clothes carefully. I couldn't go into Milltown cemetery in the standard Loyalist hit-squad gear of blue boiler suit, heavy boots, gloves and balaclava. So I chose a new look. I needed to blend in. I wanted to look no different from the hundreds of young Republicans who would go to the funeral service and pay their final respects at the Republican Plot. I had to look like them, but I also had weapons to conceal. The gun couldn't sit in my coat pocket and I couldn't string the grenades around my neck. My outfit had to perform two functions: disguise me and disguise my weapons.

In my garden shed I experimented with items of clothing from my own wardrobe. I tried fleece jackets and jeans. I tucked the guns down the waistband of my trousers but they were too bulky and too obvious. I started to use my head, making mental notes about exactly what my requirements were for the operation. I needed functional clothes that didn't look out of place. I went to a motorbike shop and bought leather gloves. I cut the legs out of an old pair of Levis and made holsters from one leg to secure a gun under each armpit. From the other leg I made a kangaroo-type pouch which I would tie around my stomach to hold the seven grenades. The pouch would be linked to the holsters with old leather ties. The grenades would be placed in the pouch, the ones with the shortest fuse settings first. I etched the Roman numeral 'V' on two five-second grenades so that in the heat of the operation I knew exactly which grenade to grab. I made a webbing holder for the grenades with two old belts. I stitched them together and laughed to myself at the thought of the young Michael Stone sewing mailbags as he did his time in the

Maze for stealing guns. The fleece top, jacket and all-weather coat disguised the bulkiness of the munitions I was carrying around my middle and under my arms. I was ready.

I checked my weapons meticulously. I cleaned both and took the Browning to a shooting range I had made for myself. It was down a storm drain and completely soundproofed. I used it regularly and there were thousands of spent shell cases down there. I put my earplugs in and used the gun, shooting round after round to make sure it worked properly. After ten minutes I was satisfied with the weapon and had no reason to believe it would let me down. I was ready for war, ready to die for God and Ulster.

I felt uncomfortable that I kept my weapons of war in my family home, but I consoled myself by saying it was the biggest operation of my life, it was right to do this because the operation was honourable and I was taking the war into the Provos' own backyard.

I kept contact with my two associates to a minimum. I had one dry run with the driver and now it was time to coach my back-up man. The original plan was that he would accompany me into the graveyard and perform a crossfire operation, but I had a change of heart. I wanted to go into Milltown alone. On 14 March I told him of my new plan. At first he didn't believe me and playfully punched me with his fist. I looked him in the eye and told him I wasn't joking: his new role would be strictly as my back-up man and he would keep position on the motorway. I reassured him by saying I needed a good man who would give accurate covering fire when I was chased by Republicans. I told him his job was still important and probably more important than going into Milltown with me. He pleaded with me to change my mind. I told him my mind was made up and that he now had a new role on the city-bound carriageway of the M1 motorway.

He looked at me, tears welling in his eyes, and begged me to give him a chance. I shook my head and said no. The lad broke down and cried. He sobbed like a baby. After the tears of disappointment dried, we talked. I explained my decision. I told him that I couldn't guarantee his safety. I told him the operation came with no guarantees. I said there was a chance both of us would die at the Republican Plot. He said he was prepared to die at my side and asked one final time if I would change my mind. I said no. He told me he would never forgive me and I told him to behave himself.

Back home, Leigh-Ann had taken the children shopping. It was the perfect opportunity for me to have a full dress rehearsal. The guns fitted perfectly in the denim holsters, the barrels pointing backwards and out. The handmade webbing to hold the grenades was also a snug fit. I took one look in the mirror and I didn't like what I saw. I was standing in my own home dressed for my war with Republicans. I was putting my family's life on the line. I was an arrogant and selfish bastard. My children and wife came a poor second to the Republicans I made it my life's mission to stalk. No one in my entire family knew I was a paramilitary. It would be a shock to them all if I were to die on active service on 16 March. Before I went on an operation, I gave myself a survival rate. Most of the time it was 50:50. I figured Milltown would be at least 60:40 against me, but could even be less. But I believed it was worth a risk if it meant the leadership of the Republican movement was wiped out.

My human side continued to seep through the tough soldier exterior. Reality was beginning to hit home. The enormity of what I was about to do was starting to sink in. I can remember every freeze-framed second of the day before the operation. Unable to sleep, I took an early morning walk in the Belfast hills. I took my dogs and sat on a bench and watched the city wake up below me. I could see the shipyard, where I worked as a teenager. I could see other landmarks, such as the City Hall and the Royal Victoria Hospital. I could see Milltown spread out before me. I knew I might die on active service and for a brief second I thought about pulling the plug on the operation. I was only human, not a robot or a monster. I didn't have ice running through my veins. I was anxious and a little scared. I was doing Milltown for innocent

Protestants and civilians everywhere. I was doing this to protect innocent people, no matter what their religion, from the evil endorsed by Gerry Adams and Martin McGuinness.

I continued walking and thinking and ended up at the home of a good friend. I asked him to take my dogs and to look after them, not to fight them, and said if he was bad to them I would be bad to him. He was puzzled and asked what was going on and why I was leaving my terriers and pitbulls with him. I told him I needed to know the dogs were in safe hands. As I walked away from his home he shouted after me, 'I don't understand what's going on, Stoner. What about Leigh-Ann and the kids?' I never answered and just kept on walking, not daring to look back.

I was now focused and in control. The big ball was rolling. The big ball was in motion and once moving couldn't be stopped. I met up with my two associates and together we did our final dry run. We drove to the M1, pulled into the hard shoulder and I went over the sequence of events with them to make sure they understood their instructions. I had to be sure in my head the two volunteers knew exactly what their job was and their exact positions during the entire operation. I warned them to be alert and fine-tuned for danger. I told the driver to cruise the roundabouts and junctions of the Westlink and under no circumstances to sit on the hard shoulder for hours on end. I stressed it was essential he keep moving to avoid being spotted by the security forces. I told them that when they were parked on the hard shoulder they should open the car bonnet, scatter some water on the ground and pretend to have a broken radiator. It was important they used their heads and not look suspicious. The golden rule was to keep moving.

As we pulled away from Milltown my back-up man once again asked me to change my mind about letting him take part in the cemetery part of the operation. I didn't answer his question, just shook my head and indicated to the driver to move off.

I knew the time of the funeral from the death notices in the *Irish*

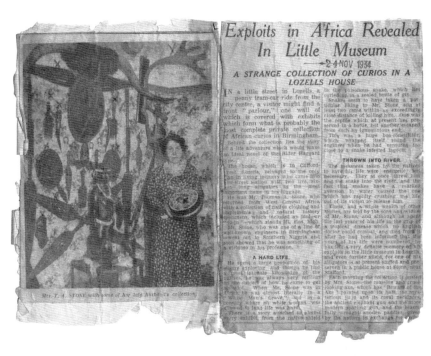

Exploits in Africa Revealed
In Little Museum
→ 2 4 NOV 1934
A STRANGE COLLECTION OF CURIOS IN A LOZELLS HOUSE

IN a little street in Lozells, a penny tram-car ride from the city centre, a visitor might find a front "parlour," one wall of which is covered with exhibits which form what is probably the most complete private collection of African curios in Birmingham.

Behind the collection lies the story of a life adventure which would make an ideal novel of the Rider Haggard type.

The house, which is in Clifford-road, Lozells, belonged to the only man in living memory who came to his street laden with two live, six-long alligators as the most important items in his luggage.

He was Mr. Thomas A. Stone, who returned from West Central Africa with a collection of native clothing and implements and natural history specimens, which included an idol—or a *jo-jo*—which stands 5ft. 6ins. high.

Mr. Stone, who was one of a line of well-known engineers in Birmingham, set out for Southern Nigeria and soon showed that he was something of a virtuoso in his profession.

A HARD LIFE.

He spent a large proportion of his life exploring. And though he had a great intimate knowledge of the natives, he was always very reticent on the subject of how he came to get that idol. When Mr. Stone was in Africa he was almost literally in a "White Man's Grave," and in a country where no white woman was known to keep life was hard.

There is a story attached to almost every exhibit, from the native shield

by the poisonous snake, which lies curled up in a sealed bottle of gin.

Snakes seem to have taken a particular liking to Mr. Stone, and at least two came within an exceedingly close distance of killing him. One was the reptile which at present lies preserved in a bottle, but another escaped from such an ignominious end.

This was a huge boa constrictor, which wrapped itself round the engineer when he had ventured too close to a snake-infested lagoon.

THROWN INTO RIVER.

The measures taken by the natives to save his life were energetic, but necessary. They at once threw him and the snake into the river, and the fact that snakes have a marked aversion to water caused the one which was rapidly crushing the life out of its victim to release him.

These, and a whole wealth of other stories, are told by the son and widow of Mr. Stone, who, although he spent the last years of his life in the grip of a tropical disease which no English doctor could combat, and died from it after he had been informed that the years of his life were numbered, has left a very definite memory of his exploits in the little museum in Lozells and even further afield, for one of his alligators is at present stuffed and preserved in a public house at Stone, near Stafford.

Each morning the collection is dusted by Mrs. Stone—the massive and cruel-looking axe, which has "Beware of the axe" painted upon its haft, the mysterious *ju-ju* and its coral necklaces, the ancient elephant gun and the more modern sporting gun, and the beautifully carved wooden paddles, given by the natives in exchange.

Mrs. T. A. STONE with some of her late husband's collection.

My great-grandfather, Thomas Alfred Stone, was a real character. He kept a pet baboon – Jacko (*pictured below*) – and two alligators. He spent many years in South Africa, laying the railway along the Gold Coast. (*Inset*) My other great-grandfather, James 'Soldier' Moore, who served with the Royal Irish Fusiliers.

Margaret Mary Gregg, who, along with her husband John, raised me as her own child.

Top left: The only picture I have of my biological parents, Mary Bridget O'Sullivan and Cyril Alfred Stone – a symbol of who I am, and a poignant reminder of the two people who brought me into this world but played no part in my upbringing.

Top right: My grandfather, Cyril Stone, who served in the Royal Corps of Signals.

Bottom: My biological father in the RAF (*bottom row, third from left*).

Top: Me aged two and five.

Bottom left: Me aged seven with my Christmas present – a Johnny 7 gun.
I am pictured with my elder sister, Rosemary.

Bottom right: Aged eighteen on the Braniel estate.

I married Marlene in 1976 but the marriage soon broke down.

Above and opposite: Mad Dog Adair. He used to visit me in the Maze before his meteoric rise through the UFF command structure – but he was more interested in the fame game than being a true Loyalist.

Bottom left: The Long Kesh First Flute with a banner of John McMichael.

Bottom right: With Bobby Philpot, one of my prison talks team.

Top: One of my efforts painted on the wall of H-Block 7 of the Maze.

Bottom: UDA and UFF banners in the Maze.

News. It was common knowledge that the security forces were staying away, but I needed to be sure. At previous Republican funerals it was normal for the RUC and British Army to be present. They were there to stop Republicans firing a volley of shots over tricolour-draped coffins, and Republicans saw this unwanted intervention as a massive insult to the memory of their dead. I checked with one of my intelligence officers, who confirmed the RUC and Army would not be shadowing the ceremony. He asked why I wanted to know and I told him I was working in the area and was making sure my personal security wasn't going to be compromised. I had a clear run and that was one less thing to worry about.

Throughout the day I paid visits to friends. There was a good chance I would not survive the operation. Every time I felt apprehensive at the thought of the operation, I forced Martin McGuinness's face into my mind. That was enough to spark the fire of hate bubbling in my belly. If you play, you pay, Martin.

I did final checks on my weapons and gave the getaway car a final examination. I had personally modified it. I welded a quarter-inch steel plate inside the boot to provide an extra layer of security. Cushions were filled with sand and placed against the back window, again for added protection. I also dropped the suspension to make the car stick to the road when we made our high-speed getaway.

I knew I had emotionally and physically switched off from Leigh-Ann. I was a mass of contradictions, wanting to be close to my loved ones and yet craving my privacy. I tried to play games with Daryl but it was forced fun. I just wanted to hold him in my arms. I was saying goodbye to a little boy I might never see again. My beautiful Lucy was just a baby and I cuddled her, fed her and got her ready for bed. Leigh-Ann was suspicious and asked me if I was feeling all right. I gave her a stupid answer, something about a father wanting to spend time with his daughter, but she just looked at me with a funny expression on her face.

I tuned into every news bulletin. The late news on BBC Radio

Ulster said large crowds were expected at the triple funeral. I knew it was going to be huge and guessed somewhere in the region of two thousand, maybe three. Bravado was beginning to set in. I honestly believed I could take on a crowd of that size and win. I really believed I could take out three, maybe more, top Republicans and get out of the cemetery alive. I was focused. I had three men in my sights and I knew that, if everything went according to my detailed plans, then this time tomorrow Gerry Adams, Martin McGuinness and Danny Morrison would be dead.

The large crowds gathered to mourn the Gibraltar dead were not my targets. I was after those who organised, supported and condoned atrocities such as La Mon and Enniskillen. I knew that some non-IRA people might get caught in the crossfire and that would be regrettable in my eyes, but that was war and in war innocent people get injured and killed.

I went to bed but couldn't sleep. I tossed and turned for hours before giving up and getting dressed at 3am. I sat with Lucy for an hour. She was sleeping gently and peacefully in her cot. I kissed her and went into the kitchen and turned on the radio. West Belfast was aflame with rioting. Republicans were welcoming home their martyrs with hijacked vehicles and flaming barricades. I looked at old baby photographs. I thought about my three sons from my first marriage, Michael, Gary and Jason. Soon Leigh-Ann was up, getting Daryl and Lucy ready for the day. She asked me why I tossed and turned and why I couldn't sleep. I lied. I told my wife I was bidding for an important tender and would know in the next few hours if I was successful. She put the kettle on and made us both a cup of coffee. We sat in the kitchen in a comfortable silence. I took her hand and told her I would see her later.

At the back door I turned to look at her and wave goodbye, but she had her head turned away, bouncing Lucy in her arms. This is my lasting image of 16 March 1988: my young wife holding our daughter in her arms as I waved an unseen goodbye to them both.

15

MILLTOWN

I UNLOCKED MY SHED AND STARTED THE RITUAL OF DRESSING FOR THE OPERATION. I DID SO METHODICALLY RATHER THAN MECHANICALLY. I strapped the handmade webbing around my middle and placed the grenades in it. I primed them by straightening the split pins and placed them in order of time delay into the webbing. I filled the speed strips – security forces issue at the time – with .357 Magnum and Winchester bullets and placed them in the pouch. I put on the denim holsters and inserted the weapons, barrel down, cocked and with the safety catch on. The leather gloves and a cap went into the pockets of my all-weather coat. I was ready for my war with the Republican movement. It was payback time, big style.

I followed my usual travelling procedure, taking a bus into town. I sat at the back. When I look back now, I find it unbelievable that I had live grenades strapped to my stomach and guns under my arms. I listened to idle chit-chat, pensioners talking about the weather, kids talking about school and young mothers coaxing toddlers to behave.

Then he arrived, a friend from my youth. He insisted on sitting beside me. I wanted to be alone with my thoughts, but he insisted on taking the seat beside me and refused to stop chirping in my ear. He even put his arm around me and said, 'What about those Provies being buried today. I hope it pisses out of the heavens on them.' I agreed. Of course I wanted it to rain. If it rained it meant I could pull the hood of my coat up over my head and disguise my long hair.

I got off at the City Hall and was surprised how quiet the city centre was, but then I remembered it was a Wednesday and half-day closing. I began walking in the direction of the Royal Victoria Hospital, keeping my eyes peeled for a black taxi, but there were none around. The vehicles, which normally clogged the city's roads, were today like the proverbial hen's teeth. I kept walking and was soon in West Belfast outside the Falls Road entrance of the Royal Victoria. Small crowds had started to gather and were walking in tight clusters towards the Andersonstown Road.

Walking in the opposite direction was an Army foot patrol. There were eight soldiers and two policemen. I nodded at one RUC officer as we passed each other, then realised what I had done. I had invited attention. Because of my cockiness I looked suspicious. I looked like a young Republican and I had deliberately chosen that look. I was fucking stupid to wink and nod at the Army because Republican youths wouldn't do that. The security forces now had an excuse to stop and question me.

I was staring trouble straight in the eye. The young policeman stopped in his tracks and repositioned the weapon he was carrying. Did he want to search me? I could see him nodding to me and whispering to his superior. What the hell was I going to say? What was I going to do? I pulled a story out of thin air. I was a gambler, I owed money, I was told to bring the weapons to a man in a blue van parked in the car park of the hospital to pay my debts. If they search me, they charge me with possession and I am looking at twenty years. I kept walking. I had my first close call of the day.

A black cab pulled up alongside me. I got in and joined two young men and a young woman. They looked at me and I looked at them. They continued their conversation, speaking quietly to one another and I was relieved they ignored me. We began our journey to St Agnes's church but didn't get very far. The road was jammed with people. The black cab pulled up outside Andersonstown leisure centre and I got out to make the walk to the church, where the funeral mass for Danny McCann and Sean Savage would take place. Mairead Farrell's funeral service was taking place in another part of the city, but she would join her dead colleagues for the slow procession to the Republican Plot. I gave the driver a pound coin, dropping it into the tiny tray. I walked into the crowd and heard, 'Hey, lad, hey, big fella.' I turned towards the voice. It was the driver. I instinctively felt for my Browning and he stuck his hand out of the window and said, 'Here's your money back, the black cabs are on us all day.'

I kept walking towards the church, keeping on the left-hand side of the road. There were thousands of people. Last night I had guessed somewhere in the region of two thousand mourners, but today I could see how much I misjudged. There were at least four thousand people here. The streets and roads were clogged with men, women and children making their slow pilgrimage to the funeral mass. I stood on the steps of the leisure centre and had a good look around. I could see two of the coffins had arrived. I could see Danny Morrison organising media crews and pointing out the best locations for cameras and reporters. I felt I was watching a really bad movie about Northern Ireland. I heard the click-click of a nearby camera. It was time to move further up and further in.

I mingled with the crowd and was shocked to discover it was a broad sweep of nationalism as well as Republicanism. Some were middle class and some were working class. There were sharp suits and tracksuits. There were thick West Belfast accents and middle-class accents. There was a guy in a wheelchair being pushed by a kind friend. I remember him clearly. I remember thinking the IRA had done this to innocent civilians. I walked on, gathering speed. There were children everywhere, playing games and chasing one another. They were shouting and laughing at the tops of their voices. I felt a surge of anger. The parents of these children were mad taking youngsters to something like this.

The *Irish News* photographer, Hugh Russell, had found himself a good place to take pictures. He was sitting on a gatepost snapping away. I kept my head down and walked on. The world's press had gathered to try to capture the atmosphere and emotion of the day. I didn't want to be in any of those pictures. I needed to stay anonymous. I mistakenly thought the funeral would be packed with men, but there were a lot of ordinary people and young girls. One came striding up to me and said, 'I know you. You're Flinto. You drink in the upstairs lounge of the Beaten Docket. I didn't know you were one of us.' I had been recognised by a waitress. I smiled at her and kept walking. By now there were more than five thousand in the immediate area around the church. The coffins of Sean Savage and Danny McCann were lined up at the bottom of the church steps. I saw Martin McGuinness and Gerry Adams arrive. Businesslike, they shook the hands of people I assume were family, surrounding the coffins.

On the road branching away from the Andersontown Road and leading to the M1 motorway, I could see a wall of Land Rovers and cops with Ruger rifles. I was faced with a dilemma. I had a perfect opportunity to assassinate both men as they stood at the coffins, but I had no getaway car. To get away, I would have to run straight into that wall of cops, who would think I was a Provo who'd taken a 'head stagger' – gone nuts – and shoot me on sight. The opportunity was there. There were hundreds of opportunities. At the entrance to the church, Danny Morrison was organising young girls into columns. McGuinness and Adams disappeared into the church and I followed them. I remember clearly the water well at the back of the chapel, where Catholics dip and bless themselves. I did a bluff 'bless myself' to cover my tracks.

The chapel was packed. It was standing room only. I positioned myself three rows from the back of the church, standing at the inner end of a pew. I watched the pre-funeral activities and the church staff making last-minute preparations on the altar. There was a strong smell of incense. I mentally searched for a place to open fire. I could clearly see the back of McGuinness's and Adams's heads. I wanted to pull a grenade out and blast the two of them to smithereens.

But the families were beginning to arrive. There was a blonde teenage girl, Danny McCann's sister. She was crying and a woman had an arm around her shoulder, supporting her, while another woman held her hand. I saw her tears and her grief and I felt sad for her. Until you witness a family's grief as their loved one is buried, you don't understand the human aspect of killing someone. When you are on active service you refuse to acknowledge that the target has people who love him and will miss him when he's gone. You try not to acknowledge the human cost. The target is a soldier, and in wars soldiers die. As I watched two families mourn a husband, father and son, I thought of my own wife and mother, who would mourn just like these people if I were killed in action.

I learnt a lesson in St Agnes's church. Republicans weep and mourn, just like Loyalists. I stored the image of the weeping blonde girl and I thought about her throughout the day but, as I watched her take a seat behind her dead relative, the soldier in me took over and I knew it was time. It wasn't part of the original plan to execute McGuinness, Adams and Morrison in their place of worship. It seemed too barbaric to do that in the confines of a church. But I wanted to do it because the INLA did it in the County Armagh village of Darkley in 1983, when they murdered three civilians as they gathered to pray.

I forward-ran the sequence of events in my head. I saw myself marching up the middle aisle, opening fire and making my escape. I saw myself throwing a grenade up the aisle for good measure. I kept staring at the backs of their heads and thought it would be so easy if only I could find a way through the sea of people. The crowds were packed five, ten and fifteen deep at the back of the church and there were thousands more outside. I knew that if I pulled the pins and lobbed the grenades into a confined space, the body count would be big. I couldn't do it. I thought of McCann's crying relative. These families were just like my family. Perhaps they didn't know their loved ones were in the IRA and had dedicated themselves to a war. My family didn't know about my life as a Loyalist volunteer, so why should these people be any different?

The blonde girl saved Adams and McGuinness in the chapel. I saw my own family reflected in her face. It was a missed chance.

The church unnerved me and I left before the funeral service started. I wondered why people were staring at me. Outside, as I made my way towards the cemetery, it dawned on me. I had left my cap on inside the church. It is a tradition that men remove their hats when they are attending a place of worship, and this is especially important when attending a funeral because it shows respect for the person who has died. It was ironic. The cap was my disguise but my bloody disguise made me stand out in the church. That meant people were now aware of me. Years later, when I was in prison, a Jesuit priest wrote to me. He was in the congregation that day and noticed me. He said he wondered why I didn't take my hat off, and did I realise that I stood out like a sore thumb? It was because I kept the hat on, he said, that he had never forgotten my face.

Outside, the remains of Mairead Farrell were approaching and a sea of people walked behind her coffin. I stood at the strip of shops and watched as she came to rest at the bottom of the steps. McCann's and Savage's coffins had already left the church and the three comrades were reunited for the final journey. McGuinness and Adams were also outside, getting into position for the slow walk to Milltown cemetery. The massive crowd, estimated by the RUC to be around ten thousand, was beginning to move. I had to be in position before the cortège and the sea of people arrived.

I walked faster than the rest of the mourners, who kept a snail's pace to accompany the remains of the three. As I approached the gates of Milltown I recognised someone. It was Tim, a former member of the Hole in the Wall Gang and the angry young Catholic who set fire to my friend's house when we were teenagers. He was with another man and they were both wearing the trademark armbands of Sinn Fein. As I passed him he said to one, 'I know that man, he's a Prod.' I reached into my coat and flicked the safety catch of the Browning but kept walking. He shouted after me, 'Hey, fella, I know you, you're Stoner.' I ignored him and kept walking at a slow pace. Directly in front of me was another man wearing an armband, and he was pointing at me and gesturing to the two behind me. He opened his mouth and spoke.

'Where you going, mate?

'I'm going to the funeral. Do you have a problem with that?'

I looked in the direction of the sangar and knew the Army was photographing everything that was happening. I knew that if I shot this guy, the soldier in the sangar was going to shoot me. I quietly laughed to myself at the irony of being killed on active service by the British Army after years of defending my community, defending them by chasing Republicans all over the country. I continued walking. The man with the armband made no further attempt to stop me.

Milltown looked different today. Nearby, ordinary people were tending the graves of loved ones. I stood at the Roll of Honour and looked at it again. I reread the names. I was moved. These were the names of soldiers and volunteers who fought and died for a cause they believed in. Soon the names of another three would be added: the three who had died for Ireland on the streets of Gibraltar. I was astounded by the formality and the glory the Republican movement afforded their dead, and the personal sacrifice each volunteer had made was acknowledged. The people tending the nearby graves started to leave. That's when I learnt another lesson, that not all Catholics supported the IRA. It was obvious these people did not want to be around when the IRA funeral began.

I took a mental note of my position and had a walk around the immediate area. I knew I had about twenty minutes before the cortège arrived. Judging from the crowds gathered outside the church, it would be unlikely the cortège could move faster than a crawl. I was aware of six men, with walkie-talkies, hovering around the Republican Plot. I looked towards the motorway. By now my getaway car and two associates would be on the move and could even be speeding past Milltown at that very second. The two had been given their instructions and were to carry them out exactly to the letter. I trusted both of them. They were good Loyalists.

As I watched the traffic whizzing by, another vehicle caught my eye. It was a white Ford Transit and was parked on the hard shoulder of the city-bound carriageway of the motorway. I found it very odd, just sitting there. What was a van doing in the exact place I had picked as my pick-up point, and why was it there given a triple Republican funeral was about to start? It was about six hundred metres away. I had seen the vehicle, so surely the occupants had seen me. For a brief second I thought it was abandoned and soon to be turned into a bomb scare by Loyalists, but if that was the case I would have known about it.

The dirty old Transit made me feel uneasy. I had no idea what it was doing there or who was in it, but I definitely knew something was up. Was it the Provos with their own in-house security? Was there a gang of men in the back getting ready to mingle among mourners and keeping an eye out for trouble? I didn't think the IRA would be so obvious as to plant a surveillance unit on a busy motorway.

I tried to forget it, telling myself it was a driver in difficulty and he would soon be gone. It would be three young men in boiler suits who would provide the answer. I watched in disbelief as they ran across both the city- and country-bound lanes of the motorway. To my surprise, out of the van jumped two policemen wearing black jumpsuits and bullet-proof vests, with their trousers tucked into their boots. They were not wearing headgear, had closely cropped hair and were carrying rifles. They were not ordinary RUC officers. They looked like a SWAT team. I could see them quizzing the young men, who were pointing across the carriageway. I later discovered the young lads were enrolled in the industrial training school on the Boucher Road but had taken the morning off to go to the funeral.

I now knew who was in the van. It was an elite unit of the RUC and they were keeping a discreet eye on the IRA funeral and spying on mourners, despite having made a public commitment to stay away. The white Transit changed everything. I hadn't a chance of making an escape with a police van parked on the hard shoulder. My associates would never pull in with that parked there. They would just keep driving, as I had warned them to do, and I would be left stranded without back-up or an escape vehicle. I ran each possible scenario through my head: I do the hit, I make my escape, they hear the shooting, see a man with guns running towards them – what are they going to do? Open fire. Armed with rifles, they would shoot me on the spot. If the Transit didn't move within the next fifteen minutes, my getaway car would not be able to pull in and pick me up. For the third time today I had an overwhelming feeling the operation was a complete mess-up.

I walked slowly back, passing the Roll of Honour, to the Republican Plot, and stood with small groups of people as the cortège and its wall of supporters drifted in. The coffins wound their way down the narrow path towards the plot. Two men tried to engage me in conversation, speaking about 'bloody Brits' and 'shoot-to-kill'. I knew they were IRA, but I didn't want to start something I couldn't finish. One had a weapon. He kept touching his chest, patting the barrel of his gun, which was disguised under a thick coat. To shut them up I spoke the only Irish I knew, the famous IRA freedom slogan *Tiocfaidh Ar La*, or Our Day Will Come. It seemed to keep them happy because they didn't persist in talking to me but carried on their own conversation.

I was now in position. The cortège was quite near and the young girls who formed the colour party led the way. It was an astonishing sight. It was stage-managed by the Republican movement, with kids bearing wreaths leading the way before Adams and McGuinness, who walked proudly as if they were gods among men. Adams and McGuinness were close. I had my chance, a golden opportunity to take both men out, but those bloody kids distracted me. Where did they come from and why were they not at school? I felt a surge of anger for their parents who allowed their children to carry flowers and wreaths for three Republican killers.

Adams and McGuinness were just three or four feet away from me as they followed the coffins, but I was locked in. I was swallowed up by the huge crowds of people and I couldn't move for photographers and cameramen pushing and shoving mourners out of the way. The moment was lost among a tide of people. I was seconds away from priming a grenade, dropping it into the crowd and making a run for it, but there were so many mourners following the coffins from all sides that I found all my exits blocked. I would have enjoyed the irony of Adams and McGuinness dying at their most sacred place, at their own cenotaph, but I couldn't make it happen. Mourners had surrounded the plot on all sides. There was a cordoned-off area for senior Republicans and the families of the deceased. I started to move back a little, searching for a better position.

It was then I noticed another van. It was a small white one and parked a short distance from the Republican Plot. It wasn't there five minutes ago. A small group of people, one a woman, got out of the van and made their way towards the plot. I could see them carrying equipment and assumed they were media, but I wondered why they were casually strolling when they should have been running for their lives. They had missed the arrival of the coffins. I reckoned their bosses would not be happy.

The driver was a fat man. He continued to sit in the van and didn't get out. He didn't seem particularly interested in watching the funeral. A young man with dark hair and a moustache approached the van and its driver. He got into the passenger seat. The Transit was still parked on the hard shoulder. The moustachioed man pointed to it in a way that suggested 'What's that?' or 'We need to keep an eye on that.'

Behind me I could hear the priest begin his service. His words rang out among the headstones. I stood at one, studying the name inscribed on it. The marble Mary looked like it was crying. Over time the eyes had been worn away and there were gullies that held rain water, which spilled down the statue's face. It was a surreal sight. I listened to the funeral service for a while before moving towards the Republican Plot. I had to pass the small van and its two occupants. I put my hand inside my coat and fingered the Browning, getting ready to pull it out. Both men looked at me as I passed them and continued their conversation.

Then suddenly there was a child beside me. I have no idea

where she came from. She looked like she was only ten and she stood in the grave, kicking and scuffing the gravel. She piped, 'How'ya, mister', and I told her to behave herself and not to play on the graves.

'Why, mister?'

'Because there's someone down there.'

'Really, mister? Hey, mister, I'm tired. I want to go home.'

I gave her fifty pence and told her to go back to her mother. Her mother was mad dragging a youngster to a Republican funeral. She should have been in school. I saw the child point in my direction and the mother look at me before turning her attention back to the service.

It was time for me to make my move. I stood on one of the grave surrounds and calculated that I was about fifty metres away from both of my targets. The Browning was no good. It could only reach forty metres before kicking dirt, and both men were just out of range. I needed to be closer, but closer was riddled with problems. I had the size of the crowd to contend with, plus the IRA's armed men, who were mingling with mourners. Behind me was the small van with the two men in it. The Transit was still on the hard shoulder.

I knew I was going to have to go into the Republican Plot to get Adams and McGuinness, and I knew I was going to have to shoot all round me to get in and out of there alive. There were women and children everywhere. There were pensioners and disabled people. I didn't want to be responsible for another Enniskillen. I didn't want to stoop to the IRA's indiscriminate tactics. There was also the risk to my own life. I didn't want to die among these people. I considered aborting the operation, but I couldn't leave by the front gates because by now I was sure Tim and his Provo pals were looking for me. There was still no sign of my getaway car. They had obviously realised the Transit was the security forces and were unable to pull up and get into position.

I remembered La Mon, Darkley, Kingsmills, the Abercorn and Enniskillen. It was time.

The priest was finishing his service. I could hear a woman wailing. Protestant women had cried like this too, saying goodbye to a husband, lover and friend. A woman volunteer began the oration and again I held back. They were soldiers and they deserved a soldier's farewell. Once she had finished her oration, three masked and uniformed volunteers would fire a volley of shots over the coffins in honour of their fallen comrades, but I was getting restless. The bodies should be in the ground by now. The ceremony and the tradition were becoming tiresome.

I wanted to panic the crowd. I needed to confuse them. I wanted them to start running in fear.

The grenades would do that. I moved towards the Republican Plot and took out two grenades with five-second fuses. I pulled the split pins and lobbed both grenades over the heads of mourners, straight at Martin McGuinness and Gerry Adams, who were fifty metres away. I was proficient in the use of grenades, and knew I could land them on the target. They flew through the air and the fly-off levers came away, causing two short cracks. I had announced myself.

I took out the Browning and fired three shots directly into the air. I was aware of a clapping in the middle distance. People turned to look at me and some began to applaud, thinking it was the start of the volley of shots. Then I saw shock on their faces as they realised I was unmasked and not the firing party. The applause trailed off and then a male voice addressed me. 'Hey, boy.' I turned around. The ignition cracks from the grenades had alerted the man with the moustache sitting in the small van. He confronted me. He had one foot out of the van, his body facing me. I lifted the Browning out of its holster, fired one shot and he fell backwards into the passenger seat. He was just twenty metres away. The driver of the van – a man named Jordan, I learnt later – was still in the driver's seat. His face was frozen in terror, but he never moved and he never spoke.

Then two loud thuds. The grenades had gone off.

To say there was wholesale panic is a gross understatement. As I anticipated, the crowd dispersed, running in different directions. I moved forward, Browning in my hand, my targets just a few metres ahead and within my sights. A group of young Republicans who were standing on the roof of the brick factory had a clear view of what was happening and began gesturing to the crowd before jumping down. Then part of the crowd turned around. A small group of young male Republicans were standing looking at me, bewildered expressions on their faces.

I wasn't moving. Adams and McGuinness were going to have to come to me. In my mind's eye I saw them defending their people. I visualised them charging down the central path, and that's when I would kill them with clean shots to the head. They would die heroes. They would die protecting their people, and the world's media was on hand to record the event. But it didn't happen. McGuinness and Adams failed to appear.

I stood where I was, took out another grenade and ripped out the pin. I had used just four shots. One to kill the moustachioed man and the three that were shot into the air. The Browning held thirteen rounds. I counted each of my shots so that I knew when to reload or change weapons.

I took four paces forward. The panic had eased a little and there was silence. Most of the immediate crowd was huddled behind gravestones. Then the shouting started and missiles began to fall. A small cluster of young men stood facing me, hurling gravel, bit of urns and anything they could get their hands on. They were good shots. It must have been years of practice stoning soldiers and the police. The moment was freeze-framed; the only animate objects were the missiles flying through the air. The men didn't move, afraid of the gun pointing at them, although they were out of range. I wondered when the IRA men would appear. I knew they were among us and it was only a matter of time before they showed themselves. That's why I didn't open fire. The crowd was not my target. I was looking around for known faces.

Then the crowd moved forward. They were shouting sectarian obscenities, like 'Orange bastard' and 'Kill him.' The operation had degenerated into sectarian taunts and was no longer a military action. I heard myself screaming at the top of my voice, 'Come on, Gerry, come on, Martin, you Fenian bastards. Show me what you're made of.' But the leaders never came forward.

I started walking towards to the motorway. I was still expecting Adams and McGuinness to show. I passed the small van. The passenger door was open and a man I now know to be Thomas McErlean was lying slumped across the seat, one leg out of the door. As I passed him I kept the Browning aimed at his head just in case he was playing possum, but he never moved. Thomas McErlean was dead. His family denied he was an IRA volunteer. I think he was another paramilitary who refused to tell his family he was involved. Meanwhile, Jordan was still in the small van. As I passed him I pointed the gun at him and saw him grip the steering wheel in terror.

The crowd was gathering behind me, throwing missiles from the safety of gravestones. Some were very near the small van and were shouting at Jordan, 'Use the van, run him over.' He never took his hands off the wheel, but I noticed him straightening his back. I thought he was a threat, so I aimed and fired. I was just twenty metres away. The windscreen shattered. Jordan had ducked. At my trial he gave evidence and said the shot would have been a bullseye and, had he not dropped his head, he would have been shot 'right between my eyes'.

The gruesome dance of death had begun behind me. A small group of men were advancing, ducking between gravestones as they lobbed missiles at me. I never returned fire. I could hear the loud cracks of gunfire, but I had no idea where the noise was coming from. It wasn't a Wild West, bang-bang-bang situation. I didn't shoot indiscriminately or waste bullets. I didn't go into Milltown and spray the place. I could have killed hundreds if I had wanted. I didn't.

I had chosen the grenades to create a diversion and to create panic. I hadn't picked the grenades to deliberately injure people. The grenades were chosen to do a specific job, to cover my withdrawal from the Republican Plot. But mourners were coming at me from all angles, so I prepared two more grenades and lobbed them left and right to try to stop the crowd from outflanking me. The Transit was still on the hard shoulder and there was still no sign of my getaway car. I had to get to the motorway. I had to take my chances. I took one final look at the crowd and began to make my way to the chain-link fence.

The Transit was gone.

My getaway car, doubtless hovering somewhere nearby, could now pull up. To reach my associates I had to negotiate the bog meadow, the strip of wasteland that separates the cemetery from the motorway. I began to jog looking around to see if anyone was following or catching me up. A small crowd of young men continued their pursuit to the bottom of the cemetery. I shot random rounds in their direction but they were out of range. They kept their heads down and no one was struck, and that's all I wanted. They weren't my targets. I just wanted to keep them back. I also saw a man in the middle distance, arms held forward in the firing position. I shot at him, and he too was out of range. I later discovered he was a photographer.

Another man, part of the small group, was nearer than the others. He was perched between two black headstones and was shouting instructions at the others who were a short distance behind him. He was wearing grey trousers. I could clearly hear him giving instructions – 'Move slowly', 'Keep down', 'Do this', 'Go there' – accompanied by sweeping arm gestures. When he stood up I shot him in the lower body. It was Kevin Brady. I later found out he was the golden boy of the Stewartstown Road brigade of the IRA who blew up two UDR men at a security barrier in Belfast city centre. Kevin Brady was not my target. I wasn't after him that day, but he made himself a target by organising his friends.

I continued to watch the crowd, count my rounds and make my way to the hard shoulder. Then my cap came off and I actually bent down to pick it up, still believing I needed to keep my disguise and then I thought, What the fuck are you thinking? The disguise didn't matter any more. My priority was to get out of Milltown. The RUC never recovered the cap and apparently it is in a glass case in a Republican club somewhere in West Belfast.

I scanned the motorway for my associates in the getaway car. They were nowhere to be seen. I got to the bog meadow with the intention of sprinting across it. As I skirted the edge of the bog, I suddenly sank up to my knees. I lost my balance and fell forward, putting both my hands out to break the fall. I was now on all fours, crawling through the muddy soup. I got to my feet and waded to the high bank running alongside the chain-link fence. The empty Browning in my hand had been submerged in the bog and the working part had been 'clashed back' and was open. It was now filled with bracken, mud and water.

I looked behind me. The crowd was still there. They had gained on me. I pulled out a grenade. I wanted to place it in the long grass, primed to explode as the crowd approached it, but it had a nine-second delay and the crowd were a bit further back than nine seconds. Instead I threw it. It landed among the crowd and exploded. They scattered in all directions as tufts of grass and lumps of earth flew into the sky. I continued along the small path that would take me to my pick-up point. All that stood between me and the hard shoulder was a shallow ditch.

The Browning was out of ammunition. I had used the thirteen

rounds. The loaded Ruger was still concealed under my arm. The crowd kept coming forward, but they had no gravestones for cover, so I had a clear line of fire if I needed it. I didn't want them to move further forward, but if they did I would shoot them. I could see a couple of men crossing the bog meadow in pursuit of me, but they were still out of range. I wanted to get out of Milltown alive. I snapped the magazine out of the Browning and threw it to the ground. I quickly inserted a fresh magazine, cocked the weapon, aimed in the direction of the crowd and took several steps forward, believing in the old war adage, 'The best form of defence is attack.'

I fired two rounds. Then the Browning seized. It was a new weapon and I had tested it in my own firing range. This had never happened to me before. I cursed the damned thing. What fucking awful timing. The gun was seized solid, frozen. I aimed again and tried to fire. Nothing happened; just the dull click that told me the weapon was now useless. I tried to release the magazine. It wouldn't budge. I whacked the Browning against one of the concrete posts that supported the chain-link fence, but it didn't free it.

Meanwhile the crowd was surging forward, but where the fuck was my getaway car? I was at the exact point I was supposed to be. I had gone over this bit hundreds of times with my two associates. There was no sign of them. I couldn't even see them on the opposite carriageway or speeding towards me on the city-bound lane. Had they got delayed or arrested? Had they got the time wrong? I remembered the back-up man's words to me when I told him I didn't want him in the cemetery. He said he would never forgive me.

A brick bounced off my head. I didn't know where the young man had come from. He just popped out of nowhere. He was full of rage, shouting, 'Come on, you Orange bastard.' I was surprised he was on his own and I think he was genuinely surprised to find himself at that spot without his mates around him when he looked back. He waved to the others, yelling at the top of his voice, 'Over here, he's over here, and he's out of ammo.' I reached into my coat and pulled out the Ruger. I had never any intention of using it. I pointed it at him and told him to fuck off. He continued to throw bricks. I repeated my request, but he stood his ground. Then suddenly he moved forward. He saw the gun. He challenged me.

I gave him one final opportunity to walk away unhurt. I put the Ruger in the flat of my hand and offered it to him, so he knew I was armed and would open fire. He stopped. He was a slight man, no heavier than ten stone. I said to him, 'Fuck off right now, just go.' He stood his ground. This lad had something many Republicans lacked. He had guts. He had more courage than Gerry Adams and Martin McGuinness put together. I admired him. He showed his true colours. He gave chase. He charged ahead.

He bent down and picked up another rock. He lifted his arm to throw the brick at me and I shot one round, hitting him once in the neck. I was on the small bank and he was in the bog meadow. I wanted to aim for his right shoulder, but because he was standing on the rough and springy grass he looked like he was balancing on a waterbed. He moved and the bullet entered his neck and travelled through his body, killing him instantly. I kept the gun on him, just in case he was ready to spring on me, but he didn't move. His name was John 'Minto' Murray. I regret shooting him. I had killed three men I had no intention of harming just twenty-four hours earlier.

My getaway car never showed. I had two grenades, a Browning that was jammed and my Ruger with five rounds left. I knew I was going to have to fend for myself and that meant hijacking a car on the motorway. Three hundred metres away I spied a man creeping along a fence that ran through the bog meadow. I took two shots at him but he was well out of range and he stayed down. I took one of the grenades and lobbed it in his direction. It slipped in my muddy, gloved hands and it travelled just twenty feet. It exploded, causing a water jet to spring thirty feet into the air. For a split second there was a rainbow and it was a beautiful thing among the mud, blood and horror. It was a surreal moment. The red-haired guy, who was wearing a green parka, kept his head down.

I was determined to get out of Milltown alive. I knew forcing a car to stop was going to be virtually impossible. They were travelling at speed, up to seventy miles an hour. I made it to the city-bound hard shoulder. I had the two guns, one in each hand, with three rounds left in the Ruger. I got on to the inner lane of the motorway and pointed the two guns at the oncoming traffic. I could feel the cars brush past my legs and looks of amazement on the drivers' faces. I looked behind me and it was a blizzard of stones, wood and gravel. The missiles were bouncing off the vehicles and I am surprised there wasn't a serious pile-up as a result of the confusion and panic.

The crowd was now over the chain-link fence and had reached the hard shoulder. I pointed the Ruger at them and fired my final three shots. Then I took out a grenade, pulled the split pin and held it in one hand. It was now live. In my other hand I had the two guns.

A car was slowing down. A young woman was behind the wheel. I eyeballed her and pointed the guns at her windscreen. I will never forget the look of horror on her face as I waved the two guns at her. She had a passenger, a young baby strapped into a carrycot on the back seat. The baby looked the same age as Lucy. I stood back and she sped off. I did not want to cost that woman and her baby their lives and I remember thinking, This is crazy. This is not you.

I knew a hijacked car was out of the question and I still hoped my getaway car would show up, the back-up man would open fire with the AK and we could make our escape. The crowd poured on to the motorway. There was more than a hundred of them and they began trying to force vehicles to stop. I was now on the hard shoulder of the country-bound carriageway, walking towards South Belfast. I looked behind me and saw a wall of Land Rovers and armed cops at the bottom of the motorway. It was a Catch-22. I could run towards the cops, but they would shoot me and I couldn't face being killed by the security forces.

The crowd was now across all four lanes of the motorway. I had one live grenade left. I knew what I was going to do. An oil tanker was speeding down the city-bound carriageway. I was going to use my last grenade to blow it up and create a massive fireball that would kill the Republican crowd. I would also be killed and so would the motorists unlucky enough to be on the road at that moment.

My throwing range was forty metres and the tanker was no further than ten, but I changed my mind. The tanker was heading towards Belfast, which probably meant he was returning to the oil depots at Sydenham with an empty tank after making his deliveries. It would be a waste of my final grenade. A year later, at my trial, the driver of the tanker stood in the witness box and under oath told how he was returning to Belfast with seventy-five thousand litres of fuel on board. He was on a local delivery loop.

By now Republicans had got to the tanker. They forced it to a standstill and started to swarm over the cab. The driver was wearing blue overalls and looked like he was in his fifties. The mob hauled him out and threw him on the ground. They punched, kicked and slapped him before allowing him to run for his life. One Republican got into the cab and positioned it so that it faced the central reservation. I knew what was coming next. They were aiming the tanker at me and were going to try to run me down. It was chaos on the city-bound side. Cars were screeching to a halt, desperate to avoid the scene. The RUC maintained their position at the end of the motorway.

16

YOU PLAY,
YOU PAY

**THE OPERATION TO KILL MARTIN MCGUINNESS AND
GERRY ADAMS WAS MILITARILY A DISASTER.** The crowd
wouldn't give up until they caught me and had lined up three
abreast. They marched along the country-bound carriageway,
singing in unison, 'I-I-IRA.' I smiled back at them. It was a wry
smile. I was smiling in the face of adversity.

The Republican mob got to me before the RUC. They hurled
bricks and stones, lumps of wood and even a road cone. They
rained on my head and bounced off my body. I was walking
backwards when I spotted the man in the green parka from earlier.
He had managed to outflank me and I could see he was carrying a
large piece of wood. I was hoping one of them had a gun and
would shoot me on the spot. I didn't want to be taken away,
tortured and chopped into pieces. I wanted a quick death, a
soldier's death. The crowd was several hundred strong, and now
part of it broke free and moved nearer to me. As they closed in I

threw my two guns down the embankment. I flicked the release pin on the last grenade, the fly-off levers came off, I tucked the grenade under my chin and put my head down. They continued to chant, 'I-I-IRA, I-I-IRA' and other sectarian obscenities.

One. Two. I am counting the seconds until the grenade explodes. The crowd moves closer. Three. Four. I feel a massive crack on the back of my neck. The man in the green parka has hit me so hard the lump of wood snaps in two and the impact forces the grenade out of my gloved hand. It rolls towards the Republican crowd. Five. Six. One person kicks it away and others jump over the grenade as it lies on the road. They are in for the kill and nothing, not even a grenade, is going to stop them. I curl up in the foetal position and continue counting. Then the kicking begins. I am wearing several layers of clothing, but their boots and fists make an impact on every part of my body. They are even kicking and punching one another in their efforts to get to me.

Seven. Eight. Nine. The grenade explodes.

There was silence for a few seconds, then I heard a voice say, 'Everyone OK?' Then feet and fists began attacking me again. I was starting to pass out when they bounced a traffic cone off my head. The sounds coming from the two hundred-strong crowd were frightening. They made indistinguishable guttural noises.

I heard another voice, 'Stand back, stand back', and the metallic click-click of a firing pin striking against an empty round and I thought, Fuck, what a way to go, to be shot with your own bloody gun. I knew it was my Ruger. After three or four clicks he knew it was useless to him, so he beat me around the head and face with it. My fear was the Browning, that they could clear the blockage. It still had eleven rounds in it.

Another voice spoke. It was older. The voice said to the mob, 'All back, all back', and I was hauled to my feet. Four men dragged me to a car and threw me into the back seat. One sat on my chest and another at my head. The other two were in the passenger and driver seat. The car was a Skoda. I think they had hijacked it, but it didn't have much engine power and it helped save my life. The mob couldn't get me off the motorway fast enough.

As we drove, the two men in the back continued the beating. I could hear the crack and thud of fists on flesh but I no longer felt any pain. I was drifting in and out of consciousness. Another voice broke into my consciousness: 'Jesus, he's dead, quick, get him to the garage', and I thought, I'm going to be skinned alive here. I am going to die a horrible death. I started to laugh and one of the men in the back said, 'The bastard's not dead, he thinks he's on a day out.' He punched me in the face. I knew they would torture me and mutilate my body before delivering the death shots. My face was caked with blood and mud. I had teeth missing, blood was pouring down my throat and spilling all over my captors and the car. I heard the voice of the man sitting on my chest saying, 'Jesus, lads, I'm covered in the fucker's blood. He's bleeding all over me. We need to get him to the garage.'

In the rush to take me to my death in a backstreet garage the four men had overlooked one thing. They had only partly closed the back door of the car. Even though I was drifting in and out of consciousness, I still managed to fight back and kick it open. My legs were dangling out of the back, dragging along the motorway. I was wearing rubber-soled Dealer boots and I could feel my feet getting warm from the friction of being dragged along the motorway. I wanted to prove that there was still a spark of life left in me and I wasn't going to my death quietly. The only image I had in my head was of a Hellman's Mayonnaise advert in which Bob Carolgees and Spit the Dog run home so fast Carolgees's feet go on fire.

The punching continued. There was nowhere left on my face and neck, so they moved to other parts of my body. I'd had martial-arts training. Tommy Herron taught me that if you strike a blow directly underneath the heart it is possible to rupture a vein and stop it beating. 'He-art, he-art,' I shouted at them. I wanted to speed up my death by encouraging them to give me a direct punch to the heart and to continue punching until I stopped breathing. They didn't understand. They thought I was having a heart attack. The truth is, I wanted to die before they got me to the garage where a gang of IRA men would be waiting to torture and kill me.

I heard the voice of the man sitting on my chest say, 'Paddy, the bastard's having a heart attack' and the passenger say, 'Don't hit him any more, we need the fucker alive.' The car screeched to a halt.

'Fuck, the peelers. They're everywhere.'

Two men lifted me out of the car and dropped me to the ground with a thud. I landed on my shoulder and neck. They were out of the car and dragged me down the embankment out of view. There was no traffic. The four hadn't given up and continued to beat me. One was a redhead. I will never forget him. I was on all fours trying to get my breath back and he ran at my head like he was taking a penalty. My head flopped back with every blow. I had one eye that wouldn't open and I wasn't sure it was still there. I thought it was kicked out of its socket. The other was still open and I could see the blue lights in the distance.

I could also see a large slab of concrete lying on the hard shoulder and two of the four men trying to lift it. I heard one say, 'I can't lift this, it's too heavy', and the other tell him, 'Bring him over to it and bash his head off it.' I was thinking, Just drop the bloody thing on my head and finish me off.

The police had arrived.

'Citizen's arrest, officer, citizen's arrest.'

I was covered in blood and unable to move. They were covered in my blood and standing by a massive concrete slab and beside a hijacked car. The RUC had arrived in the nick of time and put their own lives on the line to whisk me away from that hate-filled mob. They could have been ambushed by a West Belfast unit of the IRA who could have been on the motorway within minutes. One of them radioed for help. He knew he had a tiny window of opportunity to get me out of the area before an IRA unit arrived and tried to snatch me back.

Meanwhile a young officer, his hand shaking, pointed his gun at the crowd and me. The four men released me and moved back. The crowd, a little further back, were still moving forward and hurling missiles and the stones and lumps of wood were bouncing off the RUC men and me. The officer knew there would be a bloodbath if the IRA arrived and opened fire and they, in turn, were forced to return fire. The RUC moved quickly and while the young one continued to point his gun at the small crowd, one of his colleagues rolled me towards the Land Rover, leaving me in the recovery position. 'Are you police or are you Army?' he asked me. I couldn't speak. My mouth was full of blood and bits of teeth. He was interrupted by a teenager who said, 'Mister, I was told to give you these.' He threw down at the policeman's feet an empty magazine from my Browning and the fly-off levers from one of the grenades. The Republican mob had been picking my debris up as they followed me to the motorway. They knew they were handing over evidence. The Ruger and the Browning were never recovered and were used in Republican killings after Milltown.

Two RUC men lifted me and put me in the footwell of the Land Rover. I was like a rubber man and drifting in and out of consciousness. They saved my life. I was minutes from being tortured and chopped up. By now I was losing a lot of blood and two officers started doing first aid, slapping my face, asking my name and trying to stop me from slipping into unconsciousness. Over their radio I could hear details of an attack at Milltown cemetery. Two were confirmed dead. One young policeman tapped my shoulder and said, 'Did you hear that, you got two of them, isn't that brilliant?' I did answer him. I said, 'Yeah, fucking brilliant, mate.' It was said through a busted mouth, broken teeth and blood gushing down my throat. It was said when I was punched senseless, barely conscious and lying in a heap on the floor. I didn't sit up in the back of the Land Rover, cock my head and say, 'Brilliant, mate, yes, a job very well done.' It wasn't like that. I didn't gloat. I knew I was facing life behind bars. I was a heap of skin and bone lying in the footwell of an RUC vehicle thinking, This is fucking brilliant, just brilliant.

I could hear a heated discussion between police officers about which hospital to take me to. The Royal Victoria had the nearest casualty department, but one officer, a sergeant, thought it was too risky because it was in the heart of Catholic West Belfast and too dangerous for both them and me. An IRA active-service unit could be at the hospital within minutes. A network of sympathetic workers would keep Republicans informed of my arrival for treatment there. So I was taken to the City Hospital in South Belfast, which is surrounded by Loyalist districts.

In Accident and Emergency I was handcuffed to a metal trolley. My coat was removed and the rest of my clothes were cut from me. I lay on the trolley in my underwear. Four policemen stood guard, but I wasn't going anywhere. My legs weren't working. The doctors and nurses didn't know who I was or what had just happened. I could have been involved in a car crash, for all they knew. The doctors complained to the police that they couldn't do their jobs, but the uniformed officers refused to budge. One of the officers from the Land Rover again asked me whether I was working for the police or the Army.

The walking wounded from Milltown also started pouring in. I was lying there, almost naked, in double handcuffs, and they were looking at me. I knew it was only a matter of time before someone realised who I was. I looked around and spotted a tray with a lot of medical instruments, including scissors and scalpels. I felt helpless, unable to defend myself. I knew that sooner or later, someone would grab one of those sharp implements and stab me.

The detectives arrived and were given permission by the doctors to interview me. The police, puzzled by the unexpected and clinical nature of my attack, wanted to establish exactly who I was and who I was working for. One said, 'Where are your guns?' I told him I threw both weapons down the motorway embankment. But there was still ammo in my coat pocket. I had been in custody twenty minutes. The coat was lying on the floor. He poked at it. He didn't put his hand inside but carefully removed a speed strip and said, 'Oh fuck.' The speed strips were RUC issue. The detective approached my trolley. He took my hand, put the speed strip in my open palm and pressed my hand around it. I couldn't fight back because I was handcuffed. It was now the only ammunition with my prints on it.

He asked me who I was. I said nothing. He said he had my mates and they were badly injured. I still said nothing. If the guys had been caught, it sounded like the big lad went down fighting. He asked my name. I told him it was John Gregg. I had meant to say, 'John Smith', one of my aliases, but my father's name came out instead. The name was fed to RUC headquarters, which has a detailed database on the whole population. It came back blank.

The detective continued, 'Someone will have recognised you. Your family is in danger.'

'My wife knows nothing.'

'Who are your pals?'

'I have no pals. I worked alone.'

He leant in towards me. He was wearing a black leather jacket and when he leant forward it flapped open. I could see his Ruger. My brain said, 'Grab it and get out', but I couldn't because I was 'cuffed. He jumped back and clasped his chest.

'Who are you?' he said.

'I am in nothing.'

It was an automatic response. I said it because I didn't want members of the UFF, Red Hand and other freelancers arrested and questioned about the operation. The two detectives nodded to nurses that they were finished with me and I was wheeled into X-ray. They followed, allowing the nurse to remove one handcuff, and stood at the side of the machine protecting their private parts when it took images of my body. After I was X-rayed the detectives continued to question me but I was now beginning to focus. Again they asked me who I was.

'It doesn't matter,' I said.

'We need to question you about a serious incident that happened today.'

Silence.

'Your family is in danger. We will arrest your wife and your kids.'

'Michael Stone, 47 Ravenswood Park. My family knows nothing'.

My details were fed into the RUC database, and when the detective came back he said, 'We need more information. We need to know about your mates.' He kept insisting they were injured and I was hoping that if they were caught they'd had the good sense to deny all knowledge of Milltown.

The doctors OK'd my transfer to Musgrave Park Hospital, a highly fortified military unit. I was destined for Ward 18. Musgrave Park is where paramilitary prisoners from the Maze and Crumlin Road are sent when they are sick or injured. It is a prison within a hospital and is guarded by armed soldiers. I was handcuffed into a wheelchair and taken to the hospital in an ambulance with a police escort. A nurse and a porter also travelled with me, and as the porter pushed me to the waiting ambulance he whispered in my ear, 'The word is you got three and one of their top men, Kevin Brady, and the police are glad.' The name meant nothing to me. Brady wasn't my target. I'd been beaten to within an inch of my life and was now facing life behind bars for killing three men who were not my targets.

Ward 18 had four beds. I was the only patient. The nurses offered me painkillers but I refused them. I was concerned they might have been laced with something to make me talk. I left them

I was OC of the East Belfast brigade.

Top: I have nine children. Here are three of them, on a visit to the Maze. (*Left to right*) Michael, Jason and Gary.

Bottom: Making my move at the Republican funeral in 1988. ©*Rex Features*

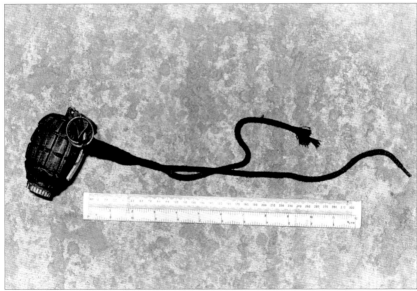

Top: A march inside the Maze, with snare drums and flutes.

Bottom: I used a Mills 36 hand grenade for my attempt on Robert McAllister's life, a World War Two weapon, brutal and effective.

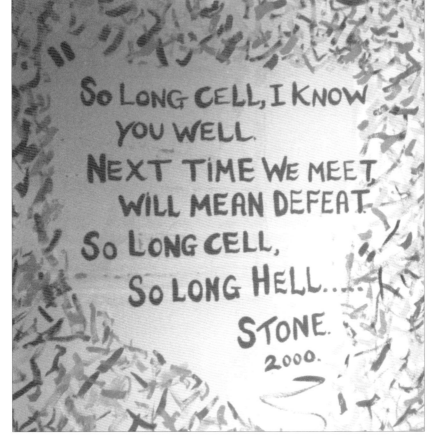

So LONG CELL, I KNOW
YOU WELL.
NEXT TIME WE MEET,
WILL MEAN DEFEAT.
So LONG CELL,
So LONG HELL....
STONE.
2000.

Top: Carrying the flame inside prison.

Bottom: A farewell to my time inside – the wall of my prison cell.

With my English Bull Terrier, Buster.

The following pages show some of my artwork. My painting became a means of expression and escape in my lonely and sunless prison cell. My art explores my personal history, the history of my community, and the history of the Troubles. Painting has turned things around for me in more ways than one...

on the bedside locker. I could hear young men chanting outside. They had obviously followed me from the City Hospital and were shouting, 'I-I-IRA, I-I-IRA. Someday, we'll get you, you bastard.' The doctors gave me another check-up and gave the go-ahead for another round of questioning. Two detectives from Grosvenor Road RUC station arrived. They introduced themselves and said they wanted to talk to me in connection with a serious incident. They asked me where I lived and I repeated my address. They asked about my mates, saying, 'Didn't they fuck off on you?' At that point I asked to see the nurse. I told her I wasn't feeling well and had a very bad headache. I told the detectives I would talk in the morning. I told them I would talk about other things too. Their eyes lit up.

The Army patrolled the corridors surrounding Ward 18. At 11 o'clock that night a Wessex helicopter hovered above the compound. It flew so low it shook the ward and the windows vibrated with the downdraught. A drip frame crashed to the floor and the glass of water sitting beside my bed tumbled and smashed into pieces. The duty nurse came running in to me and said she was frightened. The RUC officer posted at the door of the ward ran down the corridor to find out what was going on. Then the chopper took off. I have no idea what it was all about. Perhaps the Army was trying to spook me.

Next morning, before the detectives arrived, I crawled on all fours to the bathroom. It was very basic. There was a bath, a toilet and a small handbasin, but no mirror, just a small piece of reflective steel nailed to the wall. I looked at myself and the image glaring back at me was grotesque. My face was distorted, broken, twisted and unrecognisable. Quasimodo was staring back at me. One eye was clamped shut and my head was the size of a portable television. Half my face had no skin on it.

The minute I started running the taps, a massive viewfinder screeched open. An RUC officer was looking in at me. I waved at him sarcastically and he waved back. The water was cold, but I slid into it anyway. My body didn't feel the coldness. The water turned red, then brown, with blood and mud from the bog meadow. I lay back, completely submerging my body and face, and the policeman came running in. He thought I was trying to drown myself. I told him to fuck off and leave me alone. I stayed in the bathroom for an hour, running bath after bath until the water eventually heated up and the blood, matted in my hair and ground into my skin, finally came away. I made the return journey to Ward 18 on all fours. My legs were still not working.

I was offered food and milk but refused to take them. The staff gave me water and I threw it away, crawling back to the bathroom to drink from the bath taps. A box of chocolates arrived. The RUC delivered them to my ward. I told them I didn't want them. It was a one-pound box of Quality Street. They had taken the wrappers off every chocolate and kept all the purple hazelnut caramels. The chocolates ended up in the bin.

Nine officers were detailed to question me, three of them from Grosvenor Road and the other six from various city-centre RUC stations, and they took turns, in relay teams of three and four, to interrogate me. Sessions lasted up to eight hours. One senior Grosvenor Road detective told me my home was searched and they found nothing. They told me they ripped the house to bits.

'I hope you haven't arrested my wife.'

'We haven't. What organisation do you belong to?'

'None.'

'Were you on drugs?'

'You tell me, you have enough blood samples.'

They moved to another part of the ward. Within earshot one said to the others, 'They are all denying him. He has no owner. The UDA has made a statement saying they don't know anything about him. They say he is too extreme.'

So there it was. The UDA denied me and denied my

involvement in a UFF-sanctioned operation backed by two brigadiers. To this day I don't know if the cops said those things deliberately to get me to react. I said nothing. The questioning continued.

'Who are you?'

'A loner.'

'Did you act alone?'

'Yes.'

'Any more like you?'

'We are a new breed.'

The cops thought Milltown was a one-off and I was a Loyalist nutter, so I started reciting intelligence I had on Martin McGuinness and Owen Carron. I watched their mouths drop. Within the hour the RUC had set up a computer in the corridor outside my ward, and the information was fed into it. All I heard from the corridor was the senior detective shouting, 'Who the hell is this fucker?'

After a while I broke the silence and told them I was ready to make a statement and was ready to tell them everything. The detectives said they needed me to write it down. I couldn't write because my hands were swollen from protecting my face during the beating at the motorway.

The interrogation teams kept reminding me of my promise to tell them everything and I reminded them that we had a deal: I talk and they don't arrest my family. I started by saying I undertook sanctions for all the major Loyalist paramilitaries: the UDA/UFF, the UVF and the Red Hand Commando. I talked about Milltown first because it was the jurisdiction of the detectives quizzing me.

They started to ask me about the weapons. I asked them whether they had been recovered from the motorway, but they refused to say. They wanted to know where I got the two guns. I told them I stole them. I told them about the Loyalist arms hide on Shandon golf course, and a team of RUC men searched it and found nothing. The hide had been emptied many months ago. I wasn't sending the cops on a wild-goose chase. I told them to search Shandon because I wanted to have fun at the expense of the middle-class snobs who played there. The Ruger was never mentioned, although they knew it was security forces-sourced. They wanted to know who accompanied me at Milltown. I said I acted alone. I would not have any co-accused.

I told a detective about the assassination of Paddy Brady and that I shot him with an automatic shotgun using number-four cartridges, but I did not tell him what make the weapon was.

My mouth was still busted and speaking was difficult. I acted the numbskull. I made my interrogators believe I was of low intelligence. It was part of my game plan. I played a deliberate hand. I threw swerves. The detectives would ask who accompanied me on other active-service operations. I always said the same thing: 'I drove a car to Taughmonagh and picked up two volunteers, one would drive and one would be the back-up man. He would hide in the footwell of the passenger seat and I would lie across the back seat.' This was a complete fabrication. I said this to protect the active units and to divert suspicion away from those I worked with, be it in the UFF, the UVF or the Red Hand Commando. The police thought they were making progress and would send the details back to RUC headquarters to try to crack the mystery of the two volunteers. I did this to protect my associates and the freelance volunteers who assisted me in my work.

Then came the other charges: murder, attempted murder and conspiracy to murder. I gave them every scrap of intelligence I had seen on my targets: Owen Carron and Martin McGuinness. I told the detectives exactly where these men lived, what cars they had in their drives, including the colour, make and registration number. I could tell them about the layout of Carron's garden and the names of his two dogs. I watched their faces as a young officer tapped in the information. They were speechless. They just stood looking at the computer, bewildered. They wondered how a Loyalist with an address in East Belfast knew so much about Mid Ulster, Londonderry and South Tyrone. I know they were puzzled that a loner had so much intelligence at his fingertips. I didn't betray my associates. I didn't tell them about my 'eyes and ears', about my network of contacts all over Northern Ireland who had access to intelligence and sensitive information and that these people passed this information on to me.

I had one 'official' visit while lying in my hospital bed, but I don't know who my English visitors were. It was after dark. The detectives had gone. The RUC were patrolling outside my ward. The door opened and five men entered the room. Two were plainclothes RUC men, probably Special Branch. The other three had English accents and were dressed in expensive suits. One said to the others, 'So this is him', and one of the plainclothes RUC men answered, 'Yes, this is the man.' The three Englishmen looked at me like I was a specimen in a museum, turned on their heels and left the ward. The RUC officer on the door nodded at them as they passed and closed the door after them. It was obvious they were military men, but I have no idea why they wanted to peer at me.

Questions on the death of Kevin McPolin and Dermot Hackett came thick and fast. When detectives put it to me that McPolin's death had all the marks of my *modus operandi* on it, I just said, 'He was a legitimate target.' The RUC questioned and probed but they were puzzled. I imagined myself there and tried to recreate a credible version of events. One of the senior detectives said he didn't believe me. I was grasping in the dark for something to make my version of events sound like the truth. But in the end the detectives were satisfied and the murder of Kevin McPolin was added to my charge sheet.

Dermot Hackett was a different story. I had no difficulty convincing them I was responsible for killing him. I had seen his intelligence file, knew the weapons selected for the operation and had done a dry run. I had done everything bar pulling the trigger. The only question mark hanging over my confession was the trajectory of the bullets that entered Hackett's body. I told the detectives I pointed the gun out of the window, when in fact the gunman had stood up through the sunroof of the Opel Manta. The detectives didn't pursue this discrepancy in any great detail and added Dermot Hackett's name to my charge sheet.

The RUC had twenty-eight outstanding murders on their hands and wanted to close the book on them all.

On 16 March 1988, the same day as Milltown, another young Catholic died. He was called Kevin 'Mungo' Mulligan and had been in hospital for eight months after being blasted in the chest and stomach in a shotgun attack. He was working on the Beersbridge Road in a garage and was hit when he was bending down to change the wheel of a car. I wasn't responsible for this operation but the detectives wanted a confession. They said that Mulligan's death showed my MO: a shotgun at close quarters. I told them it was nothing to do with me. They got me to look at photographs showing his injuries in the mistaken belief that it would shock me into a confession. I asked them to confirm where the young lad was hit and they said the stomach and chest. I said it was an unusual place to aim, given that Mulligan was in a crouched position at a car wheel. I told them that if I had killed him I wouldn't have shot him in the stomach. I would have shot him in the head. I also told them I deliberately kept my paramilitary activity away from East Belfast because I didn't believe in 'shitting on my own doorstep'. This was not what they wanted to hear. The senior detective from Grosvenor Road slammed his file shut, then left the ward.

I was also questioned about the death of Jack Kielty, the father of the comedian and television star Patrick Kielty. My teams of interrogators insisted I did it. They tried to link every shotgun killing to me, saying the choice of gun and the style of execution automatically made me the gunman. The UFF had intelligence on the County Down businessman, and I had seen his file, but I did not kill Jack Kielty. I understand his death, in January 1988, was a joint UDA and UVF operation. There were rumours that Jim Craig, the UDA's chief extortionist, had a hand in his murder. Jack Kielty was to be a witness in a court case taken by Central Television. One of the station's programmes, *The Cook Report*, was being sued by Craig.

The RUC also questioned me about the killing of Adrian Carroll, who was shot by the UVF in 1983. The incident gave rise to a long-running legal and political controversy. Four members of the Ulster Defence Regiment were convicted of his murder, even though they protested their innocence. As with Kevin McPolin, I had never heard of Adrian Carroll. The detectives would say, 'We know you are the gunman', and I would answer, 'Aye, and I sank the fucking *Titanic* as well.' They tried to force a confession by showing me graphic photographs of other unsolved murders committed over the years. They would push the gory pictures into my face and say, 'Have a look at this, Stone, you done that. Does it not make you sick?', and I would answer, 'No, because I didn't do it.'

The RUC didn't force anything out of me. I wasn't mistreated and I wasn't beaten. I freely confessed to the four murders that I did do and they got closure on two outstanding deaths, one of which the cops knew for a fact I didn't do. My interrogators thought they could trace other murders to me and that I was just going to confess, but they had misjudged me. The RUC had been given Hackett and McPolin. They had four other murders on my charge sheet. They had five counts of attempted murder, three counts of conspiracy to murder and six counts of wounding with intent. The RUC had been given enough.

I admit, having been a Loyalist volunteer for seventeen years of my adult life, that I was involved in other military operations. But that is between me and the big man upstairs when my time comes.

I was allowed just one visit from Leigh-Ann. She was very tearful and cried for most of it. She brought newspapers but I couldn't read them. They were like string vests as every story relating to me, Milltown or the Gibraltar Three had been ripped out. I told Leigh-Ann I was sorry for putting her through this nightmare. She told me she was shocked to see me lying in a hospital bed because I had never been sick once during our marriage. She said she had been to the doctor and her family was very worried about her. She was on medication and was a 'bag of nerves'. I said it would be best if she didn't make any more visits. I told her it was for her own good that she didn't come to see me for a few months. I said I didn't want her to have to run a gauntlet of hate or endure Republican taunts. She sadly agreed.

I was formally charged on 22 March 1988 at the police office at Townhall Street. No charges were put to me at Musgrave Park Hospital. I was handcuffed and put in the back of a police Land Rover, which was right in the middle of a large, high-security convoy. The cops were panicking. They knew the Land Rover could be hit at any time.

The arresting officer preferred all the charges, including six counts of murder. He read the names of the three, Thomas McErlean, Kevin Brady and John Murray, who died at Milltown. I replied, 'I alone carried out the military operation as a retaliatory strike against Provisional Sinn Fein and IRA for the slaughter of innocents at La Mon, Darkley and Enniskillen. I am a dedicated freelance Loyalist paramilitary.'

When the charges relating to Paddy Brady, Dermot Hackett and Kevin McPolin were read out I said, 'I read their files, they were legitimate targets.' The detective's face fell. Until this very second I had not mentioned intelligence files.

Even though the UDA had let me down I still felt loyal to the association. I didn't want to compromise the UDA, so I said I worked alone. I said I was a freelance operative even though two UFF brigadiers sanctioned the Milltown operation. I said I was a lone paramilitary because Milltown was a disaster and I refused to bring the UDA into disrepute and the organisation is bigger than one man, any man. I had a deal with the hierarchy. If I were killed on active service they would bury me after claiming me. If I were arrested on an operation they would claim me and I would do my time on the UDA wings. I wasn't sure if the deal still stood. Up until this point the UDA leadership had reneged on their promise to me. After Milltown, Tucker Lyttle had forced the UDA's hand and I was collectively disowned and politically isolated.

When the charges had been put to me in the police office I was taken to a holding cell and waited three hours to be taken to my remand hearing. The cell stank of stale urine from the drunks who had been kept overnight and was a jolt to my system after the sterility of my hospital ward. I had to stand. There was no seat and no bed. Two RUC officers stood guard. I noticed there was a thirty-step climb to the remand court and the injuries to my hip and legs meant I wasn't able to walk very far, never mind climb a flight of stairs. Outside the cell was a bench on which two men, dressed in formal suits, were sitting watching proceedings.

The sergeant said, 'Big day for you, Michael.'

'I'll never make those stairs.'

'We'll help you.'

It was a big day for me in more ways than one. I knew once the remand proceedings were finished I would be taken to Crumlin Road jail and would stay there until my trial. The trial was at least twelve months away. I was getting agitated. I knew once I was brought to the Crum I would have to fight for my life, but physically I was not in any shape to defend myself. I was still carrying the injuries sustained from the beating on the motorway. I could barely walk, let alone fight. The Crum is two-thirds

Republican. The wings are mixed. I knew I was putting my head in the lion's mouth. I was fearful for my personal security. I had committed a crime in the eyes of the Republican movement and they were going to make me pay. The Republicans knew they had me once my remand hearing ended.

The sergeant's voice filled my cell: 'We'll help you', and in a voice filled with anger and frustration I yelled, 'I wish I had an AK. I'd soon be out of here. I'd cut you all to ribbons.' At these words the two suits turned their heads to look at me. They stood up and walked away. I don't know who they were.

My name was called, indicating that I was now officially summoned to my remand hearing in the tiny courtroom. I continued to hover at the bottom of the stairs because I couldn't move. I knew I didn't have the strength in my legs to climb thirty steps. I felt like my pelvis had locked and my legs were made of rubber. I told the sergeant that it would take 'an army and maybe a crane' to get me to the courtroom. He was a kind man and I regretted screaming at him that I would use an AK to shoot my way out of the place. Put your arms across your chest and stick your elbows out, he told me. He was a big man, and he and the constable carried me to the top of the stairs and put me down outside the door, allowing me the dignity of limping into court. The sergeant opened the door and said, 'You walk in there to your remand hearing and you stand tall.'

I was pleading Not Guilty to all the charges put to me. I told my legal team that I wanted my day in court and by pleading Not Guilty was giving myself a trial in front of a judge. I intended to tell the court that Milltown was sanctioned at the highest level in the UDA. I intended embarrassing the Republican hierarchy, who lied when they said they gave chase in Milltown. And I intended damning the authorities who had planted a police unit on the motorway to watch the funeral.

The remand hearing was open to the public. Republicans had

packed into the tiny gallery. The press was also present. I focused on a spot on the wall and kept my face expressionless. When the charges were read, I said, 'Not guilty.' The hearing ended and I was remanded in custody until a date was fixed for my trial at Belfast Crown Court. The same officers carried me back to the stinking cell while arrangements were made to take me to Crumlin Road. The cell was disgusting, a miserable little hellhole. I kept running Milltown over and over in my head. Every split second of the operation was freeze-framed in my mind and projected on to the dank walls like a movie. I could still see John Murray. He had a brave face. John Murray was a brave man. I also thought of my little daughter and I knew I would never see her grow up.

A male voice dragged me back from my thoughts. It was a young RUC officer, who passed a copy of a magazine through the bars and asked me to sign it. It was the RUC's in-house publication *Police Beat*. Jack Hermon's face was on the front. The officer wanted me to sign my name across his 'bald head'. I refused and told him to piss off. He wouldn't go away and chirped on and on that he wanted to prove he met me so he could show off in front of his mates. So I signed the magazine. I signed, 'Michael Stone, 1988, No Surrender', before pushing the magazine back through the bars.

Thirty minutes later I was taken from the cell and put in a Land Rover that would take me to my new home, the Crum. As I hobbled towards the vehicle, I heard a girl's voice behind me saying, 'No, I'm going to do it.' She was young and was wearing the uniform of the RUC, but she planted a kiss on my cheek and said, 'Good luck, Michael Stone, you are a true Loyalist.'

I was bemused. I thought it was a strange world, and as the Land Rover pulled away I couldn't help but think about her words. The young policewoman was right. Where I was going I would need all the luck in the world.

17

PRISONER A385

CRUMLIN ROAD JAIL: A RAT- AND COCKROACH-INFESTED VICTORIAN DUMP. IT WAS NOT FIT TO HOUSE HUMAN BEINGS, BUT THEN TO THE AUTHORITIES WE WEREN'T HUMAN BEINGS. We were the lowest forms of life, no better than the cockroaches and rats that shared our cells.

I had been in prison before and knew the introductory procedures, which included the strip-search and the medical on arrival. Prisoners are always given a grubby towel measuring just twelve by twelve inches to wear after showering and before the search. I didn't see the point of it. The towel barely covered my private parts, so I slung it over my shoulder and limped around naked. The prison doctor gave me a medical and put on his notes that there wasn't a piece of white skin on my body, which was still recovering from the motorway beating. I wasn't surprised to find out I was spending my first week in the prison's hospital ward.

In that week I had just one visitor: my mother. With us throughout her visit was a prison officer, and when I asked him to leave he refused. He hovered at my shoulder listening to every word we spoke. My mother cried. She hugged me and whispered in my ear that she understood, she loved me and I would always be her son, no matter what happened. It would be a full year before I saw her again.

After a week I was released from the prison hospital fully expecting to go on the wings. The Governor came to see me. He was carrying a clipboard and on it was an order, signed by the Secretary of State that said I couldn't enter the general prison population and would be held for an indefinite period on the Prisoner Segregation Unit. I was told that the Secretary of State would sign the order papers every twenty-four hours until a decision had been made to move me back into the general prison population. I asked him whether I was spending my remand on 'the boards' and he said yes. I limped, accompanied by four prison officers, past the noisy heart of the prison and then down below ground. I was destined for the bowels of Crumlin Road jail. 'The boards' is solitary confinement, and being on the boards means being locked up twenty-three hours a day in the PSU. Inmates who have broken prison rules or misbehaved by fighting one another or assaulting a prison officer are sent there as punishment. The internal system that decides how much time in the PSU a misbehaving prisoner should get is called 'adjudication'.

The cells in the PSU were six-by-ten-foot units of hell. They had a tiny, narrow bed along one wall and along the other wall two bits of wood sticking out pretending to be a table and chair. It was dark and dingy, with no natural light except a small slit covered with Perspex which was so badly scratched and so dirty that it may as well have been boarded up. A plastic knife, fork, spoon, plate and mug sat on the table. There was a plastic bucket in the corner. The walls were brown and a naked light bulb hung from the ceiling. The maximum period of time a person can spend on the boards was six days, unless the prison Governor asks the Secretary of State for Rule 25, an extension order used under exceptional circumstances.

I was held on the boards for one whole year. I was the first prisoner in the history of Crumlin Road to do fifty-two weeks in a row in the PSU. Every twenty-four hours the Governor, flanked by two prison officers and one principal officer, would come to my cell and read these words out to me: 'Michael Stone, the Secretary of State has ruled that for security reasons, and the security of the entire prison, you are to be kept in the PSU. For the next twenty-four hours this is where you will be housed.' Within a week I knew by heart the words that renewed the order to keep me in the bowels of the Crum. After a week I told the Governor to 'give my head peace, I know those words by heart', but he had to stick to prison protocol. I was officially told that I was being kept in the PSU for my own safety. I wasn't stupid. I knew I was on a Republican hit list. I knew prison walls couldn't protect me from a Republican wanting to settle a score. The Governor believed that if I was let among the general prison population anything was possible.

Every twenty-four hours the Governor asked me if I wanted anything. I always said no. He asked if I wanted family visits. I said no. The 'unlock' of one hour each day was weather-dependent. If it rained, I didn't get out. I found it hard being confined to a tiny cell and I missed human company. I hated having nobody to talk to. I sat within those four dingy walls and I began to think. I started to reflect, step back.

I thought about my family, and came to the conclusion that I was a selfish, arrogant bastard. I knew I was self-absorbed and put my UDA career before two wives and nine children (five born in wedlock, and four out of wedlock). I refused all their cards and letters. I wanted to be as far away as possible from the people I cared for and who continued to love me despite everything I had put them through, but I had let my mother and my entire family down. My baby daughter would grow up not knowing me. I would be a geriatric before I would be able to spend any quality time with her and by that stage she would be a grown woman with a life and family of her own. I thought about my boys. What sort of role model was I for my sons? I thought about my mother. Her health was not good. I thought about Tommy Herron and his words 'It's death or prison, kid' bounced off the dingy walls and rang in my ears. The chickens had come home to roost. Everything Herron said, none of it was a lie.

I found irony on the boards. Touts were held in the PSU and I found that funny. I took my war to the back door of the Republican movement. It was ironic that I should be held in a cell that was once home to Loyalist supergrass Budgie Allen.

In the early weeks I was treated to impromptu concerts. Small flute and drum bands would travel from West Belfast and play tunes outside the prison. I couldn't see them but I could hear them. Their music kept me connected to reality. The bands would beat their drums very loudly and chant my name. Republican prisoners hated it. I could hear them shouting obscenities back.

Even in this subterranean hellhole there were rules. Every twenty minutes I underwent a suicide watch. The screws had to be able to see you, so things like sleeping with the blanket over your head were seen as a breach of security. I was strip-searched twice a day, morning and evening, and was constantly guarded by two screws and a principal officer who stood outside my cell. The authorities were terrified some poor bastard would hurt himself even though there was nothing to hang yourself from and nothing in that dingy cell to use as a makeshift rope.

The Crum was a Victorian prison and still had Victorian fittings. The light switch was outside the cell and was an old metal one that sounded like a firework going off in a tin can when it was flicked on and off. The crack was loud enough to wake the dead and it shot a fluorescent beam into my tiny space. The prison officers flicked it every twenty minutes for the first four weeks. One day I asked them to make a decision: either keep the light on or turn it off. They said it was a suicide watch and they had to flick it every twenty minutes. I told them I wasn't going to kill myself and I would much rather kill someone else. They looked at me in astonishment. The light wasn't switched off for a full year and I used two circles of paper, coloured in with a black ballpoint pen borrowed from a screw, as an eye mask to shield my eyes from the bright light at bedtime.

I did get my own back on the screws by faking my suicide. One was an annoying little man with an English accent who worked the night shift. I rolled my grey blanket into a sausage shape and stuffed it into my jeans. I tied the jeans to a pipe that ran above the door and attached my trainers to weight it down. Through the tiny slit of the viewfinder all the screw would be able to see would be two denim legs hanging from the air. I waited. The screw came on duty. He peered through the viewfinder and hit the panic button. The 'Ninjas', the Crum's Immediate Reaction Force, bounded into the unit. The screw was screaming at the top of his voice, 'Stone's hanging in his cell. I think he's dead.' In the meantime I had taken down the jeans and got back into bed, covering myself with the blanket. The Ninjas unlocked my cell door and I sat up innocently in bed and asked, 'What's going on, are you moving me?' The screw protested that he saw me hanging in my cell, but he was disciplined and moved from the PSU. The principal officer, called 'the Beet' because of his red hair and ruddy complexion, said to me the next day, 'You wound him up, didn't you? We're going to have to watch you, Mr Stone.'

I nicknamed my little exercise yard the 'dog-run'. It was exactly like a kennel, tiny and boxed-in with a metal grille for a roof. It measured just fifteen feet by six. My dogs at home had more room than me. All I could do was walk up, turn around and walk back. I wasn't allowed out when it rained, which was most of the year.

The dog-run was disgusting. Prisoners filled paper bags with their waste and slung them out of the windows. They were called 'mystery parcels'. They burst on hitting the grille over the dog-run and the waste dissolved into a shower of excrement. The longest period I went without seeing daylight was seven weeks.

As the weeks wore on routine became the single most important thing in my life. I never lost track of time. I set my body clock by the twice-daily strip-searches. I started to lose weight. I also started to think about my future. I knew I was facing a substantial stint on the boards, but there was still a chance I would go to the wings to do the rest of my remand. Then I was looking at the Maze for my sentence. I needed to get fit. I needed to get back into shape, mentally and physically.

I began an exercise routine consisting of sit-ups, press-ups and shadow boxing. The prison officers would laugh at me, but I told them to fuck off and mind their own business. The exercise was my survival kit. I put my mattress against the wall, put socks over my fists and punched the mattress. I started to firm up. If anyone came near me, I would fight first and ask questions later. Bathrooms were called the 'ablutions'. I would take a plastic chair and sit under the hot shower for hours. I made a point of asking for a shower regularly.

The authorities hated granting my request for legal visits because that meant they had to 'lock down' the entire prison. This meant that all movement stopped, grilles were closed, doors were locked and the army was even put on alert.

About six weeks into my remand a Republican prison called Terence Clarke arrived on the boards. 'Cleeky' was doing time for his part in the capture of two Royal Corps of Signals corporals, Derek Howes and David Wood, who were murdered after straying into the funeral of Kevin Brady, one of the men I killed at Milltown. He even did a stint as Gerry Adams's bodyguard and was head of security at the funeral for the Gibraltar Three. But

Cleeky fucked up that day. He didn't see me coming. He had been adjudicated and sent to the PSU for breaking prison rules. He grew a moustache. Under the Crum's tough internal regime changing your appearance wasn't allowed.

Cleeky had deliberately broken a prison rule in order to be sent to the punishment block because he knew I was housed there. He wanted to get a feel for the layout of the place. Cleeky was opportunistic. He was looking for a chance to take me out. He announced himself to the PSU by shouting, 'Where are you, Stoner, what cell you in?' Later, when I was unlocked, I went looking for him. I didn't know what he looked like. I had only heard of him. Cleeky was legendary in the Republican movement. He was a bad boy. I found his cell card and lifted the viewfinder to take a look at him. He was sitting on his bed, and jumped when the metal flap screeched open. He thought I was a prison officer until I laughed into his cell and told him that I was watching him. Cleeky screamed back at me, 'You are so lucky, Stone. I was that close to getting you. I wanted to chop you into little pieces that day. I wanted to scatter your body all over the six counties. I wanted your dick in South Armagh and your head on a spike on the Falls Road. I didn't get my way that day. You're dead.' I could see him pretending to box me and he was shouting, 'Get your screw friends to let you in'.

I slammed down the flap and rattled the door in the pretence that a screw was opening it. I told Cleeky I wanted to 'put one in his baldy head'. He hit the alarm button and screamed at the screws, 'Officer, officer, Stone threatened to kill me.' Within seconds the Ninjas were all over the unit. Within the hour the Governor was at my cell door.

'Mr Clarke is back on the wings. He has made an official complaint and wants to press charges. Did you threaten to kill him?'

'He threatened me, so I said I would put one in his baldy head.'

'He's as bad as you. You are as bad as him. I don't want to hear any more about this incident. End of story.' The door slammed shut.

Cleeky's pal, Harry Maguire, was sent to the boards three weeks later, also for breaking prison rules. He was on remand for his part in the murder of the two corporals. I could see a pattern emerging. The Republican hierarchy was casing the place in an attempt to create an opportunity to kill me.

Maguire made his appearance when I was having a shave. Behind me, a door opened. I thought it was unusual because boards prisoners never overlap in their unlock time, but a mistake was made by a prison officer and our times overlapped. The screw who was guarding me looked uneasy. I turned around and Maguire was standing behind me. He had a mop of red hair. We eyeballed one another. I handed the ancient shaving contraption to the prison officer. There was a brush propped up against the wall. I lifted it and snapped it in two across my knee. The screw stepped back. I taunted Maguire, I gestured with my hand and pointed to the broken brush handle and asked him if he wanted to have a go at me. He refused to bite and returned to his cell, his screw walking behind him. I was charged with breaking prison property and was fined one pound.

It was impossible for me to go to the canteen to eat, so my meals were brought to my cell by the duty prison officers. The Governor wanted to avoid a fight breaking out at the food counter, or worse, a poisoning. Two screws and a principal officer were responsible for selecting and delivering my food. I told them I would only eat individual items like potatoes or meat. I refused to touch stews, casseroles and curries or any food that was cooked in the one pot. I was sixteen years old and doing time in Long Kesh when I discovered what happens in prison kitchens. Young lads would spit, piss and even put steel wool and shards of glass into the massive cauldrons of food. By the time my food got to me it was cold, but I ate it anyway. Cold food was better than no food.

Some of the screws were decent men. Much later, after we had developed a working relationship, we had a quid pro quo system, favour for favour. I would paint for them and they would smuggle in treats such as barbecue chicken. The screws got it in by putting it in a freezer bag, sitting on it to flatten it and placing it down the front of their trousers. When they were signing in for duty, they had to book in their personal weapon, go through the X-ray machine and were body-searched, but generally security was lax for prison officers. The chickens were a six-weekly treat and, after I had eaten the meat, I would take the bones in my bucket and dump them down the slop-out. I learnt a lesson: the screws could be helpful and useful. If they were prepared to put a barbecue chicken down their trousers they could smuggle anything in and that included knives and guns.

The screws helped me get messages in and out. One made the initial approach by passing cigarette papers, wrapped in cling film, containing coded messages.

My lonely prison life dragged on, but out of the blue I got a visit from the Security Officer. Unknown to me, I had been getting a lot of mail and the SO wanted to know what to do with it. He said there were at least three black bin bags full of letters and cards. He then asked about the food parcels that had been arriving, sometimes up to three a week. I told him they weren't from my family and he said he knew all about that. He said the parcels contained cooked meat and chicken, fruit and expensive biscuits. He said that, if it were any other prisoner, the screws would scoff it.

He then added, 'Off the record, we have an officer who has compromised himself by smuggling messages for Republicans. The Republicans have turned the tables and he is now being blackmailed. He saw the prison authorities. The authorities knew he was smuggling messages but wanted to see how far he would go unprompted. He said the IRA wanted to kill Michael Stone, by poisoning, before his trial and there was a hundred thousand in the kitty, all-comers welcome. You're here under Rule 25 and likely to be here until your trial. I have also heard that there might be a chance you will do your time in England.' And with that he left.

I had too much time on my hands to think. I thought about my old friend Sammy Cinnamond. He always cautioned me to 'step back' if things got rough and 'stand aside' if things started to look jaded. So the process of reassessing my paramilitary life had begun. I started at Milltown and worked backwards. I began to replay the story of my life. It was like a video. I fast-forwarded and rewound and I played and replayed key scenes in my life. Could I have chosen a different path? Could I have played things differently? Could I have lived a different life? I had pulled over from the highway of life. I was assessing and taking stock. I had had several chances to follow different routes. I had actually physically extracted myself from Ulster in the early eighties and moved to the UK for six months, but like a nail to a magnet I was drawn back. It seemed inevitable that I would end up here in a tiny box, no bigger than a dog kennel, reassessing what I had been doing since I was sixteen years old.

Disillusionment had set in. I was a counter-terrorist. I was a retaliatory soldier because Republicans had forced my hand. I am not excusing my actions, but no man in his right mind could sit back and ignore their sectarian crimes. Or was it the other way round? I couldn't decide. I realised what Sammy Cinnamond said was true. We are all expendable. I realised Loyalist prisoners are just unwanted baggage. Except for our families and our friends, who cares about us? I didn't want to be a social or political embarrassment to the UDA, but I feared that was all I was. I had heard nothing from the organisation I joined when I was just sixteen. A message on a cigarette paper was smuggled in to me. It was from the Berlin Arms, a UVF bar, and said that the papers were full of the UDA's denial of me, that I was a true Loyalist and the UVF were prepared to claim me after my trial. Tucker Lyttle had thrown me to the wolves.

Life went on. I continued to reassess my life and continued my fitness regime. The prison officers were the only human contact I had and different teams guarded me by day and by night. I didn't like the night men. They had a different attitude to the day lads. Some were ex-forces. They could be sadistic and used to wind me up by calling me Paddy.

My euphoria at surviving Milltown was fast disappearing. The PSU was getting to me and I was finding it tough to get through each day. Then a young trustee arrived. He was an 'ODC', an ordinary decent criminal, in for fraud. He was on the boards to work. Trustees have prison jobs. Then he started. 'The Battle of Milltown, that was brilliant. You'll do big time for that. I wouldn't want to be you. You know what I would have done? I would have taken a big M60 and sat a quarter of a mile back and killed the lot. What about your mates in the van? Didn't they fuck off on you? Everyone is saying your mates were the peelers.' That was it, a red rag to a bull. I got him in a stranglehold, he struggled for a few seconds and it was only when he went limp and slumped to the floor that I stuck my boot into him. A screw eventually saw what was going on and hit the alarm. They lifted the ODC up, slapped his face and took him back to his cell. I wasn't disciplined. The authorities couldn't do anything with me. I was already on the punishment block.

Then King of the Bull Roots arrived. 'Bull Root' is prison slang for a sex offender. In the prisoner hierarchy, sex offenders are the lowest form of life and are considered worse than a paramilitary tout. In Northern Ireland, if a sex offender is walking through the wing and another prisoner shouts 'Bull Root', the prisoner nearest the sex offender must attack him. It is an unwritten rule. This particular Bull Root's real name was John Clifford and he was convicted of the rape and murder of his niece, Sue Ellen. She was just eight years old and her body was put in a bin bag and dumped. Clifford bragged about the death of the little girl and that pissed off the screws. He was due for a stint on the boards and the screws asked me to 'sort him out, don't kill him, just give him a good hammering'. Clifford never appeared. The authorities wanted to keep the PSU clear of other prisoners.

I asked for a radio and was surprised, not when they gave me one but when they said I could have had the radio from day one. The authorities had kept that from me. It was small and battery-powered but even from the bowels of the Crum it managed to pick up my favourite station, BBC Radio Ulster. I discovered David Dunseith and he became my link to the outside world. I tuned in to his *Talkback* show every day. Many times I was the subject of his discussions. People are entitled to their opinions. I also listened to the news bulletins and was dismayed to discover that the Provos were still bombing indiscriminately. It depressed me to think that the war was still going on and I was locked up in the Crum. Ironically, I heard a phone-in where Cleeky Clarke's family complained and blamed me for their son's spell in jail.

I started to think about escape, despite being underground and alone. I broke it down, cell to unit, unit to perimeter fence, perimeter fence to outside. I didn't factor in the armed soldiers guarding the prison twenty-four hours a day. I would be shot on the spot. I knew there was a blind spot that the security cameras didn't cover, the razor wire was sagging and it was possible to get under it and on to the roof. The Beet spied me eyeballing the prison perimeter and said to me, 'You know, Stone, a few years ago a boy got on to the roof. He didn't get very far because the authorities got a forklift truck, they put pallets on the bucket and dogs were in the pallets. The dogs were released and bit the prisoner. Forewarned is forearmed.' Over the following days an extra line of barbed wire was erected.

I realised I was politically isolated. There hadn't been any contact from the UDA since my capture and arrest. Then I overheard a conversation between two Republican prisoners. Directly above the PSU was a workout unit, used by men who had done most of their sentence and were getting ready for release. I heard them talking about going home. I heard one say to the other, 'Twelve years tomorrow, just eight weeks left', and the other replying, 'Me too. A few more months and it will be *adiós* to the Crum.' They were leaving this stinking prison and going home to family and friends and I hadn't even been given my trial date. I hadn't even done twelve weeks. I was facing life behind bars. Was my cause less worthy than their cause? The two men had done time when their comrades were on the 'dirty' protest and dying on hunger strike. These men were no better men than me and I was no better than them. We were all part of the same problem. We were all part of the same war. Their conversation about going home and freedom pulled me to my senses. I knew I had to stay focused. I knew it was essential I stayed on top of things.

My routine was mind-numbingly boring. After the incidents with the two Republicans I vowed I would survive the PSU. I knew the boards had the potential to break men, but I was determined that I wouldn't be one of them.

I gradually built up a relationship with a couple of the day screws that worked the PSU. They would keep me informed of developments and new arrivals to the unit. They were my eyes and ears and supplied me with gossip.

Six months into my remand, the Governor said I had a visitor. He was introduced as Head of the Board of Prison Visits. In walked John Alderdice. He asked how the Crum authorities were treating me and I said it was fine. He said that any time I needed anything or needed his help, I just had to ask. I thanked him for his kindness and generosity and was very tempted to say, 'Are you still living at – ?', but didn't. When Alderdice left the room I heard the Governor say to him, 'He has been in the segregation unit for six months and I don't know how he does it.'

It was my radio that announced the imminent arrival of Sean O'Callaghan. The high-ranking PIRA man was also an RUC informer. He gave himself up after walking into a police station in Tunbridge Wells and confessing to several murders. O'Callaghan was immediately sent back to Northern Ireland and the authorities had him sent to the Crum. I quizzed my screw friends and they confirmed O'Callaghan was being put in the PSU for his own safety. He was an informer and his Special Branch handlers were expecting big things from him. His life was in danger from his own people on the Republican wings and the rumour was they would have him killed for bringing the Republican movement into disrepute.

The screws pointed out O'Callaghan's cell to allow me to have a look at him during my unlock time. He was sitting on his bed smoking a Marlboro. There were several boxes of them scattered over the bed, and plastic bags full of chocolate bars. I kept a close ear on radio bulletins, but there was no mention of O'Callaghan and there were no revelations of arms finds or new information leading to the arrest of Republicans. It was as if O'Callaghan didn't exist. I couldn't understand why a high-profile Republican prisoner had faded completely into the background. I was six months into my own remand and still the subject of heated arguments on the radio. Sean O'Callaghan was a mystery.

The screws kept me informed of his routine. They told me that his health was failing. First he was limping, so the prison authorities gave him a walking stick to help him move around his cell. The following week he had a second stick and two weeks later the prison doctors gave him crutches. Within six weeks of arriving in the Crum, he was confined to a wheelchair. The screws told me he had a bad back, wore a medical corset and was on medication.

O'Callaghan was a Republican soldier and he killed

indiscriminately. A former Special Branch detective died at his hands. He used a mortar bomb and killed a UDR woman soldier. He was an informer and the authorities appeared to be taking their time deciding what to do with him, if they were going to do anything with him at all. Perhaps he was in the PSU as part of a bigger plan, to stop me going into the dock.

In the meantime I was going to have fun at O'Callaghan's expense. I managed to read his mail. The letters were mostly from Republican supporters in County Kerry, but there were other letters from Dublin and even Belfast. Comments in them such as 'keep the chin up', 'we're thinking of you', 'you're a good lad and keep thinking of the cause' and 'we know you'll come through this' gave me plenty of entertainment. I would shout at him, 'I'm going to booby-trap your wheelchair, you Provie bastard.' I didn't trust the informer tag the authorities wove into O'Callaghan's new prison identity. He was in the PSU for a reason. I believe that reason was to kill me. I had a feeling the bad back and wheelchair were not genuine, and there was still no mention of him on news programmes.

Night and day I taunted O'Callaghan. I banged the cell pipes non-stop to hammer home my mantra: 'Se-an, Sea-aa-annn. There's only one thing worse than a Provie and that's a Provie tout. I know why you are in here, you piece of shit. Did your leadership send you in here to take me out?' His only reply was, 'Leave me alone' and 'I'm going to complain to the Governor.'

He had mysterious visits, always around midnight. His visitors didn't come in the main door of the PSU but through a side door linking the cells to the dog-run. There were three different voices, one English, one Irish and one local. I could hear the rustle of plastic bags containing his chocolates and cigarettes.

O'Callaghan spent eight long weeks on the boards before losing the plot. The boards broke him. It was early one weekday morning. The alarm went off, and I heard prison officers trying to restrain O'Callaghan and calm him down, but he was shouting at the top of his voice that he didn't kill anyone and was 'here to kill Michael Stone'. He kept shouting that he didn't kill that detective and the woman soldier. The commotion continued for hours. I was locked in my cell, so I pressed my face up against the bars to try to see what was happening, but I couldn't see anything. I could hear raised voices, official voices and O'Callaghan's hysterical voice arguing back. I asked the screws to let me out. They told me that was impossible. They told me to sit quietly in my cell and behave myself.

Four hours later I still hadn't been let out of my cell. I hadn't eaten, I hadn't showered and I hadn't slopped out. The screws told me that I couldn't go anywhere until things had calmed down. It was lunchtime when two of the three strange accents could be heard, the English and the Irish. I strained my ears to listen. Perhaps his visitors – I believed they were his police handlers – could shed light on the mystery.

One of the official-sounding voices asked O'Callaghan what was wrong with him and I could hear his answer. He didn't want to go down for life, he didn't kill those people and he was here to take Stone out. The second voice told him to settle down and not 'fuck things up'.

By four in the afternoon O'Callaghan was gone. I was allowed out of my cell. Outside his cell, lying in a heap, were bedclothes marked with tiny drops of blood that had been smeared so as to look worse than they actually were. There was a razor, a blue plastic disposable one minus the handle. The wheelchair was in the corner of the cell and several packets of cigarettes were scattered over the mattress.

I got strip-searched three times a week. They were random, and in addition to my twice-daily morning and evening searches, so I never knew when a search was coming. O'Callaghan was supposed to have the same security procedures, so how did he get the razor in? The screw said it was probably smuggled in in the lining of his medical corset and probably travelled from England with him. I asked about the wheelchair, as O'Callaghan apparently couldn't move without it. The screw said he miraculously didn't need the wheelchair when he was leaving. He walked out of the PSU like an athlete with his back ramrod straight. The walking sticks, the corset and the wheelchair were all a ploy to lull me into a false sense of security. O'Callaghan had planned to strike when I was least expecting it. He would leap out of his wheelchair and slice my throat. I asked about the blood on the sheets and was told O'Callaghan cut his skin, just enough to cause bleeding but not enough to wound himself. He wanted to make it look like he was suicidal so that he could be moved from the PSU to another part of the prison.

I could see just two possibilities. One, O'Callaghan is a tout; he kills me to get back in with the IRA, which clears the debt he owes to the Republican movement. Or two, he was placed in the Crum by the security forces to have me killed. I hope it wasn't a conspiracy to silence me, but I believe it was. I believe the RUC were unnerved when they ran checks on my conspiracy confessions. I think they did a deal with O'Callaghan: kill Stone, make it look like a fight, get yourself injured, say it was self-defence, you get your time, you get early release and we'll give you a new life on your release. After the O'Callaghan incident there was a change of prison staff in the PSU. The old team were moved, including my pal the Beet, and were replaced by officers who never opened their mouths and never smiled.

I believe O'Callaghan went straight to the Republican wings and was welcomed with open arms by Danny Morrison. In his own book O'Callaghan tells how he wanted to smuggle in a gun and kill me and two RUC officers sent in to question him. The two policemen weren't sent in to question him. O'Callaghan said the three deaths inside the Crum would be proof positive of his loyalties to the Republican movement. When he put the idea to Gerry Adams, Adams is believed to have replied, 'No, no, no.' O'Callaghan failed to mention the blade hidden inside the lining of his medical corset. He failed to mention his midnight visitors with the English and Irish accents.

Later that day the Governor came to see me and said I owed my life to the duty prison officers. I told him I owed them 'fuck all'. I told him I knew from day one that O'Callaghan was in to take me out.

O'Callaghan couldn't live with himself for being a tout, the lowest form of life, but he still went to court and nailed his colours to the mast. He announced he was an informer for eleven years and confirmed he had police handlers. He claimed to have saved lives, including those of Prince Charles and Princess Diana. After pleading Not Guilty to the charges, he was found guilty and sentenced to life. He was sent to Maghaberry but ended up in a psychiatric ward. He thought there was a plot to poison him. British intelligence admitted O'Callaghan was one of their main agents. Despite being given a life sentence, he served just eight years for three murders and his release had nothing to do with the early release scheme introduced as part of the Northern Ireland Peace Process. After walking out of Maghaberry a free man he became an overnight celebrity and now works as a security consultant against terrorism.

Following O'Callaghan's release I spoke to my solicitor. I said O'Callaghan had threatened me. I'd heard him yelling at the top of his voice that he had been sent to the Crum to kill me. I wanted to take this matter much further. I had affidavits made out and tried to pursue a private prosecution, but no one would touch it. I couldn't get anyone above my own solicitor to represent me or touch the case.

After the O'Callaghan incident I had an official visit from the Governor. He came to my cell accompanied by three prison officers and a principal officer and was holding in his hand the order to renew Rule 25. He addressed me from outside my cell. Prison staff are not allowed inside a cell. He said, 'Michael, the Secretary of State is thinking of putting you in the general prison population. How do you feel about that?'

'I intend surviving.'

'What does that mean, Michael?'

'It means, Governor, that if someone comes near me that I don't know and can't identify, I will take them out before they take me out.'

'I don't understand.'

'It means, Governor, I will kill them. I am going away for the rest of my life. If I am threatened I will defend myself and I will kill to defend myself.' He read the renewal of Rule 25 but came back to my cell the following morning. He said I would stay in the PSU until my trial.

A six-foot by ten-foot windowless box was to be my home until my trial in the spring. The Governor asked me how I felt about that and I clearly remember saying I was fine. The defiant soldier in me had already kicked in. I told him I wanted my day in court.

As soon as a Republican prisoner was sent to the PSU I went into overdrive. I was fine-tuned for signs of danger and threats to my safety. Many prisoners like to 'work their ticket', pretending to be mad in order to get into the PSU. I was suspicious of all new Republican arrivals, especially those the screws said were 'acting up' on the wings.

Tommy McGrath was the latest recruit. He was serving a double life sentence for the murder of a UDR soldier and his son, William and Leslie Corrigan, who were shot dead in County Armagh in 1976. McGrath was sentenced to life and had served some eleven years but his mind was affected. He attacked a screw in the prison hospital and the authorities sent him to the boards for three days as punishment. McGrath was the subject of a television documentary called *Indelible Evidence*. The programme revealed how the RUC caught him and got a conviction with an imprint of his teeth left on an apple found at the scene. McGrath had protruding front teeth. The programme showed how a dental expert built a cast from the tooth imprint and this nailed him to the double murder. McGrath had left his personal calling card when he murdered the father and son.

The screws said he was mad, went nuts on the wing, was carrying his excrement on his shoulder and talking to it like it was a budgie, but I needed to be sure. After O'Callaghan, anything was possible. I had a look at him. McGrath was a wiry fellow about the same build as myself. He was very twitchy and kept jumping up and down and looking out of his viewfinder. He looked like he had overdosed on caffeine or was on drugs.

Then bizarre things started to happen in the middle of the night. One night I heard two voices. One was clearly McGrath but the other I didn't recognise. I can still remember the 'conversation'.

'McGrath, we know you did it. We know you killed a UDR soldier and his son.'

'I didn't bite the apple, mister, that's a lie.'

Then I heard a third voice. It was the night screw asking McGrath if he was all right. The strange voice answered, saying McGrath was fine, leave him alone and we'll look after him. The words were followed by the crack-crack of a fist on flesh and the strange voice shouting, 'We know you did it, you lying little Provo', accompanied by the sound of McGrath sobbing. Next morning the screw told me McGrath spent the night interrogating himself. He used a deep voice when he was the RUC and his own voice for himself. In the days following his self-interrogation, he calmed down. When he was chilled out he asked for his guitar. He was quite good and sang Eagles and Johnny Cash songs.

McGrath asked to see a priest. The priest was brought to him and I could hear them chatting. McGrath sounded well. He even sounded happy, because faint laughter drifted through the unit. He played a couple of songs for the priest. It went quiet for a few seconds, then there was a bing-bong-bing, the sound of a guitar being smashed. The priest's screams could be heard all over the unit. McGrath had tried to strangle the priest with a guitar string. The alarm was hit, the Ninjas stormed in, McGrath was sedated, and the priest was taken away to recover. McGrath had used a bass string. The priest would have been decapitated if he had used a treble string.

McGrath was a tight wee guy and gave a good fight. He liked to get steamed into the Ninjas, but he wasn't well and should never have been on the punishment blocks. He should have been getting the medical attention he deserved. Soon after the priest incident, he was gone. I was told he ended up in Broadmoor, but I don't know if this is true. I just hope the young lad got the medical attention he needed.

There was another man, a young Catholic hood who was doing time in Magilligan Prison for handling stolen goods. He was held hostage by Loyalist protesters who threatened to kill him unless they got segregation. This man was given three days on the boards but I don't know what he did wrong. He walked with his head down and was a sad-looking figure. The screws asked me not to wind him up but I couldn't help myself. He had a budgie and the Governor allowed him to keep the bird in his cell. The bird tweeted a lot and the hood would tweet back at it. This went on all night, so I shouted at him that if he didn't stop the fucking tweeting I was going to kidnap the bird and smother it in onions.

The lad was on medication. The prison orderly would give him tablets every night. He only lasted two nights. On the second morning, when the screws unlocked his cell, they were confronted with a gruesome sight. He had given himself a vasectomy. He had smashed the little mirror in the budgie's cage and used the shards of glass to cut open his scrotum and had tried to slice off one of his testicles. The screw said it had unravelled like a ball of string and was hanging down his leg. This prison officer who unlocked him threw up and had to take sick leave.

There were plenty of 'screamers'. Philip Laffan was in for armed robbery. He was caught doing a smash-and-grab on a jewellery shop on Royal Avenue. He was on remand and attacked prisoners and assaulted screws. He was sent to the boards, never recovered and committed suicide.

The screws had asked me to keep an eye on Laffan, befriend him and keep him occupied until his trial, which was just weeks away. I took a look in his cell one morning and saw he was sitting on his bed naked. His clothes were in shreds and he was shoving the ripped fabric into his mouth. The screws had given him a radio, exactly like the one I had in my cell, but he dismantled it and wires and batteries were all over the floor. He had even eaten bits of the plastic.

Laffan called me 'Rambo Stone' and pleaded with me to get him out of prison. I told him I couldn't because we were in a high-security prison, but he didn't understand a word of what I was saying. He just repeated the same thing over and over: 'Rambo, Rambo Stone, you can get me out of here, please take me with you.' The screws had told me he was likely to get four years for the robbery but he would be out in two and he would serve his time in Magilligan. I told him to try to relax, to think of his wife and daughter, not to pick fights with the screws and not to eat his clothes. He got worse, but no one seemed to care. He was awake all night, shouting at the top of his voice. The night screws ignored him, but that isn't a surprise. They had ice water running through their veins.

Then, out of the blue, Laffan asked for food. He said he wanted sandwiches, so the screws allowed him to have a plate of bread and a tub of margarine. He seemed happy making his sandwiches until the screws looked inside his cell. He was naked and had smeared his body with the margarine. He was in one of his aggressive moods and attacked the screws, lashing out with fists and feet. Every time they tried to grab him, Laffan slipped through their fingers. He threw his cell bucket over them. The alarm was pressed and the Ninjas came thundering into the unit. They dumped him back in his cell.

Laffan was quiet for a few days, then asked for a pen. He told the screws he wanted to write to his wife and child. The screws asked me to keep an eye on him because they had given up. I looked in on him and his mouth was covered in ink. He had eaten the pen after covering his entire body in childish drawings. I felt sorry for him. On the day of his trial, Laffan shouted into my cell, 'So long, Rambo Stone.' He went to court and got his four years. I never saw him again. A week later he was dead, hanged in his cell.

I tell these stories because they prove what war and prison do to people. They pulp their brains. Haunted by their past, these men were reduced to shadows of human beings. I could have been any one of them, or all of them, but I made an effort to stay focused and in control.

18

PAT FINUCANE

PAT FINUCANE WAS A PROMINENT AND SUCCESSFUL LAWYER. HE WAS ONE OF JUST A HANDFUL OF SOLICITORS WHO HAD BECOME PROFICIENT IN THE OPERATION OF CRIMINAL TRIALS IN NORTHERN IRELAND'S NON-JURY DIPLOCK COURTS. He had been involved in a number of high-profile cases, at one point defending IRA hunger striker Bobby Sands. At the time of his death he was involved in the inquests and court cases that surrounded the death of two County Armagh men who were shot dead by the RUC.

Finucane lived in North Belfast with his wife and family. He was ambushed in his home one Sunday evening while he was eating with his wife and children. Two UFF volunteers sledgehammered down his front door and shot him with an automatic rifle and a 9mm Browning pistol. He was hit fourteen times in the head and body.

He died on 12 February 1989, just three weeks before the start of my trial. Pat Finucane overheard a heated argument I was having with three detectives, one of them Special Branch, when I was on remand, and I believe overhearing those angry words may have cost him his life.

Six weeks before my trial was due to start I had a visit from the police. Two of the officers who questioned me in Musgrave Park Hospital came to Crumlin Road to deliver my box of depositions. My legal team had been complaining for nine months about not having access to the evidence, which would be used during my court case.

Legal and police visits were held in a special room that was divided in two down the middle, with each side divided into five cubicles. The cubicles were tiny, no bigger than five by eight, and were separated by thin plasterboard walls. There were three plastic chairs and a shelf that doubled as a table. You had to speak in whispers because other prisoners and other people's lawyers could overhear conversations. Ten prison officers accompanied me, the prison was locked down and I was strip-searched before being allowed into the visit. As I walked the length of the room I noticed all the cubicles on the left-hand side of the tiny corridor were empty, except the last one. In the fifth cubicle were two of the investigating officers who questioned me in Musgrave Park Hospital and a third man – I didn't recognise him – was in plainclothes. He was introduced as a detective sergeant in Special Branch.

On the table was a large box containing my depositions, stacked on top of one another, two feet high. There was silence and I spoke first.

'You took your time with those.'

Silence. None of the RUC men spoke.

'My solicitor has been waiting on these. I have been waiting on them. Why did it take so long to get them to me?'

'Mr Stone, we have other charges we wish to make.'

'Fuck your charges.'

I was getting agitated. The Special Branch officer decided to contribute to the conversation. He mentioned my family and the danger I was exposing them to if I didn't co-operate with this new round of enquiries. That was a red rag to a bull. I got to my feet and yelled at the top of my voice to the Special Branch detective, 'You tell that fucker — that if he fucks with me, or my family, the shit will hit the fan.' It is an open secret among Loyalists that the man I was referring was head of Special Branch at the time.

The Special Branch detective addressed me directly.

'What do you mean, Mr Stone?'

I turned to the two detectives I recognised and spoke directly to them.

'Tell him, the white Transit van. Tell him if he threatens my family I am going into the dock and I am going to say my mates fucked off and left me.'

'What are you going to say about the white van, Michael?'

'I'm going to say my mates fucked off on me. I have been rotting in solitary for almost a year. I have to nothing to lose. I will drop everyone in it.'

The implication was that I knew the RUC men in the white van and they were my back-up unit on the day and were going to drive me to safety when the operation was over. I was angry. They had wound me up by talking about my family. I had done a deal with my interrogators and now they were going back on their word.

The three detectives stood up to leave the cubicle. As they did I shouted a torrent of abuse at them. 'Tell that fucker that if he messes with me, I will mess with him.'

I watched as the three men began their slow walk through the unit and stopped outside the cubicle next door. I was still shouting at the top of my voice and punching the stud wall. I was filled with anger that they wanted to pin other things on me after I had wiped my slate clean.

Then I noticed their attention was drawn to something or someone in one of the other cubicles. The Special Branch detective was tugging the coat of one of his colleagues. I followed their gaze and looked in. There was a man reclining in one of the plastic chairs and he had the side of his head pressed against the stud wall. His legs were extended straight in front of him and he looked relaxed. The man was wearing an expensive suit and a Crombie overcoat. I recognised him immediately as Pat Finucane, a high-profile lawyer. I looked straight at him and even asked him what the fuck he was looking at, but it didn't faze him in the slightest. He didn't answer me and he didn't even look at me. I lifted the first paper on my bundle of depositions and read it out loud as the three officers left the unit. I was shocked. Pat Finucane had overheard every word.

Days later, when I had calmed down, I had a think about what I shouted at the detectives in anger. Then I thought of Finucane, who had heard the RUC ask me about the white van and me reply that I'd go into the dock and say my mates fucked off on me. After Milltown, Sinn Fein had focused all their attention on the white Transit van and alleged I was working in collusion with the security forces. This claim was rubbish. The white van was as much a shock to me as it was to Sinn Fein when it appeared on the hard shoulder. I knew what was coming next: Finucane would make a statement. It would state that he knew, categorically, that Michael Stone, the Milltown killer, carried out the operation in collusion with the security forces.

I braced myself for the fallout but it didn't happen. Less than three weeks later Pat Finucane was dead. I heard on a late-night radio bulletin that there was a fatal shooting in North Belfast. The victim was a well-known solicitor and the UFF had claimed responsibility. Finucane was killed by three members of the West Belfast unit of the UFF. His wife was injured in the operation. A statement issued after his death by the UFF said it killed 'Pat Finucane the Provisional IRA officer and not Pat Finucane the solicitor'. The double agent Brian Nelson personally targeted

Finucane and provided the intelligence to the unit who carried out the killing. I was told by an associate that Nelson 'pushed it and pushed it hard and it was done and dusted within fourteen days'. Members of Finucane's family had strong Republican connections. His brother John was killed in a car crash in 1972. A second brother was extradited from the Irish Republic to the North. A third brother was the fiancé of Mairead Farrell, one of the IRA volunteers shot dead in Gibraltar. Pat Finucane was the first solicitor to be killed in the Troubles.

Finucane was never a UFF or UDA target, and I know that for a fact. He wasn't even a secondary target. No intelligence file existed on him, but a file did exist on his brother Frank, who was also a UFF target. I am told Pat Finucane wasn't killed because he was a Catholic solicitor or because he defended Provos or because he had family involved in the IRA. He was killed for 'other reasons'. Finucane had heard my angry words with my RUC interrogators and the Special Branch detective. RUC and Special Branch knew he overheard the shouts about the white van. It was said in the heat of the moment, it was a bluff to protect my family and frighten the RUC from making further enquiries or adding further charges, but it cost Finucane his life. I have no doubt the Special Branch detective reported back to his superiors that Finucane overheard me scream, 'I'll get in the dock and tell the court that my mates fucked off and left me.'

After Finucane's death I decided I would not go into the witness box. I would plead Not Guilty, but I wouldn't let my legal team defend me. I now knew what the authorities were capable off.

Three weeks after this visit the two interrogators from Grosvenor Road came back. The Special Branch detective was not with them. Every month I was remanded in custody, and the same RUC officers were always around and would stop me on my way from the hearing. They asked me was I still pleading Not Guilty and then said, 'Will you tell us about the white van? You know you can talk to us.' I replied, 'Behave yourselves. What about your bastard Sean O'Callaghan you sent in to take me out?' They said they didn't know what I was talking about.

Later, eighteen months into my sentence, I was told by the Maze authorities that investigating officers from the Stevens Inquiry wanted to talk to me. I agreed to the visit but had nothing to say to them. When I got to the room where the meetings were being held I noticed that there were six officers, including two of my interrogators from Musgrave Park Hospital.

'I thought this was about the Stevens Inquiry.'

'It is. They want to interview you.'

'What about?'

'Collusion with the security forces.'

'You are not Stevens officers. Why are you here?'

'Will you accept a visit from the Stevens team?'

I refused to answer. One officer continued to talk.

'You've been sentenced but we need to go over a couple of things. Kevin McPolin, was that you?'

'You tell me. How does this sound: "Dear Mr Stevens, there are few things I want to get off my chest?"'

'Michael, he's an Englishman. He doesn't understand our situation here. He doesn't understand how things work. We are all Loyalists. He doesn't think like we do. Will you see Stevens?'

'No.'

'The white van?'

'Fuck off.'

'The Ruger, where did it come from?'

'I have been done for that.'

'Did you know the police officer it was stolen from?'

'No, but I suppose you are going to tell me that the officer hung himself in his police station because he was caught stealing money for gun permits?'

I left. They sat on. Throughout the whole conversation not a word was written down. I do not know if they were wired. When I looked behind me, two of the officers were scribbling furiously in their notebooks.

Several months after that I got another visit. This time it was a request from the Samson Inquiry team. There were two plainclothes police officers and I had never seen them before. They shook my hand and introduced themselves and explained that Mr Samson wanted to meet me. 'Mr Stevens also wanted to meet me and I refused his visit,' I said. 'Tell Mr Samson that I can't help him with his inquiry.'

'There is a lot of interest regarding your statement, "I read his file, he was a legitimate target." Can you elaborate on that for us?'

'No.'

'Do we tell Mr Samson that Mr Stone refused a meeting?'

'I have nothing to say to Mr Samson.'

All files I read on targets were given to me by UFF intelligence officers and they in turn had their own contacts. I was never handed a file by a member of the security forces, although I do concede that the files were very professional both in presentation and content, especially the aerial photography. I am not aware of any Loyalist paramilitary group that had its own air corps.

19

SHOW TRIAL

**ONE MONTH BEFORE MY TRIAL I HAD A VISIT FROM MY
LEGAL TEAM, WHO BROUGHT SOME DISTURBING NEWS.**
Justice Higgins, the judge assigned to my trial, refused to speak
to them in chambers about the case. My solicitor said it was the
first time in his legal career that this had happened and it was an
unusual departure given that cases are discussed privately. He
then dropped the bombshell. The authorities were thinking of
giving me 'natural life', which, if convicted, meant I would die in
prison. I hadn't even stood in the dock, my depositions hadn't
arrived and my sentence was already under discussion.

I told my legal team to go back and give Justice Higgins and
the Crown Prosecution Service a personal message from me: 'I
will get into the witness box and I will talk about the white
Transit van.' The following day they came back and told me
natural life had been ruled out and I would get the first
stipulated sentence in Northern Ireland in eleven years. I told
them that 'thirty years is better than forty and twenty years is

better than thirty'. Within a few hours my solicitor was back, telling me that if I was found guilty I would be sentenced to thirty years. I knew four weeks beforehand what the outcome of my trial would be. My trial would be academic. But the nonsense continued.

Two weeks later I had another visit from my solicitor. He told me the CPS was going to use the television footage taken at Milltown as the backbone of their prosecution. I was shocked that the live pictures of me captured that day were going to be played before the court. I was asked whether I wanted to see it so that I would be mentally prepared for the images it would show, but I said no. The thought horrified me. I didn't want to see the events of 16 March, the day I nearly died. I hadn't seen the images the outside world must have seen a million times and I was not looking forward to watching myself in action at Milltown.

The start of the trial was fixed for 3 March 1989. I would be tried in Court Number One of Belfast Crown Court. I knew it would be a media circus and all eyes would be on me. I knew the gallery would be packed with Republicans. I was relieved to discover that Loyalists had also turned up to offer their support.

I was taken in a convoy to the city-centre court. I was placed in a holding cell with four prison officers guarding me. There was also a team of RUC men standing nearby. The holding cells are below the Crown Court. They were small rooms, separated by thin wooden partitions. In the room next to me were two young prisoners. It was just minutes before my trial started, and I can still remember what they said because it was so bizarre. All I kept thinking was, I'm not really about to stand trial, I'm in the middle of a Monty Python sketch. I can still hear the conversation.

'Hey, mate, that fucker Stone is up today for attacking those innocent people at Milltown.'

'I thought they were all IRA up at that funeral.'

'No, mate, a few of them were Provo boys but most were innocent.'

'Maybe he was after the big boys, the top men.'

'What are you in for, mate?'

'Stealing electrical goods.'

'Hoods rule. See you on the wings, mate.'

'Yeah, see you on the wings.'

A prison officer appeared at my cell.

'Michael Anthony Stone, Court Number One.'

The two hoods shouted, 'Fuck you, you Orange bastard.'

I shouted back, '*Tiocfaidh Ar La*, you wee fuckers.'

Only in Belfast would something like this happen.

I walked into court, escorted by prison officers as guards, and was surprised to see lots of faces after a year in solitary confinement. There was a massive television at one end of the court, plus three others positioned so that the judge, the defence, the prosecution and the media could see the images that would be shown. I knew once the tape started playing I would have to face the things I had done and relive my own narrow escape from death.

I had previously decided to plead Not Guilty and had made this decision because I wanted my day in court. I wanted to take the stand and ridicule the Republican movement. I wanted to mock Gerry Adams and Martin McGuinness for their cowardice at Milltown and for their wrong account about pursuing me through the frightened crowd. I wanted to acknowledge John Murray as a true Republican who gave his life for what he believed in and I also wanted to shame the authorities.

But, following the meeting with my legal team just four weeks earlier and the death of Pat Finucane, I decided against it. I would still plead Not Guilty, but I wouldn't be giving evidence. I told my legal team that I would not be going into the witness box and I would have nothing to say throughout the entire trial.

There was enough hard evidence linking me to three murders. The authorities had enough to justify their thirty-year sentence. I told my legal team that I didn't want them to question any of the charges or any of the evidence presented in court. They reluctantly agreed with my wishes.

Court Number One was finally in session and my charge sheet was read out. It took ten minutes to complete.

Murder – 6 counts
Attempted Murder – 5 counts
Conspiracy to Murder – 3 counts
Wounding with intent – 6 counts
Doing an act with intent to cause an explosion
likely to endanger life
Causing an explosion with intent – 2 counts
Possession of firearms and ammunition with intent – 9 counts
Possession of explosive substances with intent
Possession of an explosive substance with intent – 2 counts

Naturally, Republicans trooped forward in their droves to give evidence and the evidence was substantial. There were eyewitness accounts. There were reports from experts in the fields of forensics and medicine. There were damning press photographs and the dreaded television footage. There was Army surveillance footage and, finally, there were my statements. To the frustration of my legal team, my depositions had arrived only six weeks before my trial. The RUC had refused point-blank to hand them over any earlier. So to me, my trial was a joke. In my eyes, my trial made a mockery of the legal system. It was a show trial.

Then the nonsense started. Republicans wanted to give their evidence but refused to take the stand. My solicitor told me that he had the names of three women who did not want to go to court and would I mind if their evidence was read out instead? I bloody well did mind. If these woman had important evidence to give to the court, then they should give that evidence in person. My brief explained that one was old and frail. I laughed and said, 'Not too old and frail to stand in Milltown for hours.' Obviously the old woman didn't want to be seen in court. Obviously she was frightened. A large Loyalist crowd had gathered in the public area. The woman was terrified of being fingered. I allowed her statement to be read to the court.

The next day there was a flood of similar requests to give evidence in written form, some from old ladies but many from young men. I refused. These people were taking the piss out of me and were the same young men who gave chase and beat me senseless on the motorway. They would give their evidence in person. They would stand in the witness box and tell their version of events. Sometimes a familiar face would give evidence. I held back from shouting, 'I know who you are, where you live, what you do, what you drive. I've seen your file, pal, and know everything about you.' I didn't say a word.

A man called Paddy Flood took the stand. Under oath, he swore to tell the truth. He was an IRA volunteer from Londonderry who was injured at Milltown. He had shrapnel wounds in his back and buttocks. He told the judge that he gave chase at Milltown. He didn't give chase. The fact he had injuries to his back meant he had been running the other way. Flood was assassinated and dumped on the border by his own organisation. They accused him of being a tout.

At the very start of my trial, my solicitor told me the CPS was thinking of adding a further charge to my sheet: conspiracy to kill ten thousand people. I laughed at him. I really thought it was his sick sense of humour trying to break the ice on the first day of my trial. I was wrong. The CPS did want the charge. I asked him, if the IRA blow up Cornmarket in Belfast city centre on a busy shopping day and the authorities catch the bomber, is he going to be charged with conspiracy to kill a hundred thousand people? I threatened to give evidence if I was charged with conspiracy to kill ten thousand people. The charge never materialised.

I made a decision on day one to not show any emotion during the trial. I wanted to play it straight. I didn't want to smile. Not that I could. Only a monster could laugh as the grisly events of 16 March 1988 were recalled in graphic detail. I didn't want to sit hanging my head in shame, because I didn't feel shame. So I decided to fix my eyes on a spot, and I focused on that spot for the entire two weeks. It was the back of the Prosecuting QC Ronnie Appleton's wig.

Then the television was switched on and I looked up. It was Milltown. I could see the gravestones and see the crowds. I could hear the voices as clear as a bell, the thuds and cracks as grenades went off and shots were fired. I looked at the press out of the corner of my eye. I didn't turn my head to look at them because I knew they were watching me. They were much more interested in my reaction to those pictures than watching the images themselves. They would have seen the footage a thousand times. I too had seen it all before – as rerun after rerun in my own head – but now it was on a real screen and it was strange to relive it again. I found it unnerving to be back among the headstones of the ancient cemetery. The press never took their eyes off me and I knew as the images of Milltown were played, rewound and fast-forwarded, they were conjuring half-truths and exaggerations for tomorrow's papers.

The next morning one of my screw guards showed me the local papers. Words such as 'he sat impassively', 'he gulped once' and 'was unmoved during the showing of the Milltown tape' were plastered all over the pages. Did they think I was a sadistic monster? Did they think I was going to break down, laugh or cry? I was reliving the deaths I was responsible for on that day. I was also reliving my own close escape from torture and death. Of course it was difficult to remain composed. It was hard to not show any emotion. I kept focusing on the back of Appleton's head, but inside I felt emotional.

I listened to every word and studied every piece of evidence. Statements were embellished and exaggerated and people told lies. To my disgust, Republican witnesses took the stand and swore on the Bible to tell the truth. The truth never saw the light of day. On several occasions the judge reprimanded witnesses and ordered them to stick to their original statements. I wanted to stand up and shout to the court, 'This man is a Provo, I have seen his file', but I didn't say a word.

I watched the circus that was my trial from the sidelines.

It was also a court of sorrow. There were the two women I had made young widows and there were injured people and children and all of them hurt by my hand. When I saw the young girls, the mothers and the old ladies, I realised I was dealing with real people. They weren't anonymous targets. They were human beings. Initial anger at them, at why they were at Milltown that day, disappeared when I saw them. They weren't my targets.

The legal process that was my trial was academic. It was a sequence of staged events over a fourteen-day period. I knew I was getting thirty years before I stepped into the dock for the final time to hear Justice Higgins make his speech and pass sentence. The night before I was to be sentenced my legal team came to me with a tape recorder and said the media wanted 'a few words' from me. My words, if I decided to say anything, would be synchronised with the television footage of my sentencing. It was a great opportunity to explain my actions but I declined. I was going to say a few words, but not to the media. I would save them for the court.

I was brought back to Court Number One and took my seat in

the dock. The courtroom was packed with the press, with Loyalist supporters and with Republicans who wanted to watch and gloat as sentence was passed. They wanted to see me go down for a very long time.

The court rose as Justice Higgins entered the room and took his seat. He then opened his mouth to speak. My brain switched off. I heard every single word of his speech but they didn't connect with my brain. I knew what was coming. The words were irrelevant.

'Michael Anthony Stone, you have prevented your counsel from speaking on your behalf in mitigation of sentence. My knowledge of your history, my assessment of your motivation and your present attitude to these appalling offences must be derived from the evidence which I have heard in the course of the trial, including what you told the police and information given to me by prosecuting counsel.

'You have a past record of minor offences, which I shall ignore. Portions of your statements to the police are exculpatory and I have reservations about their accuracy.

'You have prevented your counsel from giving me any assistance in coming to conclusions about your motivation and attitudes. You told the police you wanted to kill main Republicans, not the women and children. When charged with the murders of Patrick Brady, Kevin McPolin and Dermot Hackett you responded in each case, "I read his file, he was a legitimate target."

'In justification for your crimes you claimed your targets were members of the Provisional Irish Republican Army, its helpers or members of Provisional Sinn Fein. Even if your victims or intended victims were active members of the PIRA, and I have no evidence about this, that would not have justified your acts.

'At no time did you express regret for those crimes. You have had ample time to reflect on the savagery and enormity of your wrongdoing but I detected no sign of remorse in your features in the course of this trial. To crown it all, you have gagged your counsel and have prevented them from speaking on your behalf.

'I conclude you do not regret your actions and you are not repentant. It is my opinion that you are pleased with yourself for having committed those crimes. You have shown yourself to be a dangerous and ruthless criminal willing to offer your services as a killer to Loyalist groups throughout Northern Ireland. The crimes which you have committed since 1984 have added to the fear and turmoil in Northern Ireland.'

I heard his words but they didn't connect on an intellectual level. They were just words floating around a packed courtroom. His words mingled with another set of words: Tommy Herron's 'It's death or imprisonment, kid.' I was facing the rest of my life behind bars. I would be an old man, two years away from my pension, before I would see freedom again.

Looking back on that day, I now see how I must have appeared to the world as Justice Higgins spoke his words. Hindsight is a wonderful gift, something I didn't have when I sat in the dock in March 1989. I handled the day as best I could.

Justice Higgins continued outlining my sentence for each of the counts on my charge sheet. I forced my brain into gear, concentrating on his words. I knew the total of my sentence but I needed to hear him speak those words.

'For each of the six offences of murder I impose the mandatory sentence of life imprisonment. You deserve severe punishment and the public is entitled to be protected from the actions of such a dangerous man. For each of the five offences of attempted murder I sentence you to twenty-seven years' imprisonment. For each of the three offences of conspiracy to murder, I sentence you to twenty-five years' imprisonment. For each of the six offences of wounding with intent I sentence you to twenty-two years' imprisonment. For each offence of causing an explosion likely to endanger life I sentence you to twenty-two years' imprisonment. For the offence of doing an act with intent to cause an explosion likely to endanger life I sentence you to twenty-two years' imprisonment. For each of the three offences of possessing explosives with intent I sentence you to twenty years' imprisonment. For each of the nine offences of possessing firearms with intent I sentence you to twenty years' imprisonment.

'I recommend to the Secretary of State that thirty years is the minimum period which should elapse before you are released on licence.'

So there I had it. I had my thirty years predicted four weeks before I went to trial. If I were to add up all my charges it would come to nearly 850 years in prison. When I was sixteen I didn't think I would see my twentieth birthday. When I reached twenty I thought I would be dead by the time I was thirty. But here I was, just weeks away from my thirty-fourth birthday, married with two children and I knew I would never be a proper, full-time father to them. I would never spend time doing normal things with them. The best they could hope for would be the occasional prison visit.

I had warned my legal team that I would say something after Justice Higgins had passed sentence. I was in the care of three prison officers and one principal officer. On the morning of my sentence, the principal officer said to me, 'I hope you are not thinking of doing or saying anything stupid.'

'I intend saying something to the court.'

'I hope you won't jump the dock, abuse the judge or be disruptive.'

I told him I would be dignified and I wouldn't insult anyone. Now it was my time to speak. I had kept quiet for the entire length of my trial. I had not given any evidence and had not opened my mouth at any stage. I took my cue from the judge's words. I heard him say, '... you took the law into your own hands

…', and waited until he finished. As soon as he stopped speaking, I stood up. The judge looked at me, then sat down again. I gave a clenched-fist salute, shouting the words I promised to say: 'Long Live Ulster, No Surrender.' I was led away by the three prison officers and as I left the court I said a silent goodbye to my two children.

At my words, the courtroom erupted. Republicans were on their feet, fists joyfully punching the air and hurling abuse. Loyalist supporters also jumped to their feet and were clapping and cheering. I remember a young guy clapping enthusiastically and calling out, 'Rambo, Rambo.' I didn't know who he was, but he was staring straight at me, smiling broadly. It was a young UFF private called Johnny Adair.

Pebbles, For Lucy, xxx

You are a twinkling star on a moonlit night,
Soft petal on a summer's breeze.
A pure white pearl in an ocean blue
My sweetheart you'll always be.
You are a magical crystal most cherished
Sweet nectar for humming bee
Your hair is the colour of gold
My Cherub you will always be.
You are a rose found in a mystical glen
Small pebble from exotic sea
Your eyes with laughter sparkle
My princess you will always be.
You are my source of strength and happiness
Precious key that fits my heart.
You are my darling daughter
I weep that we must part.
Solace of time in rain
Looking out this winter's night
From the window in my cell.
The amber light pierced raindrops
Each have a tale to tell.
Even when in prison, seasons change
A phenomenon they cannot rearrange.
And razor wire and chain and lock
Can't stop the ticking of the clock.
Amid my thoughts of loss and pain
There's solace in the amber rain.

20

H-BLOCK 7

AFTER I WAS SENTENCED THE RUC BROUGHT ME BACK TO MY SUBTERRANEAN CELL IN CRUMLIN ROAD JAIL. I was told I would spend one final night there before being transferred to my new home in the morning. I believed I would serve my time in the Maze. I had no reason at all to think otherwise. All non-conforming political prisoners go the Maze and I was a non-conforming political prisoner. The principal officer, accompanied by three screws, locked me in my cell for the last time. He said, 'Michael, the word is they are taking you to England to do your time. A helicopter has been chartered to transport you and it will arrive early tomorrow.'

I heard the words coming out of my mouth: 'Are you joking?'

'No, Michael. I am telling you this so you can prepare yourself. I didn't want you to get a shock in the morning.'

'You are going to have to hurt me to get me out of this cell. You are going to have to drug me or beat me senseless. I'm not going to England.'

I spent my last night in the PSU barricading myself in. I made a shield from the tabletop, which I'd ripped from the wall. I punched two holes into it. It would double as a shield to protect my body. I would put socks on my hands and use them as basic boxing gloves. I put the metal bed frame against the cell door, ripped up my sheets and made them into makeshift ropes. I searched my cell for something that could be used as a baton, but there wasn't anything. I never closed my eyes all night. I needed to be awake and aware. The prison authorities would have to strap me on to a stretcher, like Hannibal Lecter, to get me out of this cell alive. I intended giving them a good fight. I was in good physical shape. If I had to attack prison officers I would. I wasn't going to England without a showdown.

I asked for the prison barber. My request was granted and he was brought down with four screws in tow. I told him I wanted a 'number one', I wanted my head shaved right down to the wood. He looked at me and I repeated my request. I always kept my hair long and wore it in a ponytail. The barber cut the bulk of the hair with scissors and took a razor to my skull. He also shaved off my moustache. I was now virtually bald. I looked menacing. I looked like a POW. The four screws that accompanied him asked if they could have my hair as a keepsake. I told them to do what they liked. I was in no mood for an argument. I really couldn't care less if they wanted my hair. I was now ready to do battle with the Crum authorities. I would rather leave in a box than be transported to England.

Very early the following morning the duty Governor and six screws came to my cell. I waited for the words 'England' and 'helicopter', but they never came. Instead the Governor said, 'Mr Stone, you have been sentenced to life imprisonment. You will serve your sentence in HMP the Maze. They are integrated blocks. You will slop out. You will be transported to begin your sentence in two hours and you will go straight to the Loyalist wings.' He said goodbye and wished me 'all the best' before turning on his heels and leaving. I was relieved. I sat on the bed and rubbed my bald head, thinking, Great, just fucking great. I don't know whether the principal officer was winding me up about going to an English prison or if it was something the authorities discussed, but now it didn't matter. I was going to the Maze and to my fellow Loyalists.

A Black Maria took me to the prison on the outskirts of Belfast. I couldn't see very much from the transport affectionately called the 'horsebox', but I knew we were travelling through the city centre. I peered out of one of the viewfinders and could see shoppers and school children, life going on as normal. I actually spied a relative on Royal Avenue. I wanted to shout her name, but even if I had she wouldn't have heard me. This was my last glimpse of the outside world. I would be sixty-four before I would see or walk Royal Avenue again. I could hear a helicopter buzzing overhead and I knew it was shadowing my convoy until I was delivered to my new home. The prison officers who accompanied me on my final journey were panicking. They kept saying, 'I hope they don't hit us.'

The Maze is a prison like no other, a place of political protests and death. It is one of the most notorious jails in the world and, for me, one of the most potent symbols of the Troubles. The Maze began life in 1971 as emergency accommodation for men held under the Special Powers Act and was known then as Long Kesh. I was just a young man of sixteen when I first did time in the Kesh after being caught stealing guns. Eighteen years later I was to discover things hadn't changed a bit. The authorities keep every scrap of information on former prisoners. I was shocked when they produced a photograph of the sixteen-year-old Michael Stone. Although I was relieved to be going to the Maze and to the Loyalist wings, part of me was dreading it. The blocks were mixed, so Loyalist and Republicans shared space, which was bad news for me. I would have been very naive to think that any Republican who got within striking distance of me wouldn't have a go at killing me.

For nearly thirty years the Maze housed men convicted of killings and bombings. It was a unique prison because its entire population consisted of prisoners who had been found guilty of serious terrorist offences. There were eight H-Blocks, each with a capacity of 104 prisoners. Each block had four wings, A, B, C and D. Prisoners of five separate paramilitary groups were housed in the Maze. They were the UDA/UFF, UVF, LVF, PIRA and INLA. Although each paramilitary group had a separate wing, that wing was often opposite our political enemies. When Billy Wright, leader of the LVF, was murdered by the INLA in 1997, the LVF and INLA wings faced each other in H-Block 6.

From 1994 inmates managed their own lives, running their own regimes, cleaning rosters and dining arrangements. Access to all facilities, showers, the gym, recreation and laundry was available twenty-four hours a day and prison officers could not search the wings without a day's advance warning and clearance from the block's Officer Commanding. An OC is the same rank as a paramilitary brigadier on the outside. During my first six years the screws ran the show and made all our lives hell.

At the height of the Troubles, in the mid-1970s, the Maze housed seventeen hundred prisoners. In 2000, when it closed, it had just a handful of prisoners. I was one of them. The complex is still there; grey and drab like an old museum piece set against the County Antrim skyline. It occupied 270 acres with a perimeter fence that ran for 2.2 miles. There was nothing to look at except the exercise yard and the dull walls. The story went that, if you stared long enough, your eyesight would go, and if your eyesight didn't go, your mind definitely would.

H-Block 7, one of the three Loyalist blocks, was home to some of the hardest men in the UDA and the UFF. I started my sentence in H7 and also spent my last days in the Maze there. My prison life had gone full circle, even though I spent my eleven years constantly rotated around the Loyalist wings.

The ghosts of hundreds of paramilitaries haunt the wings, of that I am certain. When you leave for the final time, a little part of you remains behind. The Maze was a turbulent place and violent and terrible things happened within its walls. There was death by the bucketful. Republican martyr Bobby Sands starved himself to death along with nine of his comrades in 1981 when Margaret Thatcher refused to give in to their demands for political status. Sixteen years later LVF leader Billy Wright was assassinated within the prison confines by an INLA death squad. Another Loyalist, David Keyes, was found hanged in his cell under mysterious circumstances. There were the Republican 'blanket' and 'dirty' protests, the mass escape of Republican prisoners, and protests by both the UDA and the LVF. The former Chief Inspector of Prisons, Sir David Ramsbotham, said once, 'I hope the Maze is razed to the ground as quickly as possible after it is finally emptied and confined to history.' I hope it is bulldozed and erased from all our memories.

On my first day as a Maze lifer I noticed that nothing had changed. I walked into the drab reception area and was told to sign the order papers lying on the desk. Like countless men before me, I signed my name and wrote 'life' in the sentence box. Maze prisoners were divided into low-, medium- and high-risk. I was classed as another level above that, 'red-booked', and this meant I would be treated as top-risk every second of every day for the next thirty years. The red book actually existed and contained my personal details, my photograph, details of distinguishing marks, my fingerprints and my sentence. It travelled everywhere with me whenever I moved from my cell. Red-bookers were rotated several times a month from cell to cell, cell to wing and wing to block. There were four Loyalist red-bookers: two Shankill Butchers, Basher Bates and Billy Moore, Sam McAlister and myself. Eighteen

Republicans were red-bookers, including notorious IRA man Bik McFarlane.

I was strip-searched and photographed and then taken to H7. As I walked into 'the circle' (the central administrative area which was housed in the link of the 'H' of the H-block – the prisoners were kept in the two 'legs' of the 'H') I was struck by the space and light. Then the noise hit me: the cheering and whooping from Loyalist inmates and the clapping and the whistling. It was a mixed bag of prisoners and included some Red Hand Commando, some UDA, the UVF and a couple from the Orange Volunteers. I heard flutes and pipes, a small band, the Maze First Flute, had honoured my arrival with a couple of tunes. They had improvised, using five-gallon plastic water containers as drums, although they did have proper flutes.

Some prisoners didn't recognise me with the shaved head. Others knew who I was straight away, and I was picked up shoulder high and carried through the wing. It was a verbal riot. My eardrums felt they were about to explode. I felt strange without my thick ponytail, but I'd shaved my head to eliminate a weak spot Republicans, and sadistic screws, could exploit had they got close to me. It took ten years for my hair to grow back. I looked like a convict from the Russian gulags and my scalp was a mass of tiny scars sustained in the motorway beating.

UVF commander Billy Moore was the first to approach me. He said he knew I had been in solitary for a year and he knew I worked with UVF volunteers in Mid Ulster. He said the UVF leadership was willing to claim me. I thanked Moore, but told him I was loyal to the UDA. I was a UDA prisoner and doing life for a UFF-sanctioned operation. Moore was disappointed. He tried to persuade me, saying the UDA disowned me and one of their ranked men, Tucker Lyttle, said I was a psychopath with no UDA connections. Again I thanked Moore and said I wasn't a UVF man. I was a UDA man and would be until I died. Moore was a quiet and intelligent man. He was a brilliant watercolour artist and he loved horse racing.

John 'Grugg' Gregg, from south-east Antrim, the UDA's second-in-command, was the first UDA man who spoke to me and it was a gesture I deeply appreciated. Grugg was doing time for the attempted murder of Gerry Adams. We got on well because we had a common history. We were honorary members of the 'Gerry Club' because we both tried to kill the Sinn Fein leader. There was another club member, a man called Gerry Welsh, who had an interesting personal background: his mother was a Catholic woman. Grugg outlined the typical Maze routine and I saw his humanity as a genuine move in the right direction. I knew that sooner or later the UDA would formally acknowledge me.

John Gregg stepped into the breach left when Tommy Herron and John McMichael were killed. Although I had never met him before the day he introduced himself in the Maze, I felt I had found another true friend. We had a common history – both having made attempts on the life of Sinn Fein leader Gerry Adams and both regretting that we were unsuccessful in our operation.

On one occasion we discussed our mutual interest in the leadership of the Republican movement. He complimented me on my choice of weapons at Milltown, saying the Browning and the Ruger were 'good handguns' and it was 'clever thinking for close-quarters work'.

I asked him what he used and he said a Luger and a Browning. He said he was sick to the back teeth of young bucks coming up to him and saying he should have used an M60, a semi-automatic machine gun or a high-velocity rifle. Grugg told me he chose his weapons carefully and he chose them deliberately. He didn't want to risk high-velocity rounds, such as a 7.62-calibre, passing clean through Adams, wounding and killing civilians. He said he wasn't risking dead and wounded passers-by just because they were in the wrong place at the wrong time. When Grugg opened fire that day, he said he watched Adams rise out of the car seat and push his head and neck as far into the roof as was possible, leaving just his torso exposed. Even though Adams was wearing a bulletproof vest Grugg did strike him in the neck.

Grugg's choice of weapons saved Gerry Adams's life that day, purely because he wanted to reduce civilian casualties.

Another prisoner who was considerate was John Somerville. He was doing life for the Miami Showband incident. Two other men, Thomas Crozier and James McDowell, were also serving life for the 1975 attack. Somerville's brother, Wesley, died at the scene when the bomb he was carrying exploded prematurely. The men, members of the UVF, ambushed a bus carrying members of the famous band, who attracted Beatle-like devotion wherever they went. Somerville said something to me within days of my arrival and I have never forgotten it. He said, 'Prison is the most dangerous place you have ever been.' Although he was a devout Christian, he never pushed his religious beliefs on anyone. 'Brother John', as he was nicknamed, was quiet, intelligent and well-versed in politics, literature and history.

On my first day I circled the yard for hours on end. I was unnerved and unsettled. The space freaked me out and I returned indoors. After a full year in solitary, the openness of the wing and all those men wanting to chat to me made me feel uncomfortable. Everywhere I went my hand was shaken, my back was clapped and I got a playful fist on the face. Some men asked about my hair and why I shaved it off, but most wanted to hear about the Battle of Milltown. I had thirty years to get to know these guys. I had all the time in the world to adjust to my new life. For now, I just wanted to be by myself.

The sun was shining and I thought about Lucy growing up without her father, who was a selfish bastard and put the Loyalist cause before her. I couldn't have that time back and I couldn't change anything. Or could I? I was certain that I didn't want to turn into a geriatric in this place, so I started to think about escape.

My new cell was in the middle of the wing. Red-bookers were not given end cells in case they tried to dig their way out. I had no intention of digging my way anywhere. If I was going out, I was going over the top. I looked at the fences and they didn't look impossible. They were no higher than fifteen feet. I was fit. That was my trump card.

The wings were mostly harmonious, but the old UVF regime, with one figurehead commandeering all Loyalist prisoners, had been in place since the 1970s and the time of Gusty Spence. That had to change. UDA/UFF prisoners resented the UVF being in command. The Maze had a set routine. Prisoners were let out of the cells between 8am and midday, locked up 12–2pm, free to move around 2–4pm, locked up 5–7pm, out 7–8pm, and night-time lock-up was from 8pm to 8am. I spent every available minute getting my body fit. I had a good start. My year in solitary doing shadow boxing and martial arts had given me a good level of fitness, but I needed to push my body further. When I left the Maze, if I got out alive, I was going straight back to war.

I had my eye on escape. It became my priority. I spent hours in the yard looking at fences, the armed security and the layout of the place. One prisoner approached me. He was a UVF lifer. He told me to give up my plans for escape. He said he was aware of me 'eyeballing' the fences and told me it would be better if I settled down and did my whack. I told him that if I could find a way out I was going for it.

Within the week I was hauled before the Governor. He told me his name and explained that the meeting wasn't unusual as all new arrivals were given a formal introduction to prison procedure. I listened half-heartedly. I wasn't interested in what he had to say, but his closing comment made me sit up and take notice. He said, 'Mr Stone, you will settle into your new life here. You will find your routine so long as you don't harbour plans to try to escape and you keep your nose clean.' He winked at me after he finished his speech. The UVF man had told tales to the Governor. He was institutionalised and looking for gold stars that could be traded in as good behaviour. The man had served just thirteen years of his life term and was grabbing at straws. Within two weeks the perimeter fence was raised by at least fifteen feet and security was stepped up.

It was a valuable lesson. Men like this UVF lifer might be my fellow Loyalists, but some were working to their own agenda. Most of my fellow inmates were good men and good Loyalists. These were men like Grugg and Brother John. But even among our own there were rogues. Just like the career Loyalists on the outside who were bastardising the name of Loyalism, they had no interest in our collective cause. Once inside, they rewrote their personal history and created new personalities and they did it to advance their personal agenda. They were in-house informers, no better than touts.

As a red-booker I was rotated around all three of the Loyalist blocks, and every three weeks I was on the move. I couldn't get into a routine and I couldn't settle. I didn't have a 'wing' job to break the monotony as red-bookers were banned from working because of the security implications. I poured all my intellectual energy into finding an escape route. I was still war-focused and day after day my mantra was: 'I'm in my prime, I have a lot still to do, people to see and people to kill.'

It was Bill Gill, a prisoner from Loyalist Sandy Row, who helped me turn a corner in those early days. He got the name 'Beastly Bill' because he was bad-tempered in the morning, but he was a very philosophical and intelligent man. He was doing life for a 'Romper Room' murder committed in the 1970s. One afternoon, just four weeks into my sentence, he took me aside. He spoke calmly and clearly and ordered me to snap out of my quiet mood. 'You have to look at your circumstances in a different way,' he said. 'I am not doing time in this place and you are not doing time in this place. I live here and you live here. Think of it as a new phase in your life. It is boring and it's monotonous, but it is your life. You have been sentenced to a lifetime of boredom, but it is now your life and you have to learn to accept it. I don't know if you are planning to go over the wire or top yourself, but if you are staying, accept it. You can't fight it or change it.'

I never said a word. I thanked him for his advice and went to my cell. I sat on the bed and turned his words over and over in my head. For a bad-tempered old fucker, he spoke a lot of sense. I didn't like my prison life and I couldn't change it. I could only change my circumstances by escaping.

Beastly Bill came to my cell later that same day. He sat on the bed and asked me where I would go if I managed to escape. I told him I was going back to war. 'If you escape you will make it unbearable for us left behind,' he replied. His final words were: 'The fool who knows he is a fool is on the road to wisdom. I'll leave that with you.'

I was very unsettled during my first year. I found it difficult to accept that this was my life for the next thirty years. In those early months I tried to knuckle down and do my whack, but some days I just didn't give a damn. On those days I deliberately caused mayhem. I saw my reports during my regular 'assessment' meetings with the prison authorities, and they were constantly littered with references to prisoner A385 being 'rebellious' and 'disruptive'. Several of the prison officers at the Maze were bullies, whose job was an outlet for their brutality and psychosis. I liked to play games with these men, and any chance I got to wreck the place, I grabbed it.

I was a political prisoner and political prisoners had rules. That was the difference between us and ODCs and hoods. We had discipline. Discipline was rule number one on the wings. Loyalists shared the circle with Republicans, and we thought about killing a Republican if the opportunity ever arose, but we didn't. Inside the prison walls there was a set of rules: no killing. Loyalists and Republicans shared a common bond – we were all political prisoners. But all rules went out the window the day the INLA shot dead Billy Wright within the Maze.

It was not a nice place. The prison officers ruled the wings and they played games with us, picking on the quieter guys and knowing how to wind up the aggressive men. They would stride up and down the wing, rattling keys, running their batons up the grilles, creating noise and aggravation for men trying to sleep or read. Out of sheer frustration the screws got a thump or a lad would smash a snooker cue over a head, socks would be filled with a snooker ball or the galvanised slop-out buckets would be used to split open a skull or break a jaw. Then all hell would break loose, the Ninjas would storm in and the whole wing would be locked up as punishment.

During the early weeks it was like stepping back in time. The guys were caught in a fashion timewarp. There were denims with a crease ironed down the front, multi-coloured beach shirts and shiny black shoes. These were men sentenced in the 1970s and nearly twenty years later they were still stuck in that era.

The food was appalling. It was like primary-school dinners. Every three days the prison was served casserole or stew. Every three days I starved. I hated one-pot meals. Anything and everything was possible in a one-pot dinner and I refused to touch them. I'd worked in the kitchens of this very jail when I was a teenager and seen first-hand what prisoners, mostly hoods, get up to with those giant cauldrons of food. Regardless of this, something had to be done about the terrible diet. We were served things like luncheon meat with one potato and a tiny glass of milk and the authorities called this our main meal. The guys would request food parcels from home and could be seen devouring whole barbecue chickens and packets of biscuits between meals. On a Sunday, the Governor thought it was a treat to have roast chicken. Great, we all thought, until we saw it. It was a chicken leg so small it looked like it came off a budgie.

The men on my block asked me to speak to the Governor about the food. I requested a meeting and was granted one. I told the Governor the guys were starving, the meals weren't big enough and the daily selections were a joke. I told him our diet was ridiculous. If there was a salmonella scare, we got hundreds of egg dishes, if it was a meat scare then we got meat products. I told him a sausage and a spoonful of beans, or corned beef and potato, wasn't a proper dinner for grown men. I told him, just because we were in jail, that didn't mean we would accept the terrible diet. His answer was laughable: 'It's procurement, Mr Stone. There is a pecking order, hospitals, the civil service, the police and then the prisons. Whatever is left over it comes here.' I told him it was a pathetic answer and if he didn't sort out the menus and the portions, then he had protest on his hands.

I knew I was beginning to accept my new life when I had my first family visit. I felt I had aged fifty years by the time Leigh-Ann brought Lucy to see me. She was nearly two. I last saw her baby face when she was just nine months old, but now she was a blonde toddler, wriggling in my arms. I wanted Lucy to look at me and recognise me as her daddy but I realised she couldn't possibly know who I was. She hadn't seen me before and was just a baby when I was last in her life. I knew I had to give up my plans to escape and return to war. If I did get out I was condemned to a life on the run. I knew that Lucy, and her brother Daryl, had been through enough. They had already lost their father, first to the paramilitaries and then to prison. I might not be at home with them but I was going to be around. Even though I was a prisoner, serving a life term, I could still be a part of their lives.

The second turning point was when I started to take an interest in the wing and prison structure. I knew it was essential that we governed ourselves. I had travelled the prison. I had been accommodated in all the Loyalist wings and knew exactly what was going on. I started by writing letters to my family. In these I complained that the place was in a timewarp, the lads were starving and the prison was stuck in 1971. I knew the letters were being monitored and watched by the prison authorities and it was my way of getting the message across that things had to change.

Shortly after my sentence began I got the recognition I deserved when the UDA finally claimed me. I didn't get a personal apology and no one from the UDA leadership came to see me. The acknowledgement came via the front cover of the UDA's internal magazine, *Ulster*, although a network of messages unofficially confirmed that I had been claimed by the UDA. On the front of the magazine there was a photograph of me in action at Milltown and the headline 'OUR MAN FLINT'. I was relieved. The tide was turning. The UDA's old guard was disintegrating. The UDA that denied me in 1988 and told the press I was too extreme to be a member was starting to fall apart. It was a shot of optimism in an otherwise boring existence.

A new, younger breed of politically and militarily astute volunteers were beginning to make themselves known. The days of the old career Loyalists, the Jim Craigs and Tucker Lyttles, were numbered. I knew I was going to be in the Maze for a very long time. I couldn't change where I was, but the structures that governed us could be changed. There was a new breed outside. Now there would be a new breed on the inside.

Brother John and Beastly Bill were always on hand to offer support. They both took me aside and offered the benefit of their wisdom, although they had completely different theories on surviving prison life. Beastly Bill said, 'It is the short-termers and the "year men" who can't do their time. They are the ones who run risks. They are impatient and unsettled; they see their release in the distance and can't wait for the time to come. The lifers are different. They are more settled because they have no date to look forward to.'

Meanwhile Brother John said it was the opposite: 'It's the lifers who are the most dangerous. They have nothing on their emotional horizon and they are desperately searching for credit. They will do anything and sacrifice anyone to collect points. They are grasping at straws.' It was up to me to steer a path somewhere between the two. The prison authorities would dangle carrots in front of the noses of lifers. After their first big review, at ten years, the authorities would offer them the chance of moving to Maghaberry and becoming a conforming prisoner. They tempted them by saying the food was better, there was better parole and a chance to go back to school. In 1989 eleven lifers moved to Maghaberry. The prison authorities told them, Michael Stone is coming to the Maze and he will wreck the place. These lifers were scared and chose to move to Maghaberry rather than run the risk of blotting their copybook.

In my second year in the Maze I was called to see the Governor. He was new to the job and called every prisoner individually in to see him. He introduced himself as Governor Hazelly and asked me how I was doing. I knew the man. He lived near me on the Braniel estate when I was growing up. His name was Brian Hazelly. Governor Hazelly was at Lisnasharragh Secondary at the same time as me, but he stayed on and then went to university. I took great pleasure in telling him that I remembered him from school. I was delighted to ask about his brother, who I knew very well, and good-looking sister, Margaret. He didn't answer. He looked at me, slammed my red book shut and ordered the screws to take me back to my cell. I glanced back. His face was the colour of the red book that marked my 'top risk' status. Governor Hazelly took a new job in England shortly afterwards.

Within five years I was beginning to settle into my routine. As I entered my seventh year I knew I was becoming institutionalised, but I fought it.

Loyalist and Republican prisoners hated one another. It was nothing personal. It was war. On my wing there were two brothers called Lambe. Every time they walked the wing to the circle, Republicans would hang out of their cells and sing 'Baa, Baa, Black Sheep'. It was funny but it was also subtle intimidation and an unspoken threat. Then a new Republican prisoner arrived. He was a dwarf, caught red-handed with an AK47. Apparently his little legs didn't even reach the car floor. Like the Lambe brothers, this guy had to walk past the cells to get to the circle, and as he did the sounds of singing could be heard from the Loyalist side. To the tune from the Disney movie *Snow White and the Seven Dwarfs*, they sang: 'Hi-ho, hi-ho, it's off to work he goes.' Poor bastard. The whole wing erupted in howls of laughter. Even his Republican comrades laughed.

A meeting was called between the OC of the Red Hand Commando and the OC of the IRA. Our OC read out the resulting statement in the wing canteen. It said: 'Agreement has been reached. Republicans will leave our lambs alone if we leave their dwarf alone.' The laughter lasted for hours. For a very short time, it united Republicans and Loyalists. We did get the last laugh with the dwarf. We had a cutting from a magazine about a dwarf-throwing competition in America. The article was left on the bus that took Republican prisoners to the visiting block.

Life went on. It was mostly harmonious, but in April 1997 the shit hit the fan. The Prison Service implemented a number of changes in the daily running of the Maze. The changes were decided after a screw found a tunnel being built by IRA prisoners. Loyalists expected the authorities to crack down on Republican inmates, but no, they clamped down on everyone. The Northern Ireland Office announced that new rules would apply across the board. The UFF, UVF and Red Hand Commando, who had always agreed a no-escape policy with the authorities, were to be punished with the IRA. We tried to discuss these changes with the prison regime but were told they were not up for discussion. We contacted the Ulster Democratic Party, the political wing of the UDA/UFF, and asked them to use their influence to try to bring about a change of heart. The request fell on deaf ears. That left just one option: a rooftop protest.

When the prison staff tried to implement the changes, they were told, politely but firmly, that Loyalist prisoners would not be complying. All visits and paroles were immediately stopped. The command structure tried to negotiate but didn't succeed. Commanders in H1 and H2 ordered their volunteers to take control of their compounds. From a tactical point of view, it was decided that the men would scale the blocks and take position on the roof. Prisoners wore masks and carried makeshift weapons. They were divided into groups tasked with dismantling the razor wire, transferring bedding and building a kitchen. The last men sealed off the blocks to keep the Ninjas back. Once everyone was assembled, sleeping quarters and a cooking area were built. Another team of men demolished a boiler room and stored the bricks to use as weapons. Finally, we soaked the edges of the roof with washing-up liquid, to make it slippery, and used the razor wire as a first line of defence.

Meanwhile, a heavily armed riot-control team had surrounded the H-Blocks and were taking up position. We threw bricks at them and they beat a retreat to a safer position. The 11pm news read out a prepared UFF statement that also said there would be retaliatory strikes against the Northern Ireland Office and the Prison Service. Within the hour the Ninjas were moved back. By morning there was a request from the authorities for talks. They shouted their request across the yard. A hole was cut in the perimeter fence and a phone was passed through so that the talks could take place. Eventually a deal was struck and the rooftop protest was called off. The authorities now knew they had a formidable group of men on their hands and we couldn't and wouldn't be bullied.

The screws had a drinking club within the Maze compound they called the Yippee Ya Yea Club. I am convinced the screws were mad. Every weekend they dressed as Confederate soldiers and carried .45 replicas. Their women wore belle-of-the-ball dresses. They would dance and drink all night to bluegrass music. We could hear their rowdy behaviour from our cells.

The one thing that bothered me most about my sentence was that there was no chance of parole or compassionate leave. My mother had several heart attacks during my years in the Maze and many times I thought she had died. The news would come from the jail's prisoner welfare officer and not from my family. He would be clinical and to the point, saying, 'Your mother is in hospital and has suffered a serious heart attack.' That's all. I would go into my cell, close the door and cry. I wanted to go and see her but I couldn't. I wasn't a free man any more. I was a lifer and red-booked, with no chance of compassionate leave.

21

AGONY AUNT

'AUNTY' WAS MY MAZE MONIKER. I WAS NICK-NAMED THIS BECAUSE I WAS THE LOYALIST PRISON POPULATION'S UNOFFICIAL AGONY AUNT. The prisoners needed someone to talk to and turned to me in their droves. It was mostly about wives and girlfriends and dealing with the loneliness and isolation prison life brings, but sometimes it was how they found it difficult to cope with their past.

The women problems I found easier to counsel them on. I'd had two failed marriages and could share my experience. Indeed, my divorce from Leigh-Ann went through when I was in the Maze. I was taken from prison to the High Court in Belfast for the divorce hearing, and the judge even asked me if it was not possible, even at that late stage, and even though I was a prisoner, to make the marriage work!

Some of the young men blew emotional fuses because their girl had dumped them or was seeing someone else. I tried to make them see sense that it was very difficult for our women. I told them they were good men, and they should understand life goes on.

Parolees would come back with sexually transmitted diseases. Out for the weekend and desperate for sex, they pick up a girl. It would be the prisoner responsible for the wing laundry who complained to me about these young lads. He was terrified of catching something and it fell on my shoulders to talk to the offenders. I told them they had a responsibility to their wing mates. I ordered them to see the prison doctor. Beetroot-red and shamed to hell, they would get treatment. Some learnt. Others didn't and had to make repeat trips to the prison doctor. They listened to me, but they never learnt.

Prisoners would have good days and bad days. Some coped very well and others didn't. Some acknowledged their past and others were in denial. Every man copes differently, and for every man doing time it was a daily effort to stay focused and on top of things, and that included me. It was my cell door many of them knocked when they were upset or angry. Every one of us went through a whole range of emotions, including rage, anger and self-pity. They came to me because they respected me. They knew they could tell me things and it wouldn't go any further.

Some of the younger prisoners, especially the teenagers, would call me 'Da'. I did reverse psychology on some of them. If they were in for five or ten years, I would tell them I wished that was all I had to worry about. I told them I had a sentence totalling almost 850 years. They would smile at me and say, 'I thought I had problems, Stoner', and they would go back to their cell feeling better about themselves. They confided in me.

Over time my role as Aunty evolved. I became a secret-keeper. I heard 'stories' that I later found out to be true. These proved that Loyalist volunteers were not backstreet killers and thugs with no instinct for the subtleties of war. They showed there were many Loyalists who felt like me and wanted to strike at the Republican leadership and that Ireland and her people were also a target. What I heard was proof that Loyalists were active in the Irish Republic and had been for years.

There were two main types of prisoners who came to speak to me. The 'screamers' had nightmares and swore they saw the ghosts of men they killed. Then there were the men who talked non-stop about every operation they were involved in. Some of the screamers were big, macho men haunted by the faces of their targets. One, a former member of the security forces, told me he was glad he had been arrested because he finally had peace of mind. His imprisonment meant he wouldn't be able to shoot his wife and kid. He sat on my bed and told me that if he had not been scooped by the police he would have ended up killing both his wife and daughter. He was haunted by the face of one of his targets and swore he could see the man's ghost sitting on the stairs of his home, night after night.

One evening the man's wife and young daughter were in bed. As he climbed the stairs the face was staring straight back at him. He grabbed his legal firearm and riddled the stairs and hall with bullets until the magazine was empty. The sound of gunfire woke his wife, who ran on to the landing to find out what was going on. Had he not run out of bullets his wife would be dead. He sat in my cell and told me the man's face still haunted him and the ghost now peered through the bars of his cell.

Another Loyalist prisoner said that when he was on active service for the UVF he shot dead a Republican. He was doing time for a lesser offence, and was never convicted or even questioned over the death of the Republican, but he was haunted by the man's last minutes. He said he smashed in the door with a sledgehammer. The target, who was sitting on the settee, looked up in surprise to see the two-man unit in his living room, grabbed his rosary beads and shoved them into the face of the gunman. The Republican knew what was coming next. He knew he was about to die and tried to protect himself with the beads. The gunman shot him twice in the face. The UVF man said the rosary beads freaked him out. He thought he was cursed. Many of these men were driven to revisit the scene of the crime and sit where it happened. I thought this behaviour very strange.

As Aunty I was regularly given detail on countless scenarios: killings, attempted murder and conspiracy. I was well known because of Milltown and because of it men came to me with stories of brave deeds of their own. There was no shortage of spoofers and Walter Mittys who could talk a good war but that was it. Then there were the others. I knew these men had lived and breathed the operation.

Ken T was a fellow UDA man, doing time for possession of weapons and caught on a technicality. Later I made discreet enquiries among my network of associates outside and found every word of what Ken told me was true. He took an hour to recount his story. After he finished talking, tears welled up in his eyes. Ken had masterminded a plan to assassinate the Irish Prime Minister, Charles Haughey. It was all worked out to the finest detail, but at the last minute he was forced to abort the operation. I stopped Ken in his tracks, telling him I didn't want to know any more. He told me he needed to tell the story so that I understood there were others like me who wanted to assassinate the Republican leadership and other big targets.

He told me Tucker Lyttle had bad-mouthed me all over Belfast after my arrest for Milltown. Then he said, 'Lyttle was the reason my operation did not go ahead. Tucker was afraid of his life, of the consequences of killing the Irish Prime Minister, and the whole operation was compromised.' Ken hardly took a breath as he recalled his master plan. I was stunned. The plan was to kill Haughey on Ulster soil. It was the late 1980s. The Anglo-Irish Agreement, the political process that pushed Loyalists and Unionists to the brink, was already in place. Officials from London and Dublin were performing this gruesome dance signifying the end of Ulster's Britishness with the hated Anglo-Irish Intergovernmental Conferences, and there was speculation that Haughey would make a guest appearance at Castle Buildings and meet the Secretary of State. Ken said the visit was wrong. He said he did not welcome a foreign politician interfering in the affairs of his country.

His plan took shape. He would shoot down the Wessex helicopter carrying Haughey and his team as it approached the landing pad at the front of Castle Buildings. Once it hit the ground, he was going to open fire with automatic weapons. The on-board bodyguards wouldn't stand a chance if they survived the impact. Ken told me how he harnessed all his contacts to gather intelligence for this operation. He had military contacts at RAF Aldergrove. One supplied the flight plan the Wessex would follow as it made its approach over Belfast. Within a week Ken was handed a map with a clear overlay showing a variety of multi-coloured routes. He was shown one marked 'green' and told this was the route the Wessex would take. The colour was symbolic: green for Ireland and green for 'all systems go'.

The Wessex, Ken's contact told him, would make a convoluted journey. It would fly over Orangefield playing fields and Shandon golf course, both greenfield sites which provided a safe passage for the craft. It would do a horseshoe over the Castlereagh Hills and fly between two block of flats, Ardcarn and Tullycarnet. It would continue over the civil service playing fields and hover at the front of Castle Buildings before coming in to land. Ken was told that the Wessex would fly at thirty to fifty metres, and he knew he could strike the plane at that height.

Ken chose his weapons. He had an automatic rifle and several thousand rounds of ammunition, but he needed a machine gun with a high rate of fire to have any chance of bringing the chopper down. Ken was given a box of one thousand .762 belt clips. All he needed was a GIMPY, a general-purpose machine gun. He knew the Woodvale Defence Association had one and south-east Antrim had two Bren .303 guns.

He spoke to his brigadier, who was surprised but impressed with the planning that went into the operation. The brigadier agreed that a strike on a helicopter carrying the Irish PM was a spectacular show of strength and agreed that whatever happened it was an acceptable risk to run, even if the pilot was killed. Ken's military contact told him that the floor of the Wessex was fitted with steel plates and the best way of bringing the helicopter down was through the exhaust ducts or the nose. He knew the pilots would be carrying 9mm weapons and Special Branch would be on board, but he had planned for this with the machine gun. None of them would survive the automatic gunfire.

Ken did a practice run at Wincroft House in the east of the city. He ran up and down the emergency stairwell to make sure he was physically fit and he designed a rope and pulley to haul the heavy machine gun in and out of the building.

A week later, at a meeting of the UDA's Inner Council, Ken's brigadier told the assembled members about the operation. He also wanted to borrow the munitions. When the brigadier finished speaking there was silence. The Inner Council was split in two. Tucker Lyttle, Jim Craig and the brigadier for East Belfast made the first contribution, saying the operation should not go ahead. Other brigadiers on the Inner Council agreed it was a good operation and gave it their backing. A week later Ken was told the UDA would sanction the operation but wasn't in a position to supply weapons. Ken's brigadier insisted the operation needed at least two more weapons.

At a prearranged time and place Ken met the Mid-Ulster brigadier. In the boot of the car were two First World War weapons, Martini Henry rifles smuggled into Northern Ireland eighty years ago, in the time of the famous Unionist Edward

Henry Carson. They needed special bullets. The guns were antiques and should have been in a museum, but the brigadier said it was all he could do. Ken was insulted. He said he was going to stiff the brigadier, who had insulted his intelligence. Ken tried to do swaps, short guns for long, and managed to obtain two weapons for seven guns from the UVF in East Belfast. He had a contact who worked as a caretaker in the two blocks of flats, and he supplied keys to the skylights. Ken and a back-up man would be in position in Ardcarn and the second gunman would take up position in Tullycarnet. They would perform a crossfire operation as the Wessex flew between the blocks, but the operation had to be aborted. Ken couldn't get the munitions he needed.

At seven on the morning of the operation Ken stood in the rough of the fifteenth hole at Shandon golf course. He wanted to see if the intelligence was correct. It was. Right on cue the Wessex appeared. It flew over the golf course and the downdraught blew his clothing away from his body. He watched it turn into the horseshoe and fly through the two blocks of flats on the exact flight path he was given by his Aldergrove contact.

Ken walked back to the wooded area and cried. He even bashed his head against a tree in anger. The UDA had let him down. He said he was insulted because the energy, time and expense that went into researching and planning the operation had been thrown away. But worse was to come. Later that day Ken watched the main evening news. Top of the schedule was the story of the meeting at Castle Buildings. There was footage of the Wessex approaching the building and landing on the front lawn. Charles Haughey didn't emerge from the craft, but his Justice Minister, Gerard Collins, did. After the meeting the Irish officials were taken to Eglinton airport in County Londonderry. Ken later learnt the Eglinton route was unusual procedure.

Tucker Lyttle had informed his Special Branch handlers about the operation to assassinate key members of the Irish government.

Ken also found out that the security forces were waiting at the Ardcarn and Tullycarnet flats to shoot on sight the active-service unit. Tucker Lyttle couldn't cope with the size of the operation, or the implications of it, so he told everything to his handlers.

I got to hear some stories because men felt they could trust me. Throughout my trial I had no co-accused and men knew they could speak to me in confidence. There was a ritual in the Maze. Every new prisoner would be introduced to the wing, but they were never quizzed on what they did as a Loyalist volunteer. If a man was doing time he was a political prisoner, and that was good enough for me. I didn't believe in grilling a man who was caught doing his bit as a Loyalist soldier. But prisoners like to talk, to make an impression on one another, and some made a point of wanting to impress me. Some men talk because they can't help themselves. Others do it because they feel they have something to prove.

There is an old Maze saying: 'You are only as good as your last job.' This means if you killed twenty Republicans and were caught on possession, then you were in for possession and other operations didn't matter. Prisoners doing time for lesser offences like this were called 'year men'.

Milltown was the reason many prisoners liked to talk to me. They would start the conversation by asking me to recount the Battle of Milltown. I would say it was in the past and they would inevitably answer, 'I can do better than Milltown, Stoner.' I made a point of telling the prisoner that he didn't have to justify to me why he was in prison. I told him I didn't want to be his bridge to burn, especially if he was a year man and hadn't been questioned or charged with the operation. But these men would say they really wanted to tell me. They would offload their experience and leave my cell feeling better about themselves.

Year men came and went on the wings, and so did their stories. I had another UDA man – I'll call him 'R' – tell me about a plot to kill the Chief Constable of the RUC, Sir John Hermon. I balked at R's story and asked him if he was taking the piss. He said no, that at the time of the Anglo-Irish Agreement Hermon was a hate figure, chosen as a target because he had let Protestants down by prostituting himself with the British Prime Minister, Maggie Thatcher. Protestants had turned on their police force. Some officers were harassed and even burnt out of their homes. All over the province, graffiti was daubed on walls saying things like: 'Come Home to a Real Fire – Join the RUC.' It was the early 1980s. Jack Hermon's wife at the time was dying of cancer. The Chief Constable was burdened with both professional and personal woes.

I told R I didn't want to know any more about the plot to kill Hermon but he insisted on recounting the events. He said I would enjoy it. Initially the story sounded like it came straight from a James Bond script and I told R this. But, in truth, even I could see the operation was planned to the finest detail and everything that he said made sense.

He began to gather his intelligence on the Chief Constable and his movements, although because of his wife's illness Hermon didn't have much of a life. The couple lived in a special apartment at RUC HQ in Knock, in the east of the city. It was a two-storey building on a gable end and faced out towards the disused Belfast–Comber railway line. There were several private homes opposite the police complex that overlooked the apartment. R initially considered two options: a sniper and a rocket-propelled grenade. He axed both ideas because it couldn't guarantee the safety of Hermon's sick wife and her care assistant.

R had a young associate who worked in the RUC kitchens and had access to the food that was prepared for the force. The canteen worker could help him in a plot to poison the Chief Constable. R discovered through this contact that Hermon ate with his wife in their apartment every evening between six and six-thirty. He made a point of sharing a meal with her. The food was brought on a trolley to the apartment and Hermon always chose the day's special as he liked to eat the same food as his men. R had another contact, who worked in Queen's University and was willing to supply a colourless, odourless and tasteless toxin. The poison was made by the contact and R did not know what it was, but once it was ingested by the victim, death was swift. R was told to be careful handling it as it was so potent it could cause death if just a tiny drop was absorbed by the skin. He was also told the authorities would have their work cut out for them trying to establish what exactly caused death.

The Divisional Commander of the Mobile Support Unit was to be targeted in the same operation. R had intelligence that he drove a white Vitara 4WD. The spare wheel was housed on the back and had a protective cover with a picture of a rhino on it. The vehicle was distinctive, easy to target. The Divisional Commander was stationed in the barracks at Dundonald. He was to be shot in the head as he arrived for work. I asked R why he was targeting two high-ranking policemen when the RUC were not the enemies of Ulster. He said that at the time he didn't recognise the RUC as a police force any more. He called them 'Maggie's puppets'. The operation was compromised, R believes, by someone on the UDA's Inner Council. Although R didn't say his name, I knew there was only one man who fitted the bill and that was Tucker Lyttle. R finished his story by saying the canteen worker was moved to a new job after there was a sudden review of internal security at HQ and the RUC hired a new team of kitchen staff.

Over an eleven-year period, only a handful of these stories came to light. But I did learn that the Irish Prime Minister was to have been the victim of a second murder plot. 'M', a volunteer who held rank in the Red Hand Commando, told me the plan was that Charles Haughey would die in exactly the same way as Lord Mountbatten – blown to bits on his boat. He also told me that he went on active service in the Irish Republic.

M had business interests in Dublin, which gave him a legitimate excuse to explore landmarks both commercial and industrial that could be attacked. His business associate had a car and that meant M could travel wherever he liked throughout the island without attracting suspicion. He said he made the most of all opportunities and even took an unsuspecting girlfriend on holiday to County Kerry, where Haughey had a holiday home and a yacht. M said he loved Kerry; it was a beautiful landscape. The couple spent two weeks in a caravan park in Dingle.

It was 1981 and Lord Mountbatten, the uncle of the heir to the British throne, had been dead two years. M had waited two years for retaliation for this crime and knew exactly how to avenge the death of the elderly royal. He was going to wire Haughey's boat with five pounds of commercial explosive. M described it as a retaliatory strike-in-kind. The plan was to booby-trap the *Celtic Mist*. He would attach the bomb to the on-board radio using an electrical detonator. Once the radio was switched on, the bomb would explode.

M watched the boat for two weeks. He knew it would be relatively easy to breach its security and plant the bomb once it was berthed in Dingle. All he needed was a window of time. The gelignite for the operation was purchased from a quarry in Scotland and transported, by a sympathetic Ulster freight firm, to the province. Unfortunately, the journey did not agree with the explosives and when the sticks were unwrapped they were covered in beads of liquid. The long transit had caused them to sweat, which meant they were volatile and ready to explode at any time. M disposed of them. He had to go back to the drawing board and look for a new device.

M had seen a massive file on Haughey that detailed everything from his love life to his business affairs and the tapping of journalists' phones. He described Charlie Haughey as a very 'bold boy'. There were two other men in the Red Hand back-up unit, but they got themselves arrested just weeks before the operation. The pair did an armed robbery, got arrested and cracked under police pressure. Not only were they done for robbery and possession, but they were also done for membership of the Red Hand Commando and other offences. The two handguns selected for use in the operation were seized by the RUC. The operation was called off. M said it was contaminated.

He told me the Red Hand's leadership also sent two highly trained and experienced bomb makers to look at commercial and industrial targets in the Irish Republic. One included a plan to blow up the fuel depots in Ringsend. M said the shopping districts in the heart of the city were also on the list. The Jury's network of hotels was also a target, as were Shannon Airport and Dublin's Connolly Station. The Red Hand leaders saw much to be gained from striking the Irish Republic. It meant the Irish government would sit up and take notice, like it did with the Monaghan and Dublin bombings in May 1974.

M's story proves what I have known for a very long time: that Loyalist active-service units regularly made incursions into the Republic. Irish people thought they were safe, so long as they stayed on their side of the border and didn't stray into Northern Ireland. How wrong they were. They were constantly at risk; in fact they ran a daily risk for years. In truth, that risk has never really gone away. The Irish government also displayed a staggering naivety. They thought that Loyalists wouldn't dare stray into Irish soil because they had no support network *in situ*. M's story proves otherwise.

Throughout my Maze years I got to know many prisoners, and many were, and still are, die-hard Loyalists. One was a lifer from a rival Loyalist paramilitary organisation. We had managed a few grunted acknowledgements to each other over the years but never had a proper conversation, so it was a surprise to me when he actually initiated a conversation one evening in the recreation room. There was an item on the local evening news recalling the

Dublin and Monaghan bombings. It was an important anniversary: twenty years had elapsed since the no-warning blasts and the families of the thirty-three civilians killed were calling on their government to hold an inquiry.

The lifer watched the broadcast without saying a word and, when the report was finished, turned to me and said the Irish government would never hold an inquiry into the attack because it would be 'too embarrassing to both governments if the truth ever got out'. He then said that both Ireland and Britain knew who planted the bomb, and that the British knew it was one of their own – SAS soldier Captain Robert Nairac who set up the entire operation and provided the explosives and timer units for the Loyalist squad. He said the Irish were too ashamed to tell their people the truth – that they have long known the atrocity was planned and executed with the collusion of the intelligence services and Loyalist paramilitaries.

Initially, I thought this man was talking a load of bullshit and was trying to impress me but I gave him the benefit of the doubt. There was a chance he was genuine and wanted to unload something that had been on his mind for many years.

I asked him did he know Nairac and his answer astonished me. He said Nairac was a 'typical Sandhurst type but a true Brit, a real soldier', before continuing with the rest of his story. What he revealed was amazing, and I have never forgotten what he said that May evening. I will now recall the story as the lifer told me:

'I first met Nairac in North Belfast. He was in uniform and, come to think of it, so was I. He was all spit and polish, with a posh accent, but when I met him several months later in a security base in County Armagh, I barely recognised him. He was shabbily dressed and bearded. He was wearing a dirty duffle coat and had the worst Northern Irish accent I have ever heard.

'I told him his accent was an insult and Nairac just shrugged his shoulders and said to me, "Don't worry about it, Paddy." I hated that nickname. I hated that he called me a Paddy. I wasn't Irish, I was British.

'We had a few drinks together in the base Naffy and got talking about the Northern Irish situation. We discussed the escalating situation all over the province and the bombing campaign the Provos were carrying out from their safe bases in the Irish Republic. Nairac knew that I had dual membership of a Loyalist paramilitary organisation because he told me he had read an intelligence file on me. He said he liked what he read and had a proposal to put to my paramilitary associates and me. By the end of our drink, we both had an understanding and a new working arrangement was about to be forged. We agreed we had a common enemy and agreed that we had to fight PIRA.

'Nairac loved to sing Irish ballads including "Danny Boy" and the rest of those awful songs, and I had to keep explaining to him that Republicans, not Loyalists, sang those tunes. I told him Loyalists would take great exception to having anything to do with Provo songs. Again he laughed and said, "You Irish are a rare breed."'

I was fascinated by this man's story. I asked him did he know anything about Nairac and did he think he was being set up by the intelligence services. The lifer said no and continued his tale:

'I met Nairac several weeks after our drink and he outlined an operation he called "a headline grabber". He said it would be so big it would frighten the Dublin administration into tightening border security, which had been non-existent for years. He said the operation would force Dublin into clamping down on southern-based Provos who carried out their indiscriminate attacks and fled to the safety of the Republic.

'The headline grabber that Nairac spoke off was the Dublin and Monaghan bombings of May 1974. Nairac organised the entire operation from start to finish. The Dublin government know the Brits have covered it up.'

I asked him was he joking because, if what he said was true, this attack was an act of war on another country. I thought he was taking the piss but, as he continued, I had to concede he knew too much detail and the man was a player with a number of high-profile assassinations under his belt. He continued his story.

'North Belfast provided the men and transport – four cars bought at four separate auctions and garaged for eight weeks leading up to the operation. They were then checked and rechecked to make sure they were fit for the journey. Nairac supplied the explosives and it was A-grade stuff, none of this home-made crap. It was the best gelignite with quality timer units to detonate the devices. Dressed as civilians, we crossed the border and reconnoitered the towns to be targeted. All journeys were timed, from north to south and then south to north. Dublin city centre was the first target. Monaghan town was the second choice. The blasts would go off ninety minutes apart.

'Nairac insisted on priming the bombs on the northern side of the border prior to delivery in southern Ireland and that is why he took the journey timings – to get the time of detonation down to the exact second.

'On the specified day, the four cars travelled through unapproved roads to the border and were met by Nairac at a pre-agreed location. Nairac primed each bomb, one after the other, and waved us on our way. I drove one of the bombs destined for Dublin city centre.'

I asked him was he not nervous driving a car with a bomb due to go off after a certain time had elapsed. What would he do if the car broke down, or he got stuck in traffic, and did it enter his head that Nairac might be setting the whole lot of them up? All he said was: 'Nairac was a soldier. I trusted him.'

Thirty-three people died in the four blasts. An entire family was lost.

The lifer had concluded this part of his story. At first I found it incredulous that the security forces were involved in an attack on their nearest neighbour. After he went to the kitchen and came back with a mug of coffee he recalled other operations where he worked with Nairac. In one, they travelled together to Dublin's Mansion House. It was the night before a Sinn Fein Ard Fheis and they planted a device disguised in a fire extinguisher. It was the exact replica of the one that sat on the wings of the stage. The device contained 15lbs of high explosives timed to go off during the meeting. The lifer told me the bomb never exploded. He believes it was discovered and defused by the Irish Army.

There was silence between the two of us. There was nothing I could say. There was nothing more that he could add.

Labour MP Ken Livingstone was also a Loyalist target, according to M. He was a hate figure because he was over-sympathetic to Republicans. Loyalists dubbed him Green Ken, rather than Red Ken, because of his overtly nationalistic politics and opinions. A volunteer was sent to London to meet up with two members of the National Front. They weren't the 'bovver boots' and shaved-head brigade but respectable businessmen. They were organised by the Red Hand to provide transport and accommodation for the volunteer. Livingstone was a political target and would be executed as he left his place of work. The death of the Labour MP would send shock waves to the very heart of Downing Street and the security agencies.

The volunteer worked alone. He dressed as a jogger to carry out the assassination. He looked at the GLC building, on the Thames opposite the Houses of Parliament. There was no security, and every evening at five-thirty Livingstone would leave his office and walk the short distance to the Underground station. The volunteer followed him on to the train, got off when Ken did and tailed him to his home. He was surprised that Livingstone lived in a modest house. The front door opened out, an indication that there was extra security. Livingstone wasn't assassinated because Loyalists called a halt on the hit. The Inner Council had too much time to think about it and decided a Loyalist group killing a British politician was a no-no.

I recall these conversations to prove that Loyalists weren't backstreet killers. We weren't thugs. These conversations prove Loyalists sought political targets and big targets.

Other stories were important to me. A UDA man came to see me and thanked me for Dermot Hackett. I said nothing. He sat on my bed and said, 'I shot him. I want to thank you for closing the book on him. I continued to operate after Hackett's death. Did you know about me?'

'I had heard of you. Why did you shoot through the letter "O" in Mother's Pride?'

'To centre my weapon. Why did you say you killed Hackett?'

'I wanted to get Deary off, but it didn't work.'

'It was said you confessed to Hackett for the glory, to paint yourself as a mass murderer.'

'You and I know differently and after Milltown I didn't need any credibility.'

Another year man, Mad Jack, was haunted by his past and an attempted murder that went badly wrong. He turned gothic. He wore dark clothes and refused to interact with other inmates. Then he freaked the men out by walking around naked, chanting and reciting incantations. He made things worse by putting curses and spells under cell doors. When he went on a visit I had a look in his cell. Painted on the floor was a pentangle. He had dried feathers and even a starling's skull on a shelf in his cell.

'What's all that about?' I asked him.

'I have had peace of mind since converting.'

'To what?'

'Satan.'

'Satan?'

'Satan. The Dark Prince.'

'There is only one Satan around here, your OC.'

I told him to clear away the skull and feathers, to start wearing clothes, to quit the spells and to paint his cell floor. He calmed down for a while. Then it started again. This time the spells were appearing under prisoners' pillows. He was also 'mixing', stirring up trouble. The wing was at breaking point. Someone was going to be killed. The guys were even getting tooled up with makeshift weapons. The gothic had to be disciplined. He was adjudicated and asked whether he had anything to say in his defence. He said that it 'helped him get his day in'. Mad Jack was marched to his punishment. A provost marshal was detailed to discipline him and I warned the provost marshal, 'Don't kick him in the head and don't break any bones. You break one of his bones, I will break one of yours.' I told Mad Jack, 'Take your punishment. If you fight back, I will finish you off.' I knew he was on medication but I didn't know what for. Within three weeks he was moved to Maghaberry. His medical notes, shown to me by one of the wing screws, said he was schizophrenic and had been for years.

Another young prisoner, Davy, was doing time for his part in a UVF murder. The police officers who questioned him showed him the crime-scene photographs and these literally drove him mad. The graphic images pushed in front of his face were to haunt him day and night until he was sectioned under the Mental Health Act. Davy was an intelligent man who was studying at university when he was arrested. It was his first job as a UVF volunteer. The man who was killed was also a Loyalist and it was part of an internal feud. The gun jammed and the target fought back. Stuck with a gun that didn't work, the men beat the target until there was nothing left of his head and they finished him off by slitting his throat to the spine. His body was dumped in a field and lay there for weeks.

Davy cried in the middle of the night. Sometimes he howled like an animal in pain. Then the crying stopped and he developed the thousand-yard stare. He was looking through and beyond me. I had seen that look before, both times in the PSU: when Tommy McGrath was taken to a psychiatric ward, and on Philip Laffan, who committed suicide. I tried to get Davy to talk to me. I asked him about girls and he said he never had a girlfriend and was unlikely to have one now he was banged up in the Maze.

One morning Davy was running up and down the wing, banging on cell doors. His eyes were on stalks and his hair stood on end. He was shouting, 'Let me out, let me out.' I discovered that someone spiked his tea with four LSD tabs. He was a country lad, and the city men saw him as a 'culchie', a yokel, and thought they could have fun with him. It backfired. Davy wasn't the same after that. The prison doctors had him shifted to Maghaberry, then the psychiatric ward, but within in a month he was sectioned under the Mental Health Act and taken to Broadmoor. His OC never displayed any concern about the young man and was more interested in finding out what Davy and I discussed. I told him it was girls and the Battle of Milltown. I was allowed to take a look in Davy's cell. It was a shrine to rock stars and actors who had died, such as Jimi Hendrix, Phil Lynott and Janis Joplin.

Two years after he was sent to Broadmoor, I got a letter from Davy. It was a single sheet of lined paper and all it said was: 'DEAR MIC.' That was it, two words scrawled in massive, childlike letters across the page. Over the months he improved, writing things like: 'I AM GOOD' and 'EVERYTHING HAS ROUND EDGES', but his handwriting never improved. Other letters made reference to inmates such as Ronnie Kray – 'not a bad lad' – and said he wanted to 'beat the shit out of Ian Brady'.

Eventually Davy made good progress, was released from Broadmoor and sent back to the Maze to finish his time. I didn't know he was back until I saw him queuing for a visit, but he didn't recognise me. Davy was released under the terms of the Good Friday Agreement and immediately moved to England to start a new life. I heard he was doing well until he got into a dispute with his girlfriend's brother. He chased the man down a street with a knife, was arrested and sent back to Broadmoor. Davy had a record of killing with a knife. The authorities were taking no chances and had him locked up.

22

MAD DOG, DAFT DOG, WEE JOHNNY, MR SHOWBIZ

I HAVE LEARNT THAT THERE IS A JOHNNY ADAIR FOR EVERY OCCASION. HE HAS MULTIPLE PERSONALITIES AND I HAVE SEEN MOST OF THEM. There is 'Mr Showbiz', the Johnny who loves the infamy of being a high-profile Loyalist paramilitary. He will be delighted I have given him a chapter all to himself. There is 'Mad Dog', the Johnny the media prefer because he's mad and bad. There is 'Daft Dog', the Johnny that doesn't have an ounce of street sense or a political thought in his head, and there is 'Wee Johnny', the Johnny that is childlike and innocent. That's the real Johnny Adair. That's the Johnny Adair I know and the only part of his complex and deeply insecure personality that I liked.

It was 1989. I had no idea who the skinny kid was who kept shouting, 'Rambo, Rambo' from the public gallery of Court Number One after my sentence was announced. I had never seen him before in my life.

He introduced himself a year later when he was at the Maze to visit a Shankill Road life man. I had a visitor of my own and Adair bounced up to my cubicle, shook my hand and said, "Bout ya, Rambo." Throughout the visit he kept smiling at me and giving me the thumbs up. At the time he was a private in C Company of the UFF. When the visits were over he bounced back up again and asked could he visit me. I refused. He said he wanted to talk 'to the hero of the Battle of Milltown'. I told him to fuck off, that Milltown was gone, I was caught, was doing life and was no Ulster hero. He pleaded and I told him one visit, one visit only. He then asked for a photograph as a keepsake of 'a special day' and I agreed. He framed the visitor's pass and kept the photograph in his car.

Within a couple of years Adair enjoyed a meteoric rise through the UFF command structure. He now had rank and I, an unranked volunteer, was obliged to take his visits. The Wee Johnny was disappearing and another personality was forming, Daft Dog. He constantly pumped me for information and wanted to know every detail of Milltown and other operations. Adair had a grand plan. I asked him about the other brigadiers and what he thought of them. He said, 'They are old women who sit around all day talking about football, going to the bookie's and eating triangle sandwiches. I hate triangle sandwiches.'

He was right. The new school was clearing the decks and getting rid of the dead wood. Adair was part of this radical overhaul that saw fresh blood being injected into the UDA command structure. It was a good thing because the days of the Tuckers and Craigs were gone.

Adair held the position of Commander of the UFF, the military arm of the UDA, a title once held by my old friend and comrade John McMichael. Within days of the Shankill bombing, Adair was in the visitors' wing of the Maze. He asked me what I thought of the no-warning blast and I told him it was terrible, an act of war. He just looked at me, smiling. I got the distinct impression there was no regret on his part at the loss of civilians, the deaths of mothers and their children, or the fact that the very heart of his community had been bombed to kingdom come. I knew the deaths of the nine were a badge of honour rather than an unspeakable human tragedy when he said to me: 'I'm very important, Mikey. Those people lost their lives because the Provies wanted me.' When I asked him how he felt about all those civilian deaths he just shrugged his shoulders and said, 'But, Mikey, they didn't get me, did they?' and in the next breath, 'Fuck it, we'll hit back.' I told him I wasn't interested and didn't want to know what was planned but he couldn't help himself. He then said Catholics would pay dearly for the Shankill bombing but his big-body-count plan had to be aborted. Adair had planned to send out men to do a simultaneous attack on five or six Roman Catholic chapels in the greater Belfast area at eleven o'clock mass on a particular Sunday morning. His exact words were that they were to go into the places of worship and 'spray the fucking place with AKs, kill them all and let God sort them out'. But the security forces were tipped off by someone on the Inner Council and banks of Land Rovers and cops were stationed on the given Sunday at the chosen chapels.

Adair didn't get to spray the places of worship but he did get retaliation, in the attack on Greysteele. He organised the weapons, transport and volunteers for the assault on the Rising Star bar in which five people, both Protestants and Roman Catholics, were killed. Much later, from his prison cell, he bragged to me that in Greysteele, the UFF 'evened up the score' and whooped at the top of his voice: 'Yeh-ha!'

Milltown was always top of Adair's talk list and he wouldn't stop harping on about it. I constantly told him Milltown was a disaster militarily. He said, 'Men queued to join the UFF because we kicked the Provies' asses in their own backyard. You are a Loyalist hero because you didn't break or betray your comrades.' It wasn't what I wanted to hear.

Within a year he was calling me Mikey. His constant mantra was: 'Mikey, what we need is one good man to run the UDA. One good man to take overall control.' I tried to tell him that 'one man' doesn't work. I told him that it was easy to corrupt, turn or kill one man but he would refuse to listen and storm off. Mad Dog was starting to rear its head, but occasionally Wee Johnny could still be seen. During one prison visit he showed me an old photograph. He was on stage, in a band. He was a skinhead with bovver boots, braces and jeans to his knees. There was a Mickey Mouse tattoo on his forearm. He told me he 'always fancied being a pop star'. Another Johnny Adair personality had surfaced: Mr Showbiz. He knew he would never make it as a pop star, so he turned his paramilitary career into the showbiz fix he craved.

Then the visits suddenly stopped. There was a double-page spread in the *Guardian* with a headline that dubbed him 'Mad Dog'. He had taken a journalist on a tour of West Belfast. He did the driving and in his car was the photograph of him and me that that he had taken on his first visit. He called it the 'prized photo of me and my mate Mikey Stone, a real Ulster hero'. Adair did start to visit me again. 'All right, Mikey?' 'All right, Mad Dog.' He squirmed in his seat and said, 'Don't call me that. That bastard Dominic McGlinchey is called "Mad Dog". I'm not a mad dog.' But secretly he was thrilled. The name stuck and Wee Johnny had a new identity.

Years later Adair was remanded to the Maze on a newly introduced charge, directing terrorism. He was housed in H1, the remand block. I was on H2. The minute he moved in, all discipline went out the window. He held weekend rave parties. There were drugs. Adair would pour bags of ecstasy tabs over the wing's pool table and tell prisoners to help themselves. Some UDA remand prisoners freaked out. They weren't interested in the parties and drugs. They couldn't sleep and they feared the authorities would tar them with the same brush as Johnny Adair and his cronies. I moved those men on to my wing. I doubled and tripled prisoners in cells in order to accommodate the remand men.

Adair's mantra was: 'We're not sentenced, you can't touch us', and it was true. I tried to appeal to his human side. I brought him on to H2 and showed him the clean and tidy cells and the kitchen. I told him that we are all Loyalist POWs. I told him we weren't criminals or scumbags and he should behave. He just said, 'Fuck ya, Mikey.' Johnny Adair had become a law unto himself. I advised him to fight the directing terrorism charge, not because I liked the man but because it set a new legal precedent. Adair didn't fight it. There was too much evidence, taped conversations he'd had with the RUC bragging about operations, and he couldn't fight it.

Adair would plead with his Special Branch pals: 'Ah, lads, don't do this to me, you're supposed to be my friend.' This evidence came to light on a local current affairs show. Johnny was already sentenced and every Loyalist on the wings couldn't wait to see the damning programme – except Adair. There was silence in the Big Cell, which doubled as a telly room. No one spoke, made tea or went to the bathroom for the entire show. The sound of jaws hitting the ground could be heard all over the block. Adair was bragging to the Branch and pleading with them. It was obvious he was on first-name terms. After the show, Adair couldn't face any of us. He knew he would be ridiculed. It took him almost four weeks to surface and face any of us. He knew everyone would see him for what he was – a tout.

The ironic thing is, Adair has never cut the mustard as an operator. He was more interested in the fame game than being a true Loyalist. He was more interested in the profile his fame would give him than the Loyalist cause.

Adair changed three months into his sixteen-year sentence. He was the first person to go down for directing terrorism. The change in his physical shape happened after he trailed me, like a lost puppy, to the gym. I trained for two hours every day. Adair would follow me in and stand and watch. Then he started to work out, but his stringy arms couldn't lift the weights. He started on the steroids and began to change shape. He bulked up. His body was swollen and he had boils on his back.

I was called to see the Governor. He wanted me to use my influence to have a word with Johnny. I told him it wasn't my problem, Johnny was a grown man. The Governor told me Johnny had been smuggling in steroids. Tests were run by the authorities which showed the substance was lethal. It was used to fatten cattle and banned in the EU. The Governor told me that prisoners could die if they continued to use the substance. I knew Johnny was using it. He was taking it three ways, in tablet and liquid form and by injecting. I went to the library and read up about steroids. I took the book with me and went to have a word with Adair.

He was smuggling in the drug in an artificial arm that a Prisoners' Aid worker brought in for him. When I confronted him he said he took the 'odd tablet'. I showed him the book and told him that the stuff 'shrinks your genitals to a chipolata and two peanuts'. He stormed off. Two days later he said he wanted to show me something. In his cell, he dropped his trousers. I quickly moved to the open door. I didn't want to be anywhere near him when he was standing in the buff holding his genitalia. He said, 'Fuck, Mikey, you were right, look. I have nothing left.' Although he was bloated, his skin was breaking out in blisters and spots and his genitals had disappeared, he didn't stop using the drug and continued injecting straight into the muscle.

Johnny was obsessed with sex and enjoyed a unique sex life in prison. He had his conjugal visits from girlfriends and he had a prison lover, a man called Harry. They were called 'the girls' because they wore pink posing vests and lycra shorts. Adair pierced his nipples using ice and a dart, in his own cell, telling me the piercing increased sensitivity. He got himself an intimate piercing 'down below' because, he said, his boyfriend really liked it. He also shaved off all his body hair, including anal and pubic.

Loyalist prisoners nicknamed him 'Willy Watcher' because he would stand and stare open-mouthed at men in the communal and open showers and make comments about the size of their manhood. I constantly told him I wasn't interested in his sex life, but all he would say was, 'I like talking to you, Mikey.' He asked me once if I'd ever 'done it with a man' and I was quick to point out that it wasn't my scene. He then blabbed about doing it with a man, a man and a woman, two women and finally two men and two girls. He said he liked the sex games he played with 'Big Aggie', who would tie a lead around his manhood and drag him around the room, calling him 'Bad Doggy'.

Adair was getting on my nerves and there was no escape from him, even on visits. I swapped my conjugal visits from Saturday to Wednesday and he copied me. One day his head poked around my cubicle and he said, 'My girlfriend wants to meet you, she has a tattoo.' I then heard him saying to the girl, 'Go on, show him, show him.' The girl was wearing a tiny denim skirt and she pulled it up. She wasn't wearing underwear and she had no pubic hair. Johnny's name was tattooed in fancy writing across her pubic area. His eyes were on stalks as he said, 'That's true love, isn't it, Mikey?'

Adair's favourite film was *Highlander* and he used to ask me who I thought would be the best actor to play him in a movie. I'd tell him to get a life and he'd say, 'Ah no, Mikey, what about that Bruce Willis or Arnie Schwarzenegger?'

He loved the pop group Bros and sang their hit 'When Will I Be Famous' over and over. He hadn't a note in his head – he sounded like a cat stuck in a lift shaft. He also had several prison nicknames. Willy Watcher, for obvious reasons, then he and his pal Harry were 'the girls', again for obvious reasons, and then there was Spartacus. He gave himself that title after I told him about a television show on the history of ancient armies. The programme was about the Spartans and how they were encouraged to take lovers among their men so that during battle soldiers would never be sacrificed or left behind. When I told Adair this story, his eyes lit up. It was as if he had found the meaning of life. He loved the story, like a child loves a nursery rhyme, and he would tell it and retell it to his henchmen. Daft Dog was in love with the legend of the ultimate warrior.

The Governor would always send for me when there was a 'man management' issue on the Loyalist wings. One day in his office he told me to take a seat and took out a video. He said he wanted to show me something. The Governor switched on the video and it showed Adair's wing and the prisoners walking around, going into the showers and into their cells with a blow-up doll under their arms and a towel covering their modesty. I started to laugh, but the Governor pointed out that if this got into the papers it wouldn't be 'Prisoners Have Sex With Rubber Doll', it would be 'Stone and Adair Have Sex With Rubber Doll'. I went to see Johnny and asked him about 'Sexy Suzy' and told him I had seen the video.

'It's the lads' bit of fun,' he said.

'What about diseases and hygiene?'

'They rinse her under the hot tap.'

I told him to burn it or I would kidnap Sexy Suzy and burn her myself. A week later she was destroyed in the exercise yard.

Johnny never gave up pumping me for information. I told my fellow OCs, 'When that wee guy gets out there will be trouble because he wants to be top dog', and my predictions have now come true.

In 1997 Tony Blair was made Prime Minister. Adair pinned his pop band photograph on the kitchen noticeboard and declared to the men on his wing, 'Tony Blair was in a pop band and became the Prime Minister of the UK. I am Mad Dog Adair. If it's good enough for the PM, it's good enough for me.'

The LVF leader Billy Wright was beginning to establish a profile. Johnny Adair's alter ego Mr Showbiz didn't like that. He would rant, 'Who does that fucker Billy Wright think he is? He's keeping all of us in jail,' and then swing the other way, calling him a hero. He would sit in his cell writing his signature over and over. I asked what he was doing.

'I'm practising.'

'For what?'

'Signing autographs when we get out of here. We are going to do some fucking, Mikey. All the women love heroes. We'll never have to look for a shag ever again. The girls will be queuing up to get us in the sack. There's me, Billy Wright and you, and we're the real heroes of Ulster. We're not like the rest. We are famous.'

'No, we're infamous.'

'What does that mean?'

'We are famous for being bad and, you know what, infamy gets you killed. Johnny, when they kill me and throw me into a rubbish skip, the last thing I will see before I die is you, already dead.'

'Don't say that, Mikey.'

He walked away, head down and hands in his pockets. I didn't see him for two months.

I was beginning to feel like Adair's personal counsellor. He would confide in me, I would tell him some home truths and he'd disappear for weeks on end. But one thing was certain: he always surfaced when he needed or wanted to talk. The childlike Johnny always felt the need to impress me. It was the big kid, the impressionable teenager part of his complex personality. When I saw 'wee Johnny' rearing his head, I was prepared to give him the benefit of the doubt. Then he hit me with it: 'Have you ever killed a woman, Mikey?'

I asked him was he serious or was he acting the prick and he said, 'No, Mikey, have you ever killed one, you know for a laugh, when they piss you off?' I told him to 'catch himself on' but there was no stopping him.

'Do you remember the Langley Street club? You get all sorts of women in there, women wanting to meet and play with the boys.' I asked him what he meant and then he dropped the bombshell. 'Mikey, let's put it like this. If they ever dig up that section of the Westlink, you know the bit that runs along the bottom of the Shankill Road, well I am fucked.' He burst out laughing. My cell door opened and Adair's right-hand man, Harry, poked his head around the door. He wanted to know what Adair was laughing at and Adair answered, 'I was just telling Mikey about the girls under the Westlink, you remember the two from Langley Street.' Quick as lightning, Harry pulled Adair out of my cell and marched him up the wing. The two were arguing with one another and I could hear their heated words. Johnny shouted at his pal, 'I don't know why you are getting annoyed, you don't even like girls.'

I have thought about this incident many times and it has left me cold. I have four sisters, I have daughters and I have female friends. I can't decide if Adair had let slip something very sinister and very real or if it was bravado, but I honestly believe the real Johnny has a secret buried under the concrete of the Westlink.

Wright was assassinated by an INLA death squad just days after Christmas in 1997. Billy was doing his time in H6 and the INLA shared the block with the LVF prisoners. I had warned Mogg, the Governor, that something bad would happen if the INLA and LVF were housed in the same block. I asked him if he understood the hatred. His exact words were: 'We'll be all right.'

Wright was murdered on a Saturday and I knew something was up after the alarm went and all movement in the prison was stopped. Men had been queuing for prison visits. Prison life had been going on as normal, but when the emergency alarm went everybody had to stand where they stood. OCs got permission to move around the wings and I went straight to my other OCs, then went to see Adair. He was sleeping after an all-night drug-fuelled rave. I shook him awake. I told him Billy Wright had been shot dead. 'Who's Billy Wright?' he answered. I reminded him of his hero story. When he finally came round, he said he wanted retaliation. I told him it was nothing to do with the IRA and we couldn't get near the INLA.

Adair ran a scenario past me. He said, if he got an RDG grenade in, would I wire it to one of the pec decks in the gym? I said nothing. But the potential incident was just violent retaliation and reminded me of an attack in the Crum when the Provos wired an old cast-iron radiator and killed two Loyalist remand prisoners.

Four weeks later the Governor asked to see me. He said the death of Billy Wright was a serious incident and asked whether I had plans to hurt Christopher 'Crip' McWilliams, the INLA gunman who assassinated Wright. I told him that, if McWilliams smirked or made funny comments about Billy, I would punch him. I said I wouldn't kill him. Mogg threw a file on his desk detailing the exact scenario Adair had put to me in the exercise yard, word for word. Only two people knew about wiring the gym with a grenade, and that was Johnny and myself. Adair had touted. Johnny Adair doesn't know how to keep his trap shut.

Adair was obsessed with Brian Nelson, the UDA double agent nicknamed Agent Orange, but he just couldn't keep his trap shut. He loved to brag about how much Nelson's secret service pals passed him top-weight, A-grade intelligence about possible targets. Pat Finucane was one of them, and other possible victims were Francisco Notarantonio and Gerard Slane. Adair sat in my cell and linked himself, C Company and Nelson to the death of the prominent lawyer with just eleven words. He told me: 'I like Nelson, sure, didn't we whack "fork" Finucane for him.' The fork is a reference to the evening meal Finucane was sharing with his family when the two-man unit opened fire.

It didn't end there. Johnny confided in me that C Company couldn't fail because he and Nelson worked hand-in-glove. I always knew his big mouth would be his downfall. He said, 'C Company couldn't go wrong because British intelligence was doing our targeting for us.' Then his mood changed. He got angry and agitated and said the Intelligence Agencies had 'pissed' all over him. He was enraged that he had gone down for directing terrorism and Nelson had been given a deal, which included a new identity and life in England. He fumed: 'After all I had done, Mikey, I didn't think the bastards would stroke me like that.'

In 1998, Mad Dog threatened to kill the Secretary of State Mo Mowlan after his request for early release was turned down. We were both in H7: Johnny was in D Wing and I was in A wing. The incident happened in the circle. The Governor had just handed Adair a memo from the NIO, which said the Secretary of State was refusing his early release because he continued to be a 'major threat' to society. I had also received the same correspondence. Adair was furious and even though he was accompanied by nine prison officers and surrounded by witnesses, he shouted at the top of his voice, 'I'll put one in her baldy head. I'm serious, Mikey, she's fucked.' Adair, OC of West Belfast, had vowed to kill the Secretary of State. He made a sick reference to the fact she was recovering from a brain tumour and sometimes wore a wig. Mad and Daft Dog was now a Sick Dog. I told him to shut his mouth but he didn't listen. He didn't understand that his threats had just legitimised the Secretary of State's decision to keep him locked up.

Adair had a chip on his shoulder about Mo. When she was shadow Secretary of State she came to the Maze to talk to us about the Loyalist ceasefire and the Peace Process. Adair was on the team and for the first ten minutes of the meeting chewed his nails constantly. It obviously irritated Mo, famous for her down-to-earth, touchy-feely approach, who got out of her chair, walked around the table and slapped Adair hard on the wrists. She told him to stop biting his nails because it was a disgusting habit. Johnny blushed from the top of his bald head to his feet. He has never forgotten that incident.

By 1999, Adair was determined that the position of Supreme Commander was his – whatever it took. He resorted to intimidation and threats of execution. He harassed North and South Belfast. The only brigade he couldn't get near was mine – East. He wore the OC for North Belfast down and now had one of a possible two OCs in his back pocket. South Belfast was harder to crack, so Adair waited until the hardmen of this brigade were on visits before sending in his henchmen to trash and burn cells. In response to the destruction of prison property, the authorities would lock down the prison and everyone was punished. Adair was a law unto himself. The South Belfast OC and myself rang out to our brigadiers looking for help. We both knew it was only a matter of time before someone was killed. I explained the situation to my man and he initially wanted me to barricade the wings. I told him that wasn't an option because it showed the UDA/UFF had massive internal problems. I asked my brig whether, theoretically, if I had to take Adair out, I had permission. His answer was: 'Do what you have to do.' I had been given official clearance to kill Johnny Adair.

I was incensed that Mad Dog was trying to take over the wings. If he had succeeded, none of our lives would have been worth living. It would have been hell on earth with him in charge. I had men coming to me saying they would have asked for an immediate transfer to Maghaberry. I would have also been prepared to give up my paramilitary prisoner status to become a conforming prisoner if Adair had succeeded in his game plan.

I was pleased the UDA had given me the nod, not because Adair would lose his life but because the organisation had acknowledged the fact that Mad Dog was on a path which would lead to the UDA imploding and destroying itself.

I prepared a homemade weapon. It was an old toothbrush with razor blazes inserted into the handle. I was going to cut his throat. The minute it was done, I would be handing myself into the prison authorities, saying Johnny and I had had a falling-out and I had killed him.

It didn't happen. Adair never came on to A Wing. He wouldn't dare.

My last conversation with Adair took place six weeks before my release. He shook my hand and asked to talk. He was the Wee Johnny that I liked until he opened his mouth.

'Mikey, what the UDA needs is one good man to run the organisation.'

'It won't work. No one man is bigger than the UDA, no one man is bigger than Loyalism.'

I told him that the Del Boy image had to go. He smiled at me.

'Look, Mikey, the bottom line is, Loyalism doesn't pay the bills.'

'What about the men who have died?'

He shrugged his shoulders and said, 'Fuck them.'

'Johnny, when we get out we are both going to have to watch our backs. You have made enemies among Loyalists.'

'You've made enemies too.'

'I know. Are you going to kill me?'

'No, Mikey.'

'Because if you are, join the queue.'

23

THE ARTIST FORMERLY
KNOWN AS RAMBO

**BACK IN 1989, MY YEAR ON REMAND IN THE CRUM HAD
STARTED TO IMMOBILISE ME.** My lonely life in the bowels of
Crumlin Road jail was slowly turning my brain to jelly. I
maintained a tough physical routine to keep my body in shape but
my mind was dying because of lack of intellectual stimulation.

I had my radio but it wasn't enough. I craved human company.
The day screws were the only contact I had. I needed to find
something that would flex my brain and stimulate my mind. I had
to find a pursuit that would occupy acres of my time or I would go
mad. I was fed up with books and magazines. I wanted a hobby
that would allow me to switch off for hours on end. I was six
months into my remand when I made a request to the Governor
for some watercolours, brushes and paper. He smiled at me but
refused. I didn't like his smile. It was loaded with sarcasm. He said
he was fascinated that a convicted terrorist, doing life for six
murders, wanted to paint. Every week for six weeks I made the
same request and every week I was refused. I wanted to paint. I

knew it would give me a creative outlet in my drab cell. I knew it would break the monotony of my long days on the PSU.

Painting was also a bridge to my past. The last time I was interested in art I was a boy of seven. I have always enjoyed painting and sketching. My first artistic creation was a sculpture of a collie dog made from toilet-roll holders, scraps of fabric and paint. It won a prize and went on display in the school foyer. As a young schoolboy art was my best subject and I was also interested in woodwork, but not for long. My enjoyment of these and academic subjects was ruined by one of my school teachers. After he beat me I lost all interest in learning and developed a hatred for educators. The day that teacher hammered the eight-year-old Michael Stone for giggling in the schoolyard was the day he also destroyed my budding talent and interest in art.

As a teenager I was more interested in using my fists and feet than a paintbrush and, by the time I became a young UDA volunteer in 1972, brushes and paints were completely forgotten about. As a young man I did some street art, though not much. In Loyalist districts, street painting is a part of growing up. It didn't matter if the end result was good or bad, it was the contribution that mattered. My first and only street painting was of King Billy on a white charger.

After refusing to allow me artist's materials for weeks, the Governor of the Crum suddenly had a change of heart. I didn't get a tray of watercolours and brushes. Instead I was handed a reporter's spiral-bound notebook and a pencil stub, just two inches in length. Each page on the notebook was numbered and I was told I had to account for every single page at the end of the day and hand in the pencil. If I didn't co-operate I would forfeit my new art equipment.

'Why the tiny pencil?'

'In case you use it to escape.'

'You mean, use it to dig my way out of here?'

'No, Michael, in case you stick it in an officer's eye in an attempt to scramble his brains.'

'Why are the pages of the notebook numbered?'

'So the authorities can account for every page and in case you try to escape with it.'

'You mean make a paper plane to fly out of here?'

'In case you draw escape plans or smuggle messages out.'

'But I don't have any visitors.'

'Don't be smart.'

I was allowed the pencil and paper for two hours every day, directly after lunch. Then both had to be handed back to the duty screws. They would only leave after checking every single page in the notebook was accounted for. I started by drawing the cell from every angle. I lay on the floor and sketched the ceiling corners, the brickwork and the peeling paint. I sketched the miserable furniture and my cell door. I even sketched the graffiti: 'Budgie Rules' and 'Budgie is a Wanker signed Christopher Black.' Both Budgie and Black had been held together in this very cell at the height of the supergrass trials.

Some screws were kind. They would slip blank paper, nicked from a printer or a fax machine and ripped into envelope size, through my viewfinder in return for a sketch. It was a quid pro quo. Looking through the tiny slit, I would draw them sitting in their chair. It was awkward but I didn't mind. Sketching kept my brain alive. Sometimes I drew the night screws while they slept. These men had an easy shift because most of the time it was just them and me down there and they got their drawings the following morning, before the change of staff. The screws were delighted. Some would even get me to autograph a sketch to prove to their mates that I did draw it. I refused to write paramilitary slogans such as 'Milltown 1988' or 'No Surrender'. The art was a new phase in my life.

The boiler room, the noisy unit that housed the Crum's ancient heating system, was next to the PSU. The heat turned my subterranean cell into a sauna. There was no air. The cell was unbearable. I preferred to be naked because it was too warm for clothes. I took the opportunity to draw my leg and ankle muscles and the bone structure of my feet. When the Governor saw I was enjoying my new hobby he gave me permission to use proper paints and paper, and when I got my hands on the materials the passion for painting was ignited.

My first experiments with paper and paint were, in all honesty, not very good. I have always enjoyed Salvador Dali's work, but my experiments in his surrealist style left a lot to be desired. They were just explosions of colour – Spanish reds, oranges and yellows – which I deliberately chose to mask the greyness of my prison cell. I was unable to grasp his distinctive idiom, but I didn't care. My painting was a means of expression and escape in my lonely and sunless prison cell. I grew as a painter, leaving behind those crude splashes of colour to develop a style of my own influenced by David Hockney, Max Ernst and Pablo Picasso. I wanted my art to be a human work in progress, a reflection of the first thirty years of my life. I now had the focus and intellectual stimulation I craved. I knew my art would help me survive the rest of my remand.

After my trial and sentence I continued my new pursuit. In the beginning I wasn't interested in art. I found it difficult to settle into my new life as a red-booker and I was disruptive. My plans for escape took over my life and my art equipment lay unused in a corner of my cell. Frustration and boredom made me take up my brushes. The Maze had art classes and proper equipment. It even had visiting artists and experts from Bosnia, America and London who gave masterclasses. The classes were under-attended and I more or less had the studio, the equipment and the artist to myself. There was also the Prison Arts Foundation, which helped pay for proper equipment. There was also the option of studying art to both O Level and A Level, but that would have bored me and taken me away from the practical stuff.

There were no canvases, so I improvised. I ripped the backs out of bedside lockers and pulled wardrobe doors from their hinges. I used bed headboards. They were made of hardboard and were perfect for painting on. I tore up my coarse linen sheets and tacked them to the back of my improvised canvases. My cell furniture had to be replaced regularly, but the prison authorities never charged me with destroying prison property. If a prisoner wanted a painting, he donated his cell furniture and bedclothes. The screws turned a blind eye. I lived with my art. I even slept on some of it. Those makeshift canvases represent my life first as a paramilitary and then as a prisoner. The colourful paintings explore my personal history, the history of my community and the history of the Troubles.

The authorities allowed me to keep an easel in my cell and there was always a work in progress on it. Initially it was a novelty to the prisoners I shared the wing with, and there was a constant stream of critics and admirers to my cell. In the early days the men would sneak into my cell for a look when I was on a visit or elsewhere. They were too embarrassed to voice their opinions to my face. Much later they would just stride in, have a look, criticise or praise the piece and then leave. The art became a focus of their lives as much as my own. The canvases were a talking point.

I helped with the prison's cottage industry, painting hankies with UDA insignia. They were sold for a fiver each and sold all over the world. The money raised went to Prisoners' Aid.

In the early days I did a lot of still life. I would borrow food from the canteen and position it on the table in my cell or the windowsill and paint it. Fruit and jugs of water weren't the most exciting of subjects, so I went one step further. I started painting from my imagination and my own figurative style was born. The guys especially liked my paintings of a woman reclining on a bed or lazing by a poolside, and they would, without fail, ask for a customised version for themselves. They would say, 'Go on, Stone, give us a couple of girlie paintings.'

'No. I don't do nudes, and anyway my memory isn't that good.'

'This should give you a bit of inspiration,' they would say, pushing a top-shelf magazine into my hand. I asked them what they wanted me to do with the magazine and they would point out a photograph and say, 'Stick my wife's head on that.'

I didn't paint nudes and I made that very clear to my wing mates. I would paint a wife or girlfriend, but she wouldn't be naked. Arms would cover her modesty. The men liked their paintings and so did their wives. At one stage every man on the wing had a picture of his girl. The screws also liked the figurative women. I had an unspoken deal with the screws: I did them a painting, they gave me a drop address, the painting was sent out and they brought me a couple of five-glass bottles of spirits. I don't drink. The spirits were for the lads' weekend wing parties. The authorities noticed I was sending out a lot of big parcels. Everything leaving the Maze had to be scanned through a device similar to the ones used at airports. They banned me from painting anything bigger than two by two feet because it wouldn't fit in the X-ray machine.

I had an individual sign-off. It used to be my signature but that stopped when young lads in the UVF forged it and passed off their artistic creations as mine. All Loyalist prisoners, UDA/UFF, UVF and Red Hand Commando, came to me for hand-painted cards. They would send them to their kids, girlfriends or wives at birthdays, Christmas and anniversaries. When I changed my sign-off to a thumbprint they copied me, but I didn't mind. They were earning a few quid on the cards. There was no harm in it.

When I was released from prison in 2000 I refused to apply for a prisoner resettlement grant. I didn't want to be dependent on Social Services handouts. I continued to paint and took up residency in a little studio in Ballybeen in East Belfast. The studio was in an old shop owned by the former UDA Supreme Commander, Andy Tyrie. Locals called it 'out of date Andy's'.

Then I started to teach art to troubled kids. I taught twenty local children aged between eight and sixteen and ended up learning more about myself. The kids always wanted to know about my past. They wanted to know about the Battle of Milltown. I told them I regret I had to fight a war and I regret taking a human life. I told them exactly how it was. I didn't glamorise or dramatise the events of my life. I deliberately talked to them like they were adults. These kids injected a much-needed shot of realism and humour into my new life as a free man. For the first few minutes they would call me Mr Stone, then it was Rambo, then Flinty and finally Stoner.

They would be very direct in their questioning and the boys especially wanted to know what it was like to kill a man. I told them it's not like James Bond or Bruce Willis and there are no actors with fake blood and a director shouting 'cut'. In films people don't really bleed, lose limbs or fall down dead, but they do in real life. I told them when you shoot a person they bleed and they die.

Teaching art to youngsters has opened up a new world to me. The kids start off wanting to do paramilitary and street art, the flags and the gunmen. I coax them into political art and mythology, Harland & Wolff shipyard and the legends of Cuchulain. Some are problem kids and are so disruptive Social Services won't touch them. They are aggressive, territorial, tough little street fighters – just like me when I was sixteen years old and thought I was the king of the Braniel. Some have been brought to the attention of the paramilitaries for anti-social behaviour and have either been beaten or shot. These are the kids I enjoy spending time with because I know what motivates them. I know what makes them tick.

Occasionally I come across a youngster who is talented. One girl was fifteen years old and from the day she walked into the studio she was painting abstract and post-modern work. She came from a problem home. She is now studying fine art at the University of Ulster. I am very proud of her.

My painting has turned things around for me in more ways than one. It has given me an income and a purpose. Five years ago, when I was a UDA prisoner doing life for murder, if someone had said my paintings had commercial value and would sell, I would have laughed in their face. I never thought anyone would be interested in owning something painted by Michael Stone. These are, after all, the hands that ripped pins out of grenades and pulled the trigger of a gun. I know that some look at and buy my work for ghoulish reasons, but there is nothing I can do about that. I have since been signed up by the Blockart company, which markets and distributes my work globally. This allows my work to be viewed and purchased by a worldwide audience.

24

LOYALIST CEASEFIRE

BY THE TIME OF THE FIRST IRA CEASEFIRE IN 1994, I HELD THE RANK OF OFFICER COMMANDING OF THE EAST BELFAST UDA IN THE MAZE. There had been rumblings about an end to Provo violence, but the UDA/UFF and the UVF needed more than rumour to be convinced. The UDA would not contemplate calling a ceasefire without making sure the Provos were genuine. The first stage was to sound out prisoners' feelings on a Loyalist ceasefire through a vote. In the wing canteen, a show of hands was taken and just three prisoners thought Loyalists should lay down their arms. I wasn't one of the three. There was hostility to the idea of a Loyalist ceasefire. The general feeling was that Loyalists had the IRA on the run, so why should we let them off the hook?

The second ballot came soon after. I pushed for a secret ballot. When it came to the vote, I abstained. I needed more time to look at the bigger picture and I wasn't completely satisfied with what the IRA were saying. Johnny Adair was now OC of West Belfast.

Many prisoners came to me asking how they should vote. I told every single one of them the same thing: that they had to make up their own mind, that I couldn't tell them what to think and feel, that it was their voice and their choice. In truth, I was undecided. My head was alert for danger signs but my heart wanted to support a ceasefire. I wanted my family to grow up without the fear of indiscriminate bombs and bullets, but I was still suspicious of the Republican movement and decided not to use my vote.

However, after much manoeuvring and politicking the ballot was passed. Loyalists would lay down their arms. In the historic setting of Fernhill House, the Combined Loyalist Military Command declared its ceasefire. The CLMC represented the UDA/UFF, the UVF and the Red Hand Commando. The ceasefire was announced by UVF figurehead Gusty Spence, who read a prepared announcement to the world's media which said sorry for the hurt caused to victims of Loyalist violence and pledged to resolve political and cultural differences.

The next big hurdle was the referendum on the Good Friday Agreement, signed in 1998, four years after the ceasefires and after the IRA's first ceasefire had broken down. I could live with the Good Friday Agreement so long as the message got across that Loyalists were genuine and were behind the principal of it. Loyalist prisoners weren't ignorant apes selling our souls from our cells and taking the lead from Republicans. We had opinions and our own agenda. If the Good Friday Agreement wasn't accepted by Loyalist prisoners, then we would go back to war.

I set political wheels in motion. I organised visits from political figures, across all parties and all persuasions, to come and talk to us and see. My prison talks team consisted of Johnny Adair, Bobby Philpot and Glen Cunningham.

Letters, drafted by me and signed by the talks team, were sent out to people in all walks of political and civic life. The only parties who did not get an invite were Sinn Fein and the

Democratic Unionist Party – Sinn Fein because they were the political wing of our enemy and the DUP because they had repeatedly called for the death penalty. Loyalist prisoners never referred to the DUP's leader, Ian Paisley, by name. They called him 'cow head'. Politicians and leaders from all walks of life wanted to talk to us and included the then Secretary of State, Mo Mowlam. Mowlam had previously met me in prison in early 1997 in her capacity as Shadow Secretary of State, and she promised that if Labour were elected to government, and she was Secretary of State, she would come back in her formal capacity. She kept her promise. I distinctly remember her taking off her shoes, putting her feet on my leg, and asking me to rub her sore toes. Our meetings were amicable and constructive, and I like her because she dispensed with formalities and there was no bullshit.

We also had meetings with the leader of the Ulster Unionist Party, David Trimble, the leader of the Social Democratic and Labour Party, John Hume, and Archbishop Robin Eames. Trimble was a genuine, intelligent and streetwise man. I still think he is a good Unionist, but sadly he doesn't have a thing in common with people like me. He is what I would call a UK Unionist rather than an Ulster Unionist. He should join Robert McCartney's one-man party. I knew Loyalist prisoners wouldn't be able to do business with him. He spoke at us rather than to us.

John Hume was an impressive politician. To me he is the ultimate pan-nationalist bogeyman, but I was prepared to give him the benefit of the doubt, as he was prepared to give me. He agreed to talk to us and that was a positive move. John Hume was a surprise. He was smart and articulate and he was enthusiastic, intelligent and diplomatic. I liked him. I can still remember what he said. 'Michael, you can't eat a flag. You can fight for it and you can die for it. You can't eat it.' His words have stayed with me. I asked him if Sinn Fein were genuine and he said he believed they were.

Johnny Adair was the wrong man to have on the prison talks

team. He had to be there because he held rank, but he did not have a political thought in his head. I had rules. I insisted the men wear a shirt and jeans. There would be no lycra shorts and posing vests, which Johnny liked to wear, and no gold jewellery. But at the meeting with John Hume, Adair turned up in a posing vest, then shamed the Loyalist cause with his only comment to Hume. He rubbed his hands together and laughed his manic laugh, saying, 'Hey, John, I bet you don't like those pipe bombs being thrown up your drives.' It was a reference to the device left outside the home of Dr Joe Hendron, a prominent SDLP politician. The entire team wilted. Adair's sectarian comments were undoing our good work. Hume never acknowledged the remark. The expression on his face never changed.

After Adair's embarrassing words, we resumed business. I put various scenarios to Hume and he said, 'We live in the United States of Europe. We are all Europeans.' He made an impression on me. I remember thinking, You are a good politician – it's just a pity you are a nationalist and not a Unionist. Hume told me he really believed the IRA's war was over and I trusted him. The night before, I had telephoned the *Belfast Telegraph* with the mobile I kept in my cell and journalists had gathered at the gates of the Maze to quiz Hume when he left. We both agreed that the meeting was 'informative and constructive'.

After Hume left and Adair cleared off to his wing, the three of us talked about the Adair comments. We all agreed he was the wrong man for the public face of Loyalist prisoners. Philpot asked if he'd been hearing things about pipe bombs and nationalists. I said no. He locked himself in his cell for two whole days in disgust.

Eric Smyth, a Shankill Road DUP councillor, did meet us, although a meeting wasn't planned. The prison talks team had deliberately ignored the DUP because of their stance on capital punishment, but while Smyth waited to see a UVF prisoner, we exchanged ideas. Smyth's son had been kneecapped by Loyalist paramilitaries for dealing drugs. Johnny Adair played a blinder in embarrassing us all by saying, 'What about your son and his knees? Are they better yet?'

'My son broke the law and the Lord's law and I have to live with that, but, Mr Adair, he is not as big a drug dealer as you.'

Johnny just gave one of his manic laughs and called him a 'raker', a bit of a chancer. After a few minutes he piped up, 'John White is after your seat in the elections.'

'My seat is safe. Everyone in the Shankill knows White won't win that seat, for obvious reasons,' Smyth replied, winking at Johnny. White had been dubbed 'Co-Co' by Loyalist prisoners, and the meaning is obvious. He then turned to me and said, 'Michael, I am a Christian man and you are a Loyalist. You are not like those scum drug dealers and we could have done business', and with that he was gone. A few months later he greeted the US President Bill Clinton in Belfast.

The Reverend Roy Magee was a gentleman and so was Church of Ireland Archbishop Robin Eames. Archbishop Eames agreed to meet us and we had the meeting in my wing canteen. He informed us about the possibility of a scheme of 'phased release' for prisoners. He said he believed there would be a sliding scale for different offences such as murder, attempted murder and possession. He looked at me and apologised, saying he didn't think anything could be done for me. I answered that it didn't matter, so long as my men got out. Archbishop Eames was wearing his official ring: a ruby set in a gold band. He was also wearing a gold cross around his neck. Again, Adair, unable to help himself, opened his big mouth. This time the Archbishop was out of range, but Adair's words were embarrassing: 'I thought I had some gear, but did you see the size of that fucking ring and the necklace? There must be a few quid in that religion racket.' There isn't an answer to this sort of comment. Johnny Adair was a lost cause.

Gary McMichael made several visits to the Maze to talk to prisoners during the ceasefire and Good Friday referendum, but Loyalist prisoners never rated him, especially Adair. They rubbished his attempts to follow in his father's footsteps. In my eyes he could never be his father's son. John McMichael was a focused military man and an astute and intelligent politician. Gary McMichael was never a volunteer or street fighter and he couldn't grasp what motivates men like me because he could never be like me. He didn't have it in him. Loyalist prisoners resented him.

On the other hand, they rated Ray Smallwoods. He was one of the chief political strategists of the UDP, the UDA/UFF's political wing, and had done time for attempted murder. He was sentenced to fifteen years for the shooting of Bernadette McAliskey and her husband Michael at their home in Coalisland, County Tyrone. Ironically, an undercover unit of the British Army happened to be on hand and saved the couple's life and arrested the UFF unit. Smallwoods was released and threw himself into politics, taking up where John McMichael had left off.

Smallwoods was shot dead by the IRA just weeks before the 1994 IRA ceasefire. His death left the UDP like a coop of headless chickens and it was up to Gary McMichael to lead the party, but he couldn't deliver. McMichael Junior was good for occasional soundbites, but that was it. Once, he criticised Johnny Adair for going to Drumcree at the height of the Orange protests. I heard the call Adair made from the mobile phone he kept hidden in his cell. They were choice words. 'I'll kill that fucker Gary McMichael for interfering in my business.' McMichael never raised the subject of Johnny Adair and Drumcree again.

During the campaign for a yes vote in the 1998 Good Friday referendum, there was a rally in the Ulster Hall, organised by the UDP. On the Monday before the Friday rally, a meeting was held in the prison gym. It was packed with prisoners and about forty outsiders. Key members of the UDP were present, including Gary

McMichael and John White. There was a heated argument when one East Belfast prisoner, Harry, said he wanted to go to the rally and speak on behalf of all Loyalist prisoners. His request did not go down well with them.

My brigadier asked me to go to the rally. I had my first parole coming up and my father was unwell. I said my family came first, but my brigadier said that the UDA was split between the hardliners and the moderates and that, if I went to the rally in support of the principals of the Good Friday Agreement, I could unite the organisation. I spoke to John White. I told him about my parole and that I would be going to the rally out of respect for the UDA. I told Gary McMichael exactly the same thing and said that, if my going to the rally was going to cause problems, then he should let me know.

On the Friday afternoon I saw my father and was then taken to the Ulster Hall. The UDA had provided a man called George Legge to be my bodyguard for the evening. Inside I was greeted with thunderous applause. The press was present and the flash of cameras also caught my eye. The banners were eye-catching. There was one, painted with the words 'Michael Stone Says Yes' and a second one, draped over the balcony, which said, 'Trust and Honour'. Sixteen hundred Loyalists rose to their feet as one, to acknowledge my presence. To get to the stage I walked along a small corridor and was confronted by a confused and speechless Gary McMichael. He was accompanied by a West Belfast UDA commander. I reminded McMichael of the conversation we had in the Maze that if he had a problem with me being at the rally he was to let me know. He couldn't remember the conversation.

The stage was packed. John White was there, other UDP representatives and VIPs were there and there was a small band from the Shankill. I gave an open-hand salute to the crowd. The open hand meant I had nothing to hide. It was a peaceful gesture. I was formally welcomed on stage by Jackie McDonald, who shook my hand and showed me to my seat among the VIPs and officials, but I chose to sit at the back with the bandsmen.

John White addressed the crowd. He said Loyalists 'like Michael Stone and Johnny Adair have made today possible'. The audience was also told that after thirty years of Republican violence to achieve a united Ireland, the IRA had lost the war. They heard that the IRA lost their war because Loyalists made it impossible for them to bomb Protestants into a united Ireland. The scales of conflict had tipped and the UFF had forced the IRA on the run.

After the rally there was a meeting in the Avenue One bar. I was briefed that the LVF were about to call their ceasefire on the stroke of midnight. From a small upstairs room I gave an interview to local radio station Cool FM, which was broadcast on the 11pm news. I reiterated the UDA/UFF's commitment to the principles of the Good Friday Agreement. I also said that it was my understanding that the LVF, the only Loyalist paramilitary group not on ceasefire, was about to announced their commitment to the Peace Process. The LVF ceasefire was announced on the midnight news on Downtown Radio.

On the Monday, I was returned to the Maze. The Governor wanted to see me. He said that I was 'all over the papers' and informed me that the law had been changed during my brief absence. He said, 'From this day, Mr Stone, prisoners on parole cannot attend events with more than twenty people present.' I laughed at the Governor and asked him, did that mean the cinema, ice skating, ice hockey or the leisure centre? He never answered.

25

UNCHARTED
WATERS ·

**I WALKED FROM THE MAZE A FREE MAN ON 24 JULY 2000.
I WAS FORTY-FIVE. I HAD SERVED JUST TWELVE YEARS,
INCLUDING MY YEAR ON REMAND, OF MY THIRTY-YEAR
SENTENCE.** I expected to be a pensioner, an old man of sixty-
four, before I could leave my cell in H7 for the last time. I was one
of the last prisoners to leave the Maze, thanks to the Good Friday
Agreement. The Early Release scheme was one of the concessions
the fledgling Peace Process brought political prisoners like me,
and the 'phased release' part of the scheme meant all political
prisoners remaining after June 2000 would be automatically
released. I was included in this bracket.

It was a monumental day for my family. The Sentence Review
Commissioners had originally given me a date of 22 July and I had
been preparing for that day for months but the authorities fudged
the date and told me my actual release would be two days later. I
lost a legal challenge aimed at securing my rightful release day.
The High Court dismissed my application for a judicial review

outright. I was the only man left on my wing and it was a long and lonely weekend. I had my release day fixed on my emotional horizon and I thought it would never arrive. So to occupy my time, I built the biggest bonfire the Maze has ever seen.

On Monday morning I walked into the reception area of the Maze for the final time. The authorities did the usual security checks. I was strip-searched and fingerprinted for the last time. They took a Polaroid showing exactly what I looked like on my release, and clipped it to my file. My release papers were read out to me and I was asked whether I understood everything contained in it. I nodded that I did. The Governor stressed that I was the property of the Secretary of State and that my licence could be revoked at any time until 2019. I signed the papers and the Governor added one final thing. He said that I was not eligible to apply for a firearm until two years after my release. I had seen enough of guns. I wouldn't be applying.

The Governor shook my hand and wished me well. Several of the screws I got to know on the wings rushed into the reception area to say their farewells. One had a Sureshot camera and insisted on taking a photograph, but I told him I didn't 'do' photographs. He insisted and persisted and I eventually relented. Then suddenly there were fifteen uniforms squeezed all around me. I said my goodbyes to the Governor and the prison officers and walked, a grateful man, through the metal turnstile. Right up to the very last second I expected Jeremy Beadle to jump out and tell me it was an elaborate hoax. But it was no joke. I was going home.

The press had gathered at the main entrance to the prison. I knew they would be there and had prepared a short statement that a UDP spokesperson would read out to them. Contained in this was a reiteration that my war was over, that all deaths in war are regrettable and a request to live the rest of my life peacefully and quietly with my family and friends. There would be no triumphalism. It would be dignified and sensitive to the feelings of the families. It was my intention to go straight home to see my family after the formalities with the media were finished.

But the statement was never read. I was given unpleasant family news and was ushered away from the Maze. I was told my son Gary was on the run from the RUC, that he was wanted in connection with an attempted murder. There had been a street fight and Gary and his friend had laid into each other over a car they both owned. Gary's pal had fallen awkwardly, hit his head on the kerb and ended up with a fractured skull. The incident happened two weeks before my release date but my family didn't tell me because they didn't want to spoil my big moment. The moment was destroyed. I didn't want to hang around talking to journalists and mingling with well-wishers. I wanted to go straight home and find out about my son.

I greeted the press with a solemn face. There was no smile and there was no speech. No sooner had one Stone been released from prison than another was in trouble and on the run. I was taken in a people carrier to the city via South Belfast. En route we changed to a 4WD to take us into East Belfast and the Gael Lairn centre on the Newtownards Road. The convoy took me past a newly painted mural on Templemore Avenue. It was me but it didn't look like me. I looked more like the cartoon character Super Mario Brother. Underneath were painted the words: 'His Only Crime Was Loyalty'. It was an honour, because in Loyalism you have to be dead before gable ends and walls are dedicated to you.

As we joined the Newtownards Road from Templemore Avenue, the UDA stopped the traffic to let my convoy of cars pass through easily. Inside the Gael Lairn centre the small conference room was packed with journalists and camera crews. Although it was a strain, given the news I had just received, I did say that all deaths are regrettable, and I expressed my regret to the families of the men I killed and my regret that I'd had to fight a war.

There was a brief stop-over in the Avenue One bar. I went through the motions for the sake of all those who had made an effort for my benefit, and was then taken to the Tullycarnet estate, where my sisters had organised a party. Despite my wish for things to be low-key and for my family to be mindful of the security implications of my release, there was a massive hand-painted banner strung across the house saying, 'Welcome Home Michael'. Balloons were tied to bushes and trees, and music was coming through speakers and blaring out all over the street. There were hundreds of people there, including some from the Braniel who had come out to wish me well and welcome me home.

After the celebrations I had to start readjusting all over again. I knew that life wasn't going to be easy. I knew I would be more of a prisoner on the outside than I was inside the Maze. I had made mental preparations for that. Before my release I had organised several safe houses in the Dundonald area. People were very kind and opened their homes to me in those early days. From the bottom of my heart, I thank them all. To protect me, and by default to protect themselves, they had every conceivable security device attached to and installed in their homes. There was bullet-proof glass, steel doors, infrared sensors, cameras and even dogs. Although the dogs were there for my protection, I loved them as pets. The last time I had stroked a dog was the night before Milltown.

When prisoners are released they begin their new lives by signing on and claiming benefits. They are given a start-up grant of around one thousand pounds for their fresh start. Because I was living from safe house to safe house, I wasn't able to sign on and I lived from hand to mouth in those early days. Political prisoners and paramilitaries don't get a pension. There are no financial rewards for giving your life to paramilitary organisations.

My first real home was with Suzanne Cooper, my former fiancée. I'd met her when I was in prison, and she was a rock of kindness and support. Suzanne had her home modified with extra security so that we could have a normal life together. The doors were reinforced with plates of steel. We had infrared sensors, trip switches and bullet-proof glass. We had matching 'his' and 'hers' body armour. We had two brutes of Alsatians bought as guard dogs to protect our lives and our home.

I had been there just one week when the RUC informed me that I was on a dissident IRA hit list. The police announced themselves by parking a fleet of Land Rovers at the bottom of my drive. The dogs were going mad. The officers wouldn't come to my door and I wouldn't go to the Land Rovers, so I lifted the phone and rang Strand Road police station. They eventually came to the front door. One officer said, 'Michael Stone, we have received reports that you are to be murdered this weekend. It has come from a reliable intelligence source who added that the killers know your exact address.' I thanked them and they left. I didn't leave the house for a month.

I worked hard at getting my life back to normal, but it took longer to adjust than I bargained for. It was small things, like readjusting to living with another person and sharing a bed. After twelve years in prison I was institutionalised, though I fought it.

Suzanne and I parted a few months later and I moved to a small flat on the Ballybeen estate. At nine in the evening, as I waited for a taxi to take me to a club, there was a knock on my door. It was an RUC car and in the back was Suzanne. She said she had been looking for me all day and warned me not to go out. The RUC officers confirmed that the INLA unit from Bawnmore wanted to shoot me in the car park of a well-known establishment. A taxi driver had seen me the week before and the information got back to the INLA. The RUC then said, 'We have been to this, this and this address but eventually we found you.'

In November 2000, just four months after my release, the Labour MP Kevin McNamara invited me to address the British Irish

Committee on Northern Ireland. It was an honour to be asked to represent my community in the Houses of Parliament. I felt humbled that I was invited to speak at a meeting within the historic walls of Westminster. I went there to speak in support of the Belfast Agreement. British politicians needed to be warned that Ulster's path to peace was, and still is, strewn with difficulties. I wanted to stress that the Agreement was worth fighting for because there was no alternative except a return to the past. Kevin McNamara wasn't able to attend. He got a better offer, an audience with the Pope.

I told the Committee that what I did I did in the name of my Britishness. I told them I did what I did because I am a British citizen. I also had a warning for the group. I told them working-class Protestants felt disenfranchised by the new political structures: the Assembly and the Executive. I assured them I was personally committed to the Peace Process because it was the only one we had and I would do everything I could within my own community to make it work.

Before addressing the Committee I had spoken to several politicians privately. I was saddened that some of these Conservative MPs shunned my visit, saying my early release was 'a disgrace' and it was 'doubly disgraceful' that I was allowed into the grounds of the Houses of Parliament. The Tories argued that a triple killer, who took life in a graveyard, had no place in politics and no place in democracy. My argument is that we do have a place because we lived and breathed a war for thirty years.

I had prepared a short speech to deliver to the Committee and it contained the following words: 'My war is over. I know it will cause great hurt and resentment to many people that I am free today. I want to make a contribution to the Peace Process. I want to do something constructive, not destructive for a change. I deeply regret the hurt I caused the families of the men I killed. I regret that I had to kill. I believed, at the time, it was necessary. There is nothing I can do to take away the pain I have inflicted.

There is a lot of hurt out there and I am responsible. Much of that hurt comes from my actions as a paramilitary. I don't see myself as a criminal. I committed crimes as an Ulsterman and a British citizen and that was regrettable but unavoidable. I committed horrendous acts of violence in the name of Ulster. I support the principles of the Good Friday Agreement but, as I have seen on the streets since my release, there is alienation within the Loyalist-Unionist community. We all need to work together and do everything we can to make this work.'

Committee members shook my hand and thanked me for my honesty. I was told I was very open about the crimes I committed and very honest about the appalling action I took in the name of Ulster. I told them I was speaking at the Committee so that British politicians understood where I, and many like me, were coming from. I told the Committee that I was not proud of my paramilitary past but I was proud of being British. I also said that I was as British as all the politicians gathered for this meeting.

After the meeting I was given a tour of both houses of Parliament. I had tea and scones in the Common Room. The Tory MP Anne Widdecombe shook my hand, but she had no idea who I was. I found the history of Westminster overwhelming. As I walked the ancient corridors I knew I belonged in Belfast. I am a homebird and that is where I belong. I decided to go straight back and do everything I could to make the Peace Process work. I had to sell it to my community and I believed I could. It wasn't the perfect solution, but it was the only one we had.

Northern Ireland has enjoyed a relatively peaceful time since 1998 and I am thankful for that. In July 2001 there was a UDA rally in the heart of Loyalist West Belfast. I was invited but refused the invitation. I wanted to keep my head down and get on with my life. I wasn't interested in rallies and shows of strength, but I was put under pressure. The West Belfast brigadier told my brigadier,

'Order him to go', but my brigadier said, 'No, he has done his time, it's his choice.' And I relented.

It was a summer's day and thousands of people had gathered for the unveiling of new murals in Johnny Adair's heartland. The West Belfast brigade had spent thousands on the wall paintings. It was supposed to be a family day. Hundreds of children were running around dressed in 'Mad Dog Adair' T-shirts and with their faces painted to resemble the Union Jack. When these kids spotted me, they asked me to sign the back of their T-shirts. I did. But it wasn't 'Michael Stone'. It was 'Mickey Mouse' or 'Donald Duck'. I did that not to upset the kids but to piss Adair off. One of the new murals depicted LVF leader Billy Wright, who had been rubbished in prison by Adair. He had called Wright a 'wanker' and said his death was 'no loss' to Loyalism. I smiled at the irony of Wright's image appearing on a wall in the Shankill estate.

John White, Adair's right-hand man and self-styled spokesperson for the UDA, was also present, and he moved through the crowd like Moses parting the waters. He approached me and shook my hand. He said he was relieved I had agreed to attend the rally. He said it showed supporters the UDA was united and still 'The Best'. I spied Adair in the crowd, hovering near the stage, and he was wearing a 'Simply the Best' T-shirt. Even his Alsatian, Rebel, was wearing one.

I noticed the crowd was running around and they looked like they were panicking. I thought to myself, Oh no, something has just happened. Meanwhile White asked me to go on stage. I refused. Under no circumstances, I told him. I was here as a spectator. He tried to blackmail me with rubbish such as, 'The speeches can't be made until you go on stage.' I told him to catch a grip, then looked at the stage and saw Adair had already taken his place. I told White I was only present out of respect for the UDA, not for the West Belfast brigade of the UDA. I said that the UDA didn't begin and end with West Belfast and I was here because I was still loyal to the organisation. He gave me a false smile and said he could personally guarantee there would be no volleys of shots or guns on stage and it would be disrespectful for a leading Loyalist to refuse to join fellow Loyalists on stage. He walked away.

I noticed there was a commotion and the crowd was beginning to disperse and running towards the Shankill Road. An LVF colour party, invited by Johnny Adair to the West Belfast rally, produced guns and fired shots at a UVF bar called The Rex. People were injured, but news of the gun attack hadn't filtered through to the Shankill estate. Meanwhile, I was told that if I didn't get on stage it would look like there was a massive split in the UDA. So I agreed, for internal politics' sake, and was shown a seat beside Adair. He couldn't sit still. He was in a high state of excitement and was like a child bouncing around the stage, breathlessly listing who was here and who had come to pay homage at God's Own Country. He kept saying, 'This is fucking great, Mikey, fucking great', and rubbing his hands together. When Adair was overexcited he always rubbed his hands maniacally.

Mr Showbiz sat on stage like a king presiding over his people. He was overwhelmed by it all. His voice was chirping in my ear, 'Will you hold my hand, Mikey?' I didn't have time to react. I didn't even have time to turn and look at him. He grabbed my hand and, with his hand wrapped around mine, punched the air. It was the show of strength I didn't want to be part of and was told wouldn't happen. The crowd erupted and Adair, a broad smile on his face, shouted, 'Wasn't I right, Mikey? Didn't I say we were famous? You're used to all this, the fame, aren't you, Mikey?'

White made a speech, and as soon as it was finished I left the stage. I knew the guns and volleys of shots would be next. As I made my way through the crowd I met an associate from East Belfast. He said we had to get out of the Shankill urgently because all hell was about to break loose. The noise of gunfire filled the air and, when I looked behind me, I could see not one but several people firing. One was a woman wearing a micro-mini combat skirt who was struggling with her gun. She continued to fire, but she was lowering the weapon while it was on fully automatic, and she seemed as if she would drop it, sending bullets everywhere. People were beginning to duck and look for cover, but in the end no harm came of it.

We were on the fringes of the crowd when a former prisoner approached me. We had never really bothered with each other in the Maze, so it was a surprise to be hugged by the man and asked how I was. The man was wearing a T-shirt and had bare arms. I didn't like this. I learned a short while afterwards that he was the gunman who had shot up the Rex. The bastard was trying to set me up by planting evidence.

My associates took me to a bar in East Belfast. I undressed in the yard while two pals hosed me down. Another friend brought a shirt and trousers. I scrubbed my skin with Fairy Liquid to destroy the evidence the gunman had planted on me. I was just out of jail. I couldn't afford to be implicated in any paramilitary business. I had no intention of going back to prison and I didn't want to play any role in an internal Loyalist blood feud. This man had deliberately tried to discredit me. The newspapers had a field day about my appearance at the Shankill rally. I told my brigadier that I wouldn't be doing anything like that ever again. I was out on licence. I was owned by the Secretary of State. My life belonged to the authorities and just the newspaper reports alone would have been enough to have me sent back to prison, no questions asked. My brigadier said he understood.

This event was the start of a bitter and bloody feud between the UDA and the UVF, and Adair had started it by inviting the LVF to the rally. The feud lasted several months and a number of men were killed.

Recently I bumped into someone I didn't think I would ever see again. It was my Milltown back-up man. After I was arrested he fled to England, but with the ceasefire and fledgling Peace Process he felt able to come home. We met in a bar on the outskirts of Belfast and he explained to me what had happened on the day. He said he was aware of the white Transit parked on the hard shoulder and, following my instructions to the letter, ordered the driver to keep moving. He also said that an RUC surveillance unit was monitoring the vehicle as it circled and cruised the motorway. The driver had a scanner that could pick up police airwaves. He then said circumstances got out of control and the car was unable to get to me. I wanted to believe him, but inside I didn't.

Twelve years on, he was still very angry and very emotional. He asked me again why I wouldn't let him take part in the cemetery part of the sanction. Again I told him that it was because I couldn't guarantee his safety. His answer shocked me. He said, 'You stole that operation from me. I have never forgiven you.' I have always had a nagging doubt that my back-up man deliberately abandoned me. I don't want to think that he betrayed me, but I know he left me on the motorway. I know he let me down.

26

PAST, PRESENT AND FUTURE

ONE OF THE REASONS I SPLIT WITH SUZANNE WAS BECAUSE I WAS WORRIED ABOUT HER SAFETY. I am fatalistic about life and I believe that shit happens. I was not willing to risk her. I believe when the IRA come for me, they will come armed with heavy artillery. It won't be a small weapon. It will be something to make a big mess, something that guarantees I don't survive. I also think they will use one of the weapons from Milltown as their death card, probably the Ruger. The Ruger will be their way of saying, 'We got our man.' I think Republicans have this little fantasy that I am sitting in a fortified prison, armed to the eyeballs, with a knife between my teeth, just like the Rambo character. I say to them, 'Catch a grip.' Like Republican prisoners and like Republican killers, I am trying to get on with my life. I can't be always looking over my shoulder. But at the same time paranoia is what keeps you alive.

It has been difficult to reintegrate, but my art has given me a purpose and an income. The thing with art is that it transcends politics, religion, culture, nationality and identity. Art is now my passion. I could happily paint till three in the morning and I have withdrawal symptoms if a day passes without me putting a brush to canvas.

I have always been an optimist about peace in Northern Ireland, but I have genuine fears for the long-term prospect of peace holding. If it all blows up again, then the new breed of Loyalist will take the war to the Irish Republic. That is a fact. It is not speculation. I believe we are all marking time. I believe Republicans and Loyalists are waiting for things to fall apart and then the paramilitaries will step back into the breach.

I find the current sectarian unrest depressing. East Belfast's Cluan Place and Short Strand flashpoint shows that wounds haven't healed and the sectarian bitterness is as ripe now as it was in the 1970s. It is back to the bad old days. I remember the 1970s, when Loyalists would go hunting the streets for Catholics. I don't want to face that ever again, but I fear we might. Naturally, I fear for my family and friends.

I acknowledge that while in prison I was cocooned from the realities of street politics, but now the reality of the situation has hit me. I don't want to seem alarmist, but the situation is simmering and coming slowly to the boil. I have said in the past that my war is over. My war *is* over, but if civil order broke down I would obviously have to defend my family and community. That's not war-mongering, that's a reality. If I could have stood with just one Loyalist it would have been John 'Grugg' Gregg, the leading south-east Antrim UDA man.

For the third time in my life, a close friend has been taken from me. John Gregg died in early February 2003 after Johnny Adair ordered and organised his execution. I will remember him fondly and with sadness as I remember my two other associates, Tommy Herron and John McMichael. Grugg loved his music and football. It is ironic that Adair's henchmen would strike as he made his return journey from a Rangers match, a team he has followed all his life. His favourite groups were UB40 and Madness and he used music – the Maze First Flute and pop groups – to keep young men on his wings from the mental wards. His Christmas and Halloween parties were legendary. The lads loved him because he was like a big father figure who kept them busy, occupied and settled.

In the months leading up to his death, we had several discussions about Adair and his quest to resurrect the old position of Supreme Commander. It was widely known in Loyalism that Grugg had Adair by the tail, and it was also no secret that Adair had marked Grugg as enemy number one. History repeated itself. The John McMichael and Jim Craig relationship was being played out all over again. Grugg, like McMichael, knew he was marking time. Sadly his time ran out just weeks into the New Year when he was ambushed and killed by Johnny Adair's C Company using AK47 rifles.

The last time I saw my friend was the night before he was buried. Even in death he was impressive. He was wearing the uniform of his beloved Clough Fern Flute Band. He was their bass drummer. I will miss him, as I still miss John McMichael and Tommy Herron.

In certain areas of Loyalism the chickens have come home to roost. There have always been disagreements and blood feuds. Former paramilitary associates and friends find themselves at one another's throats. There has been a spate of killings and attempted killings. Criminal elements within West Belfast UDA have sought to capitalise on these events in order to gain overall control of the UDA.

Johnny Adair, the former brigadier of West Belfast UDA, was expelled from the organisation by the Inner Council for treasonable activities, namely supporting and condoning actions taken by the rival LVF. The Inner Council also found that his criminal activities involving drugs, prostitution and extortion were unacceptable. We are Loyalists. We are not criminals. The houses, the holidays, the gold and the flash car have nothing to do with true Loyalism. Adair's answer was always: 'Aye, Mikey, but Loyalism doesn't pay the bills.'

In prison, Adair constantly harped on about 'one good man to run the UDA', and he was talking about himself. I told him repeatedly that it wouldn't work, that no man is bigger than the UDA and no man is bigger than Loyalism. He didn't listen.

His associate John White was also expelled for treasonable activities and for supporting Adair's aspirations to become Supreme Commander of the UDA. The position has always been precarious. The enemy or the security forces can assassinate one individual or turn him into one of their informers. On one occasion, at a meeting of the Prison Council (the UDA/UFF's prison version of the Inner Council), White, the prisoners' spokesperson at the time, declared to the assembled company, 'I am the UDA. There wouldn't be a UDA without me.' I told him to behave himself, but he insisted that he was the 'only person holding the UDA together'. I have always said, 'The tail cannot wag the dog. The tail is the prisoners, the body of the dog is the body politic and the head and teeth is the UDA/UFF, and if you fuck with them the head will turn and bite off the dog's tail.' White stormed off. He was seen by many as the unacceptable face of Loyalist prisoners because he carried out the savage mutilation of two people, one a woman. Old-school Loyalists didn't like his style.

I acknowledge that there are those who think I am being hypocritical in condemning his past actions, but I, too, am of the old school and believe in a clean kill, not a prolonged, frenzied attack.

After their expulsion, Adair and White set up a fiefdom in the Lower Shankill. Former Loyalists and associates were attacked and intimidated from the area as Adair carried out a purge of any perceived enemies. He had a number of good men in his ranks who were too frightened to speak out against him for fear of retaliation.

An incendiary blast bomb was planted at White's home. The security forces defused the device. In retaliation for the attempt on White's life, Adair's men sought to assassinate John Gregg by booby-trapping his car. This is ironic, given that Gregg attempted to kill the Sinn Fein chief Gerry Adams.

Adair, through his criminal egomania and disrespect for Loyalism, has bastardised the UDA and Loyalist cause for self-gain and notoriety, just like Jim Craig and Tucker Lyttle were doing twenty years ago. During those months before Adair was thrown back in jail, I feared for the young men under his control who, out of misplaced loyalty, were placing their own lives and the lives of their fellow Loyalists on the line.

To the Wee Johnny I knew in the 1990s when he was a private in C Company, I say, you are now the unacceptable face of Loyalism. Give it up, Johnny, or start a new life in another country or you are going to end up in that rubbish skip before me ...

My priority is to stay alive. When my time comes, and it will, I hope I am on my feet and moving forward. I accept that I will die as I lived and, to be honest, I wouldn't want it any other way.

Quis separabit.

GLOSSARY

CLMC (Combined Loyalist Military Command) Organisation formed in 1991 to represent the UDA/UFF, UVF and Red Hand Commando. It declared the Loyalist ceasefire in 1994.

INLA (Irish National Liberation Army) Extreme Republican paramilitary group, established in 1974 after breaking away from the IRA.

LVF (Loyalist Volunteer Force) Dissident faction of the UVF formed in the late 1990s by those opposed to the Loyalist ceasefire.

PIRA (Provisional Irish Republican Army) The largest Republican paramilitary group. Formed in 1970 after breaking away from the IRA (Irish Republican Army) following disagreement at the Ard Fheis (annual general meeting) of Sinn Fein, the political wing of the IRA. In 1994 the PIRA declared its first ceasefire, which was later broken and then restored.

RIR (Royal Irish Regiment) A regiment of the British Army established in 1992 after the Ulster Defence Regiment and Royal Irish Rangers merged.

RUC (Royal Ulster Constabulary) The police force of Northern Ireland formed in 1922, and called the Police Service for Northern Ireland since 2001.

SAS (Special Air Service) Special-forces unit of the British Army, first deployed in Northern Ireland in 1976.

UDA (Ulster Defence Association) The largest Loyalist paramilitary force, formed in 1971 and proscribed in 1992.

UDR (Ulster Defence Regiment) Regiment of the British Army recruited exclusively in Northern Ireland. Formed after the disbandment of the B Specials (an exclusively Protestant part-time paramilitary force), which it replaced in 1970.

UDP (Ulster Democratic Party) Formed in 1971. The political wing of the UDA.

UFF (Ulster Freedom Fighters) Cover name for the UDA, first used in 1973.

ULDP (Ulster Loyalist Democratic Party) Forerunner of the UDP, formed in 1981 under the auspices of John McMichael.

UVF (Ulster Volunteer Force) Second-largest Loyalist paramilitary group. Established in the mid-1960s, but claims heritage dating back to the First World War. Proscribed in 1975.

VUPP (Vanguard Unionist Progressive Party) Established by William Craig in 1973, the former Minister for Home Affairs in the Stormont government.